Back to the Sources

Back to the Sources

Biblical and Near Eastern Studies

In Honour of Dermot Ryan

Edited by
Kevin J. Cathcart and John F. Healey

GLENDALE

First published in Ireland by
THE GLENDALE PRESS LTD.
1 Summerhill Parade
Sandycove
Co. Dublin

British Library Cataloguing in Publication Data

Cathcart, Kevin J.
Back to the sources.
1. Christianity
I. Title II. Healey, John F. III. Ryan Dermot
220.6

ISBN 0-907606-61-X

Cover by David L. Murphy
Typeset by Wendy A. Commins, The Curragh
Make-up by Paul Bray Studio
Printed by Billings & Sons, Worcester

CONTENTS

PREFACE

The idea of a volume of Biblical and Near Eastern essays dedicated to the late Archbishop Dermot Ryan and written by former students and colleagues of his was conceived some years ago. It is a matter of great sadness to us that this has to be a memorial volume rather than one to celebrate what would have been Dermot Ryan's 65th birthday.

We gratefully acknowledge substantial contributions towards the cost of publication from the following: Most Reverend Dr. Desmond Connell, Archbishop of Dublin; Most Reverend Dr. Maurice Couve de Murville, Archbishop of Birmingham; the National University of Ireland; University College Dublin and the Irish Biblical Association.

We thank the Chester Beatty Library for permission to publish photographs of some of its manuscripts and the British Library for permission to publish the Arabic text of BL Ms Or 13,017, folios 24v–29v. Dr. Pat Donlon's assistance in the selection of photographs of the Chester Beatty papyri is gratefully acknowledged, as is that of Ms Carene Comerford who prepared large parts of the typescript for the printer.

Finally, the editors wish to express thanks to Mr. Thomas Turley of the Glendale Press for seeing the volume through its production.

Kevin J. Cathcart

John F. Healey

ABBREVIATIONS

AnBib	Analecta Biblica
ANET	*Ancient Near Eastern Texts*, J. Pritchard (ed.) (Princeton [3]1969)
b.	Babylonian Talmud
BB.	*Baba Bathra*
BETL	Bibliotheca Ephemeridum Theologicarum Lovaniensium
BetM	*Beth Miqra*
Bib	*Biblica*
BKAT	Biblischer Kommentar: Altes Testament
BThB	*Biblical Theology Bulletin*
CBQ	*Catholic Biblical Quarterly*
CBQMS	Catholic Biblical Quarterly Monograph Series
CHB	*The Cambridge History of the Bible*
CSCO	Corpus Scriptorum Christianorum Orientalium
DBS	*Dictionnaire de la Bible Supplément*, L. Pirot et al. (eds.) (Paris 1928-)
EstBíb	*Estudios Bíblicos*
ET	*Expository Times*
GCS	Griechische Christliche Schriftsteller
HeyJ	*Heythrop Journal*
HTR	*Harvard Theological Review*
HUCA	*Hebrew Union College Annual*
IDBSupp	*The Interpreter's Dictionary of the Bible: Supplementary Volume* (Nashville 1976)
IEJ	*Israel Exploration Journal*
j.	Jerusalem Talmud
JAOS	*Journal of the American Oriental Society*
JBL	*Journal of Biblical Literature*
JCS	*Journal of Cuneiform Studies*
JJS	*Journal of Jewish Studies*
JPTh	*Jahrbücher für protestantische Theologie*
JQR	*Jewish Quarterly Review*
JR	*Journal of Religion*
JSOTSupp	Journal for the Study of the Old Testament Supplements
JTS	*Journal of Theological Studies*
KTU	*Die Keilalphabetischen Texte aus Ugarit*, M. Dietrich, O. Loretz, J. Sanmartín (eds.) (Neukirchen-Vluyn 1976)

Meg.	*Megillah*
MGWJ	*Monatsschrift für Geschichte und Wissenschaft des Judentums*
OBO	Orbis Biblicus et Orientalis
OLP	*Orientalia Lovaniensia Periodica*
Onq.	*Onqelos*
Or	*Orientalia*
OrChr	*Oriens Christianus*
OTPseudepigrapha	*The Old Testament Pseudepigrapha*, J.H. Charlesworth (ed.) Vol. 1 (1983); Vol. 2 (1985)
OTS	*Oudtestamentische Studiën*
PEQ	*Palestine Exploration Quarterly*
PIBA	*Proceedings of the Irish Biblical Association*
PL	*Patrologia Latina*, J. Migne (ed.)
PTA	Papyrologische Texte und Abhandlungen
PVTG	Pseudepigrapha Veteris Testamenti Graece
Qidd.	*Qiddushin*
RB	*Revue Biblique*
RechBib	Recherches bibliques
RechSR	*Recherches des Sciences Religieuses*
REJ	*Revue des Etudes Juifs*
RevEtSem	*Revue des Etudes Sémitiques*
RSO	*Rivista degli Studi Orientali*
RSV	Revised Standard Version
SC	Sources Chrétiennes
SD	Studies and Documents
Shabb.	*Shabbat*
SJT	*Scottish Journal of Theology*
SPap	*Studia Papirologica*
SVTP	Studia in Veteris Testamenti Pseudepigrapha
Tg.	Targum
Tg. Neof.	Targum *Neofiti* 1, A. Díez Macho (ed.)
Tg. Onq.	Targum Onqelos, A. Sperber (ed.)
Tg. Ps.-J.	Targum Pseudo-Jonathan, M. Ginsburger (ed.)
TWNT	*Theologisches Wörterbuch zum Neuen Testament*, G. Kittel (ed.)
UF	*Ugarit-Forschungen*
Yer	Yerushalmi
ZDMG	*Zeitschrift der deutschen morgenländischen Gesellschaft*
11QtgJob	Qumran Targum to Job

DERMOT RYAN
(1924-1985)

Dr. Dermot Ryan, Pro-Prefect of the Sacred Congregation for the Evangelisation of Peoples and former Archbishop of Dublin and Primate of Ireland, was born on 27th June, 1924 and died on 21st February, 1985. His early education was at Belvedere College and in 1942 he entered Holy Cross College, Clonliffe. After taking first class honours in Hebrew and Aramaic at University College Dublin, he then spent a year as a theology student in Maynooth before going to Rome in 1947 when the Irish College reopened after the war. In 1949 he was awarded a B.D. at the St. John Lateran University, Rome. Fourth year theology was spent in Holy Cross College, Clonliffe and Dr. Ryan was ordained to the priesthood there in 1950. Returning to Rome in 1951, he obtained the Licenciate in Sacred Theology at the Gregorian University in 1952 and the Licenciate in Sacred Scripture at the Pontifical Biblical Institute in 1954. He was also awarded an M.A. Degree in Eastern Languages with first class honours from the National University of Ireland in 1954, for a thesis on "Rpum and Rephaim. A Study in the Relationship between the *rpum* of Ugarit and the Rephaim of the Old Testament".

After service as chaplain in the Mater Hospital in Dublin, Dr. Ryan became Professor of Fundamental Dogmatic Theology at Clonliffe in 1955, joining the staff of U.C.D. as a part-time Professor in 1957. In 1969 he was appointed to the full-time Chair of Semitic Languages at University College Dublin, a position he held until his appointment as Archbishop of Dublin in December 1971. He was ordained Bishop by Pope Paul VI in Saint Peter's Basilica on the 13th February, 1972, thereby making history, as he was the first Irish prelate for several centuries to be consecrated by the Pope in Rome. For the next twelve years he devoted himself unsparingly as spiritual leader of Ireland's largest archdiocese. These twelve years witnessed a time of unprecedented growth in urban

Dublin, making huge demands on the resources of the diocese. During this time the number of parishes grew from 134 to 189. The archdiocese has one of the largest, and certainly the youngest, populations of any in Europe. A Veritas Publication, published shortly after his death and edited by Desmond Forristel, testifies to the range of concerns to which he turned his attention. It contains a selection of his writings and addresses on many different occasions during those twelve years as Archbishop.

His involvement in commissions, committees and various other societies also testifies to the scope of his leadership, scholarship and administrative skills. He was a founder member of the Catholic Biblical Association in 1968, which was later renamed the Irish Biblical Association. He was instrumental in the setting up of the Boylan Series of Lectures to pay tribute to one of Ireland's great scripture scholars. His publications at this period include *Mother of the Redeemer* (1959), *Sacraments Foreshadowed* (1964), *The Mass in Christian Life* (1965), and commentaries on the Old Testament Books of *Hosea*, *Amos*, *Micah* and *Zechariah* in the *Catholic Commentary on Holy Scripture* (2nd ed. 1969). He was Vice-President of the Irish Episcopal Conference, a member of the Episcopal Commission for Universities and of the Joint Commission of Bishops and Major Religious Superiors. He also formed part of the Steering Committee for the Ballymascanlon Interchurch Talks, and was a member of the Working Party responsible for the Ballymascanlon document entitled: "Church Scripture Authority". He served on the Standing Committee of the Irish Episcopal Conference, and was a member of the Maynooth Trustees and Maynooth Visitors. He was chairman of the Trustees of the Chester Beatty Library from 1978 to 1984, and chairman of the Board of Management, Mater Misericordiae Hospital. He was also Governor of St. Vincent's Hospital, Fairview, and chairman of the Executive Committee and of the Board of Governors, National Maternity Hospital. In addition to these he also served as Governor of Jervis Street Hospital and Chairman of Our Lady's Hospital for Sick Children.

His appointment as Pro-Prefect of the Sacred Congregation for the Evangelisation of Peoples in Vatican City on 9th April

1984 was greeted with acclaim within and without Ireland. For he had become known internationally through his participation in the World Synod of Bishops in Rome in 1974, 1977, 1980 and 1983. He was one of the best known "foreign" bishops in Rome through his chairmanship of the English language groups at the Synod. He spoke fluent Italian, French, German and Latin, as well as English and Irish. He had a deep knowledge of the Church in Europe and had travelled there extensively on holidays. In January 1983 he was invited by the Archbishop of Paris to give an address in Notre Dame Cathedral on "Handing on the Faith in a Large Metropolis". His sudden and untimely death in Rome in February 1985 came as a great shock, not only to the Church in Ireland, but also to the Church Universal. For in his short time in Rome, he had already effected much. It was widely expected that he would soon have become a member of the College of Cardinals. He was to have been shortly conferred with an honorary doctorate in laws by the National University of Ireland.

This volume of essays is dedicated to his memory particularly as a biblical scholar and as former Professor of Semitic Languages in University College Dublin. With the exception of Professor Kevin J. Cathcart, who succeeded Dr. Ryan in the Chair of Semitic Languages at University College Dublin, all the other contributors are former students of Dr. Ryan or former part-time teaching colleagues.

BIBLICAL THEOLOGY AND THE HISTORY OF ISRAELITE RELIGION

John J. Collins, *University of Notre Dame*

One of the primary ways in which teachers influence their students is by the questions to which they direct their attention. One such question, often posed by the late Dr. Ryan, is a classic dilemma of biblical studies: is it possible to write a theology of the Old Testament, as distinct from a history of the religion of Israel? In the 1960's this question arose especially in the context of the debate occasioned by G. von Rad's *Old Testament Theology*,[1] a work which in Dr. Ryan's view was really an exercise in the history of the religion. In his view, Biblical Theology could not be an independent discipline, but only a subsidiary part of a dogmatic theology.[2] This position was at odds with the prevailing wisdom of the time, both in the American "Biblical Theology Movement" and in the great European theologies of Eichrodt and von Rad. Indeed the whole history of Biblical Theology was founded on its separation as a discipline from Dogmatic Theology[3] and in the 1960's the possibility of basing Biblical Theology on historical critical method was generally taken for granted.

The Influence of Dogmatics

Two decades later, however, the scene has changed considerably. It is now widely acknowledged that the independence from dogmatic principles, which Biblical Theology professed, was largely illusory. J.P. Gabler's foundational essay of 1787, which called for the distinction of Biblical from Dogmatic Theology, nonetheless saw the role of the former as laying a firm foundation for Dogmatics.[4] When historical criticism developed its independence from Dogmatic Theology in the 19th century, Biblical Theology was generally abandoned in favour of the History of the Religion. "Could dogmatics teach New Testament theology to see the facts correctly?" asked Wilhelm Wrede in 1897. "At most it could colour them."[5] The revival of Biblical Theology after 1920, however, was marked by the reintroduction of dogmatic principles, despite professions to the contrary. Walther Eichrodt was typical. He announced his intention to "avoid all schemes which derive from Christian dogmatics," yet he held that the "profoundest meaning" of the OT could only be perceived in the light of its "essential coherence with the NT."[6] G.E. Wright based his theology on critical historiography and archeology, yet saw theology as a "recital" which involved "a projection of faith into facts."[7] In the recent words of Brevard Childs, "the presence of Christian assumptions is implicit in virtually every modern Old Testament theology and even in the allegedly objective religions of Israel."[8]

The tension between these Christian assumptions and historical criticism was pointed out by a number of critics in the 1960's, notably by Langdon Gilkey and James Barr.[9] The criticisms were drawn together by Childs in 1970 in a manifesto which marked a watershed in modern Biblical Theology.[10] The problems went beyond the short-comings of individual theologians, and concerned the compatibility of historical criticism with dogmatic theological presuppositions. It is not that historical criticism is free of presuppositions or is purely objective,[11] but that one of its principles is methodical doubt, which holds that any conclusion can in principle be questioned in the light of new evidence or arguments.[12] It therefore disallows the possibility of dogmatic certainty. This aspect of historical criticism was especially problematic for any attempt to base Biblical Theology on historical fact,[13] but it also undermined the certainty of other theological convictions, such as the essential coherence of the Old Testament with the New.

Much of the criticism of the so-called Biblical Theology Movement of 1920-1970 has come from within theological circles. There is also increasing criticism of theological interpretation of the Bible as such. A major criticism here is that biblical theologians engage in unnecessary mystification, by "explanation by reference to the inexplicable."[14] So we find proposals that biblical sociology should replace Biblical Theology[15] or scholars devote themselves to literary study without feeling a need to pursue theological questions.

The proposal of Childs, that the context of the canon play a normative role, opted for one horn of the dilemma which the Biblical Theology Movement had tried to straddle, by taking an explicitly confessional starting-point. As his critics have pointed out, the idea of canon is extrinsic to the biblical texts.[16] It is a dogmatic construct, imposed on the Bible from without. Quite apart from the specific problems associated with Childs' notion of canon,[17] the very appeal to dogmatic principles cuts off the possibility of dialogue with those who do not share those principles. Moreover, Childs is certainly vulnerable to the charge of mystification. In his view "understanding derives ultimately from the illumination of the Spirit. . . . There is no one hermeneutical key for unlocking the biblical message, but the canon provides the arena in which the struggle for understanding takes place."[18] Hence he is deliberately vague on the procedure of interpretation, apart from the fact that one is to focus on the canon. Without denying the limits of human understanding, most scholars find it possible to give a much fuller account of the process of interpretation without resorting to such "explanation by the inexplicable." Childs has rendered a considerable service to Biblical Theology, however, by clarifying the antithesis between the critical study of religion and biblical theology based on dogmatic presuppositions. Not all practitioners of Biblical Theology have perceived the tension between historical criticism and dogmatic theology as sharply as this, or conceded the force of the criticisms, but intermediate positions have been undermined nonetheless.[19]

An Alternative Proposal

The contemporary biblical scholar then is often confronted with a choice between the explicit appeal to dogmatic considerations, à la Childs, on the one hand, and the Bible without theology, à la Gottwald and Oden, on the other. I would like to suggest, however, that there may be another alternative. Biblical Theology need not be conceived as a normative discipline, but as an area of Historical Theology, which is one source among others for contemporary Dogmatic or Systematic Theology.[20] As an area of Historical Theology it necessarily overlaps with the history of religion. Within the history of the religion, it focuses on the portrayal of God in one group of texts, the Bible.[21] While the material to be explained is canonical, the context of interpretation is not restricted, as it is in Childs' canonical approach. Biblical Theology can make full use of historical, sociological and literary research, and so can be integrated fully into the mainstream of biblical research.

Any attempt to construct a biblical theology on this basis must evidently guard against the problems which beset the Biblical Theology Movement. Confessional statements about God's activity in, and purpose for, history go beyond the bounds of such historical analysis.[22] We can only say that a community construed God's activity or purpose in a particular way, and consider why. Again, socio-historical criticism does not permit us to draw conclusions about the divine nature. We can only say how various groups in Israel imagined God, and how their belief shaped their life.[23] From this perspective we can discuss how Christianity adapted the Hebrew Bible as its Old Testament, but we are not justified in making claims about the essential or necessary unity of the Testaments.

This model of Biblical Theology has clear advantages in so far as it facilitates dialogue with other areas of biblical study and provides a context for discussing the basis of theological beliefs. Properly followed, it is not open to the charge of mystification. Two objections, however, require consideration. On the one hand, can such an enterprise be really considered theological? and on the other, is there a need for Biblical Theology and does it really add anything to the non-theological study of religion advocated by Gottwald and Oden?

What counts as "theological" depends, of course, on the model of theology we are willing to accept. Anyone who regards theology as essentially confessional, or who sees the role of the theologian as "awaiting in anticipation a fresh illumination of God's Spirit,"[24] can hardly be expected to accept the approach proposed here. On the other hand, anyone who regards theology as an academic discipline, which is analytical rather than confessional, must surely accept the analysis of biblical God-language as a valid contribution. This model is designed for the academy rather than for the church, but its practical value should not be underestimated. J.A. Sanders has argued that Scripture ("canon" in his parlance) "functions, for the most part, to provide indications of the identity as well as the life-style of the on-going community which reads it."[25] It is "adaptable for life" and has in fact been adapted in a great variety of ways, beginning already in ancient Israel. The socio-historical approach to Biblical Theology lends itself well to rendering the Scriptures adaptable for life. The typical historical-critical procedure is to reconstruct the situation in which a text was composed. Such reconstructions are necessarily hypothetical, but they provide ways of imagining how a text might have made sense in a real-life situation. They thereby provide analogies for ways in which it might be appropriated in the present. The primary goal of Biblical Theology as proposed here is understanding rather than praxis, but it can also enhance, and certainly does not lessen, the applicability of a text.

The need for Biblical Theology arises from the fact that theological language is an important part of the text and is of crucial importance for most readers of the Bible. The very fact that this language is often taken uncritically ensures the need for a critical Biblical Theology. Its contribution to the history of religion is to ensure that the theological aspects of the texts are adequately explained, and neither glossed over as irrelevant nor too hastily translated into the categories of whatever discipline is of primary interest to the historian (cf. Gottwald's sociological reduction of Yahwism). This model of Biblical Theology, then, tries to guard on the one side against the mystification and apologetics of which the discipline has often been rightly accused, and on the other against the disinterest of secular critics in an important dimension of the text. Our concern here is to distinguish this critical approach to Biblical Theology from the confessional-dogmatic approach, most clearly represented by Childs. The value of this approach for the history of religion can best be judged by the light it sheds on the text.

The Case of Daniel

The theoretical issues confronting Biblical Theology may be illustrated by consideration of some aspects of the Book of Daniel. This book is usually relegated to the periphery of Biblical Theology and in many ways it is atypical of the Hebrew Bible. For that very reason it allows us to focus on some problems which are often glossed over in treatments of Biblical

Theology which focus on the more central texts of the Torah or Prophets.

The primary difference between the canonical approach of Childs and the socio-historical approach advocated here lies in the choice of context in which the book is viewed. For Childs, the context is the canon of Scripture itself. For a socio-historical approach the literary context is provided by the other writings of the time, especially the emerging genre of apocalypses,[26] while the historical context (for the complete Hebrew-Aramaic book) is the persecution of Antiochus Epiphanes and the Maccabean revolt. We will consider the significance of these different contexts for three problems: the pseudepigraphic attribution of the book, the portrayal of God and the hope for resurrection.

Pseudepigraphy

For anyone who accepts the results of historical criticism, the first problem posed by the Book of Daniel is that of pseudepigraphy. Few would now pose this problem in such extreme terms as the 19th century conservative Pusey: "It admits of no half-measures. It is either Divine or an imposture . . . The writer, were he not Daniel, must have lied on a most frightful scale."[27] It is now generally recognized that pseudepigraphy cannot be simply equated with deception. Yet, as Childs observes, "the issue continues to trouble the average lay reader,"[28] and some Biblical theologians too. Childs proposes to solve the problem by arguing "that the author of chs. 7-12 understood his role as one of filling in the details of the early visions of Daniel through the study of scripture and thus confirming Daniel's prophecies in the light of the events of contemporary history."[29] According to Childs, the author "had no new prophetic word directly from God. Rather he understood the sacred writings of the past as the medium through which God continued to make contemporary his divine revelation. His own identity had no theological significance and therefore he concealed it. It is basically to misunderstand the work of the Maccabean author to characterize it as a ruse by which to gain authority for himself, nor was it a conscious literary device. Rather, it arose from a profoundly theological sense of the function of prophecy which was continually illuminated through the continuing reinterpretation of scripture."[30]

This attempt to resolve the problem of pseudepigraphy has two aspects which require comment, one exegetical, the other theological. The exegetical claim is that ch. 7-12 are an amplification of the early visions of Daniel through the study of Scripture. The evidence offered in support of this claim is slight indeed. The strongest case involves the parallelism of chs. 2 and 7. In Childs' view ch. 7 attests to the truth of the four kingdom schema with reference to the new circumstances of the Maccabean period. This statement is true enough as far as it goes, but it does scant justice to ch. 7, which is presented as a vision in its own right, not as an interpretation. (Contrast Dan 9 in this respect.) The motif of the four kingdoms is overlain with the new imagery of beasts rising from the sea and a heavenly judgment scene. This imagery is not derived from Dan 2 and can be only partially explained from older Scripture. Childs' inner biblical exegesis leaves unexplained the contrast between the turbulent sea and the man-like figure who comes on the clouds, a contrast best understood against the background of ancient myth.[31] Ch. 2 provides one of the building blocks for Ch. 7, but the latter is a new and independent vision. Even in Ch. 9, where Daniel draws explicitly on older Scripture, the interpretation is not inhibited by the plain sense of the text (seventy years become seventy weeks of years) and so can scarcely be said to be bound by Scripture at all. The primary purpose of Dan 7-12 is to interpret the crisis of the Maccabean period. The interpretation of older Scripture is one means to that end.

The theological issue which Childs addresses here is the scandal of pseudepigraphy, with its implication of deception. It is not clear that his solution really alleviates that problem by construing the visions as elaborations of Dan 2. While the dream and interpretation in that chapter are surely older than chs. 7-12, their association with Nebuchadnezzar and Daniel is nonetheless fictional (at least according to the critical consensus which Childs appears to accept). In short, the problem of fictional attribution arises already in the oldest stratum of the Daniel tradition. It is not clear why a pseudepigraphic elaboration of an older, legendary, oracle should be less problematic than a new pseudepigraphic vision.

A socio-historical approach to the problem of pseudepigraphy places it in the wider context of the ancient, and especially the Hellenistic, world. It was a widespread phenomenon and its motivations were diverse.[32] The notion of forgery was certainly known and condemned in antiquity, but not all false attributions were made with the intention of deceiving. The composition of speeches in the name of famous individuals was an accepted convention of Greek historiography. Speeches in the name and style of great orators were composed as rhetorical exercises. The motivations associated with pseudepigraphy could differ from genre to genre. The case of an apocalypse attributed to Daniel or Enoch may be different from that of a letter attributed to a recent historical personality like Paul. There has been much speculation on the psychology of apocalyptic pseudepigraphy. It has been suggested that the authors saw themselves as heirs to traditions stretching back to Daniel or Enoch, and that their work was attributed to the source of the tradition by a concept of corporate personality[33] or that the visionary's *alter ego* is identified with a famous visionary of the past because of the nature of the experience.[34] There is ultimately no way to verify such theories, but at least they show that Childs' theory is not the only one which allows that the authors may have acted in good faith.

The effects of apocalyptic pseudepigraphy are more accessible than its motives. There can be no doubt that attribution to a famous ancient visionary enhanced the authority of the message, and indeed was necessary to permit the presentation of past history in the guise of prophecy. We must suppose that the common people accepted the attribution, or the message would lose much of its effect. On the other hand, the immediate circle of the authors must have been aware of the manner in which the works were actually produced. In view of the urgency of the message, we may assume that the authors and their immediate circles considered the literary fiction justified and that it did not detract from the religious value of the revelation. There is no self-conscious reflection on the need for a "noble lie" such as we find in Plato.[35] Yet, however we understand the psychology of the apocalyptic writers, the phenomenon of pseudepigraphy helps underline the fact that their works are fictions, works of imagination, whose truth is of the same order as that of Plato's myths.[36]

There is no inherent reason why designating Daniel as fiction should pose a problem for Biblical Theology.[37] The fact that Daniel contains so much historical material, both garbled (chs. 1-6) and accurate (ch. 11) confuses the reader's generic expectations. A socio-historical approach frankly recognizes the fictional, imaginative character of the book, and denies that its theological value is thereby prejudiced. That value must be assessed in terms of the substantive content of the book, rather than of the literary form in which it is presented, although appreciation of the literary form is crucial for our understanding of the theological content.

The Portrayal of God

Childs makes a valid point when he insists that "the witness of the book is theocentric" and adds that "Neither the faith of Daniel nor that of a Maccabean author can be made the object of the biblical witness when it is divorced from the hope which evoked the obedient response."[38] It is somewhat surprising, then, that he has little to say about the portrayal of God in Daniel and contents himself with general statements about "the purpose of God" to allow Israel to languish for a time and to bring in the kingdom suddenly, by divine intervention.

There is, naturally, much more to be said about the God of Daniel.[39] The main lines of the portrayal are in accordance with other Old Testament books: God is the universal judge, who is sovereign over the kingdoms of the earth. There are also some distinctive aspects. God appears more remote from humanity than in the older books because of the increased prominence of angelic mediators and God's purpose has taken on a deterministic character. While older prophecy frequently allowed the possibility that God would "repent" (e.g. Amos 7, Hos 11), this possibility is no longer envisaged.[40] Biblical theologians who seek to extract a consistent picture of God from the Old Testament often disregard these aspects of Daniel's God as atypical. Childs speaks vaguely of "theological tension"[41] and seems to leave its resolution to the Spirit.

For a socio-historical approach, the issue is not whether there really is an irrevocable divine plan for history, but why the author of Daniel portrayed God in this way. This question must be viewed in the context of the cosmological views current in the Hellenistic age. Many scholars have posited influence of Babylonian determinism on apocalyptic literature and on Daniel in particular.[42] Deterministic cosmology, possibly influenced by Babylonian conceptions, was propagated in the Hellenistic world by the Stoics. Closer to Daniel, very similar views of God and history were developed in the early apocalypses of Enoch, some of which, at least, ante-date Daniel. Daniel, in short, was a child of his time. The book's conception of God cannot be regarded simply as a projection inspired by the Maccabean crisis, but it was evidently found appropriate and meaningful in view of those circumstances.

The problem presented by the deterministic God of Daniel is essentially the same as that presented by the mythology and cosmology of the New Testament, so eloquently addressed by Bultmann.[43] The portrayal of God is imbedded in a dated, time-conditioned view of the world which is no longer accepted. Bultmann proposed to interpret the theocentric myths in terms of an anthropocentric understanding of human existence. For all his insistence on the theocentric character of Daniel, Childs is not as far from this position as we might expect. Like Bultmann, he abstracts from most of the particulars of the biblical text, and affirms only the general trustworthiness of God. The appropriate human response is faith and obedience,[44] but the precise object of these virtues is left vague and indeterminate.[45] There is, of course, a fundamental difference in attitude. Childs leaves the application of the text to the guidance of the Spirit. Bultmann, in contrast, sought to de-mystify theology and placed the emphasis on human decision. The point of analogy, however, is that both finally disregard the particularities of the biblical text.

Any theological approach which wants to appropriate the message of a biblical book must abstract to some degree from its particular circumstances. Childs is right that such a process of abstraction was entailed by the process of canonization, and Bultmann is right that apocalyptic cosmology is no longer accepted by anyone in the modern world. Yet the historical particularities retain more of their significance in a socio-historical approach than they do for Childs or Bultmann. The

Book of Daniel provides a case-study which is potentially "adaptable for life" (in Sanders' phrase). To apply it properly we must appreciate that it is not a general philosophy of life, but a reaction to specific circumstances. Daniel's obedience to the food laws in ch. 1 is located in a very specific situation: it enables him and his companions to preserve their identity in the Diaspora. The virtue of the act cannot be divorced from the circumstances in which it takes place. Again, the characterization of Gentile kingdoms differs noticeably between chs. 1-6 and 7-12. The portrayal in ch. 7 is specifically a response to the Antiochan persecution, and is only justified in analogous situations. Not every Gentile kingdom is appropriately identified as a beast from the sea. The applicability of the visions requires an analogy between our situation and that of the author, and the specificity of the author's situation is therefore important.

The portrayal of God cannot be taken as revealed truth but is a way of construing the world which led to a particular course of action. That portrayal must now be evaluated both in terms of its credibility in view of modern science and in terms of the values which it supported. In any case it provides a model for imagining God which must be adapted in the light of new circumstances. The fact that Daniel's portrayal of God is inconsistent with other biblical portrayals is no longer problematic if we look on the Bible as a store of models appropriate to different contexts rather than as a consistent whole.[46]

The Hope of Resurrection

Our final theological issue from the Book of Daniel concerns the belief in resurrection in ch. 12. As is well known, this is the only passage in the Hebrew Bible which speaks unambiguously of the resurrection of individuals for reward or punishment. Childs minimizes the novelty of the belief, claiming that "the Old Testament provided the grounds on which both later Jews and Christians developed their understanding of the afterlife."[47] This is an oversimplification. The Old Testament contains some significant precedents in the notion of the fullness of life in the presence of God, in the Psalms, and in prophetic passages which speak of the resurrection of the corporate people (Ezek 37; Isa 26: 19) and these surely facilitated later adoption of the belief in resurrection.[48] Yet it remains true that the predominant witness of the Old Testament is to the expectation of mere survival of the shade in Sheol[49] and Ecclesiastes, one of the books closest in date to Daniel, bitterly disputes the notion that the lot of humanity is any different from that of the beasts (Eccles 3:19-22). There can be no suggestion that belief in resurrection was implicit in the Old Testament before Daniel.

It would be too simple to attribute the origin of the belief in Daniel simply to reflection on Scripture. Such reflection played a part, as can be seen from echoes of the terminology of Isa 26 and 66.[50] Yet it now appears that the idea of resurrection was first developed in Judaism in the Enoch tradition (*1 Enoch* 22), where it is presented in the context of mythical geography and is indebted to Babylonian and Greek traditions.[51] Daniel has a point of affinity with the Enoch tradition when it associates the risen sages with the stars (cf. *1 Enoch* 104). It is very probable that Daniel was influenced by the non-canonical Enoch material as well as by the texts in Isaiah. Moreover, the belief in Daniel cannot be divorced from the historical context of the Antiochan persecution, in which people suffered death for their faith. In view of the early development of the Enoch tradition, the belief in resurrection cannot be regarded simply as a reaction to the persecution, but the historical situation surely prompted Daniel's acceptance of the idea.

In the context of the Book of Daniel itself, the belief in resurrection is not presented as a reflection on Scripture but as part of a revelation. The revelation poses its own theological problems. In part it consists of prophecies after the fact (11:2-39), in part of erroneous predictions (11:40-45) and finally of the eschatological prophecy. The non-fulfillment of the concluding predictions did not discredit the book in antiquity, as Childs has rightly noted. The fact that the eschaton did not come as the author expected does not prove that it will not come at all. Like the use of pseudepigraphy, however, it should warn us not to take the predictions at face value. They are works of the imagination, attempts to make sense of historical experience. Whether they construe reality correctly, in their hope of justification after death, must await eschatological verification. For the present we can only discuss how the belief arose and how it functioned.

The function of afterlife is especially clear in the Book of Daniel. It is the hope which empowers the martyrs to lay down their lives in the time of persecution.[52] In the context of the Maccabean crisis it offered one model of conduct. There were other models available, including that of the zealot Phinehas from Num 25, cited in 1 Mac 2:26 as the paradigm of the Maccabees. There is no guarantee as to which model is the right one in any given situation. What Daniel offers is a way of looking at the world in which non-violence and martyrdom make sense. The attractiveness of that vision is not necessarily undermined by the knowledge that it is a work of imagination rather than univocal fact, an object of hope rather than of knowledge.

Conclusion

If nothing else our discussion has shown that the alternatives of Biblical Theology and History of Religion are a good deal more ambiguous than they appeared when Dr. Ryan posed them to his students twenty years ago. There are various models of Biblical Theology, coloured in different degrees by dogmatic presuppositions. It can be viewed as a normative discipline or as an area of Historical Theology. On the other hand the History of Religion may or may not be construed so as to address theological questions. Childs may fairly claim to have overcome the inconsistency of the Biblical Theology Movement by making his dogmatic presuppositions fully explicit. In doing so, however, he has shut his Biblical Theology off from dialogue with other areas of biblical research, especially sociology, and thereby diminished his ability to explain the text. His work is also open to the charge of undue mystification. The proposal advanced here moves in the opposite direction from Childs and fully embraces historical criticism. The History of Religion approach, then, is not an alternative to be avoided but an ally to be utilised. While it may be difficult for any Christian to avoid dogmatic prejudices and apologetics in addressing theological questions, it is not impossible and it is an ideal worthy of our aspirations. Such an approach will not satisfy those who see theology as an essentially confessional enterprise, but it does affirm the possibility of a Biblical Theology which is consistent with the regnant historical-critical method.

Notes

1. *Old Testament Theology* (2 vols.; trans. D.M.G. Stalker; New York 1962-1965).
2. I am not aware that Dr. Ryan's views on this subject were ever published.
3. J. Sandys-Wunsch and L. Eldredge, "J.P. Gabler and the Distinction between Biblical and Dogmatic Theology: Translation, Commentary and Discussion of his Originality", *SJT* 33 (1980) 133-158.
4. B.C. Ollenburger, "Biblical Theology. Situating the Discipline", *Understanding the Word. Essays in Honor of Bernhard W. Anderson*, J.T. Butler, E.W. Conrad and B.C. Ollenburger (eds.) (JSOTSup 37; Sheffield 1985) 43.
5. *Über Aufgabe und Methode der sogenannten neutestamentlichen Theologie* (Göttingen 1897). Trans. "The Task and Methods of New Testament Theology", R. Morgan, *The Nature of New Testament Theology* (London 1973) 68-116.
6. W. Eichrodt, *Theology of the Old Testament* (Philadelphia 1961) Vol. 1, 31-33.
7. *God Who Acts. Biblical Theology as Recital* (London 1952) 117.
8. *Old Testament Theology in a Canonical Context* (Philadelphia 1986) 8.
9. L. Gilkey, "Cosmology, Ontology and the Travail of Biblical Language", *JR* 41 (1961) 194-205; J. Barr, *Old and New in Interpretation* (New York 1966).
10. *Biblical Theology in Crisis* (Philadelphia 1970).
11. Modern hermeneutics has repeatedly insisted that there is no interpretation without presuppositions. See especially H.G. Gadamer, *Truth and Method* (New York 1982) and P. Ricoeur, *Essays on Biblical Interpretation*, L. Mudge (ed.) (Philadelphia 1980) and the comments of P. Stuhlmacher, *Historical Criticism and the Theological Interpretation of Scripture* (Philadelphia 1977).
12. On the principles of historical criticism see Van A. Harvey, *The Historian and the Believer* (New York 1966) 13-19, adapting the work of E. Troeltsch, "Ueber historische und dogmatische Methode in der Theologie", *Gesammelte Schriften II* (Aalen 1913) 729-753. Of crucial importance is Troeltsch's principle of criticism, according to which historical assertions can claim only a greater or lesser degree of probability and must be always open to revision.

13. See J.J. Collins, "The 'Historical' Character of the Old Testament in Recent Biblical Theology", *CBQ* 41 (1979) 185-204.
14. R.A. Oden, *The Bible without Theology* (San Francisco 1987) viii.
15. N.K. Gottwald, *The Tribes of Yahweh* (Maryknoll 1979) 667-709.
16. Especially J. Barr, *Holy Scripture. Canon, Authority, Criticism* (Philadelphia 1983) *passim*.
17. See J. Barton, *Reading the Old Testament* (Philadelphia 1984) 77-103.
18. *Old Testament Theology* 15.
19. Many biblical theologians appear to work with dogmatic presuppositions which are not adequately articulated. Rolf Knierim's view of "The Task of Biblical Theology", *Horizons in Biblical Theology* 6 (1984) 25-57, is to establish "the criteria of accountability of what is to be confessed." These criteria are not derived from frequency of attestation in the Old Testament or because they occur in particular settings but "because of the decisive theological arguments themselves" (48). Knierim does not explain however what makes these arguments decisive.
20. Such a position is advocated by S. Ogden, "The Authority of Scripture for Theology", *Interpretation* 30 (1976) 242-261, among others.
21. I have proposed this view in an essay "Is a Critical Biblical Theology Possible?" at a meeting at the University of California, San Diego, in May 1986, to be published in the proceedings of that meeting, edited by Baruch Halpern and William Propp.
22. The work of P.D. Hanson, *Dynamic Transcendence* (Philadelphia 1978) and *The Diversity of Scripture* (Philadelphia 1982) makes full use of critical scholarship but still construes theology as a confessional activity, in a manner reminiscent of G.E. Wright's "projection of faith into facts". In an academic context this is open to the charge of mystification, although it may be quite appropriate in an ecclesiastical setting.
23. Some of the more literary approaches to Old Testament Theology are open to criticism on this point, e.g. D. Patrick, *The Rendering of God in the Old Testament* (Philadelphia 1981); T.E. Fretheim, *The Suffering of God. An Old Testament Perspective* (Philadelphia 1984). This is also true of some attempts to apply Process Theology to the Old Testament. See W.A. Beardslee and D.J. Lull, *Old Testament Interpretation from a Process Perspective*, *Semeia* 24 (1982).
24. Childs, *Old Testament Theology* 15.
25. "Adaptable for Life: The Nature and Function of Canon", *Magnalia Dei. The Mighty Acts of God; Essays on the Bible and Archeology in Memory of G. Ernest Wright*, F.M. Cross et al. (eds.) (Garden City, N.Y. 1976) 537. See also his *Canon and Community* (Philadelphia 1983) and *From Sacred Story to Sacred Text. Canon as Paradigm* (Philadelphia 1987). Sanders' approach is sometimes confused with that of Childs because of the confusing label "canon criticism", but in fact it is quite different. Sanders' approach is sociological, in so far as he treats the text in terms of the needs of the community. Childs also professes to base his approach on the

actual function of the text in the religious community, but there is no evidence that "the canonical form" of the text was a matter of concern for anyone in ancient Judaism or early Christianity.

26. See J.J. Collins, *The Apocalyptic Imagination* (New York 1984).
27. E.B. Pusey, *Daniel the Prophet* (Oxford 1865) 75.
28. *Introduction to the Old Testament as Scripture* (Philadelphia 1979) 616.
29. *Ibid.* 616.
30. *Ibid.* 618.
31. On the imagery of Daniel 7 see J.J. Collins, *The Apocalyptic Vision of the Book of Daniel* (Missoula 1977) 95-106; J. Day, *God's Conflict with the Dragon and the Sea* (Cambridge 1985) 151-167.
32. See B.M. Metzger, "Literary Forgeries and Canonical Pseudepigrapha", *JBL* 91 (1972) 3-24.
33. So D.S. Russell, *The Method and Message of Jewish Apocalyptic* (Philadelphia 1964) 133-134.
34. So C. Rowland, *The Open Heaven* (New York 1982) 245.
35. Plato, *Republic* 382C, 414B, 459D.
36. On the concept of myth in Greek apocalypses see H.D. Betz, "The Problem of Apocalyptic Genre in Greek and Hellenistic Literature", *Apocalypticism in the Mediterranean World and the Near East*, D. Hellholm (ed.) (Tübingen 1983) 577-597.
37. Compare the general proposal of Paul Ricoeur "to place the originary expressions of biblical faith under the sign of the poetic function of language." (*Essays on Biblical Interpretation* 103).
38. *Introduction to the Old Testament as Scripture* 621.
39. See M. Delcor, "Le Dieu des Apocalypticiens", *La Notion Biblique de Dieu* (BETL XLI; J. Coppens [ed.] Leuven 1974) 211-228.
40. On the "repentance" of God, see especially Freitheim, *The Suffering of God* 45-59.
41. *Understanding the Old Testament as Scripture* 622.
42. So Delcor, "Le Dieu des Apocalypticiens" 215.
43. E.g. "New Testament and Mythology", *Kerygma and Myth*, H.W. Bartsch (ed.) (New York 1961) 1-44.
44. Cf. Bultmann, *ibid.* 44.
45. E.g. where Daniel is specifically obedient to the Jewish food laws (Dan 1) Childs does not specify what obedience requires.
46. On the contextual approach to Biblical Theology see J. Goldingay, *Theological Diversity and the Authority of the Old Testament* (Grand Rapids 1987) 29-58.
47. *Old Testament Theology in a Canonical Context* 245.
48. See also H. Gese, "Death in the Old Testament", *Essays on Biblical Theology* (Minneapolis 1981) 34-59.
49. See B. Vawter, "Intimations of Immortality and the Old Testament", *The Path of Wisdom. Biblical Investigations* (Wilmington 1986) 140-160.
50. G.W.E. Nickelsburg, *Resurrection, Immortality and Eternal Life in Intertestamental Judaism* (Cambridge, MA 1972) 17-20.

51. J.J. Collins, "The Place of Apocalypticism in the Religion of Israel", *Ancient Israelite Religion*, P.D. Miller, P.D. Hanson and S.D. McBride (eds.) (Philadelphia 1987) 549. Reflection on the disappearance of the biblical Enoch may also have played a part in the development.
52. J.J. Collins, "Apocalyptic Eschatology as the Transcendence of Death", *Visionaries and Their Apocalypses*, P.D. Hanson (ed.) (Philadelphia 1983) 61-84 (originally in *CBQ* 36 [1974] 21-43). Compare Childs, *Introduction to the Old Testament as Scripture* 622.

THE LAST OF THE REPHAIM

John F. Healey, *University of Durham*

In a memorial volume such as this I feel uninhibited in beginning my contribution on a personal note. Indeed, in this particular case, a personal note is especially appropriate, since I am taking up a subject on which Dermot Ryan himself wrote.

I encountered Professor Ryan in 1967 in University College, Dublin, where I had decided upon Hebrew as a worthwhile pursuit secondary to my intended Philosophy degree. In that period immediately after Vatican II biblical studies were enjoying a new-found popularity among Roman Catholics, though few were willing to go to the length of actually learning Hebrew. Fortunately there were several of us knocking on the door of the Professor of Semitic Languages more or less at the same time, at the end of a long corridor in U.C.D.'s old premises in central Dublin. Inside we found not a forbidding professor but a warm-hearted pastor who was concerned with our personal well-being as well as our academic development. This combination of personal and academic care for students was a characteristic of Dermot Ryan's which I came greatly to admire. They were two sides of the man: Father Ryan was the pastor, Professor Ryan the academic.

Professor Ryan trained us in a highly professional way, so that at the end of three years we really knew our Hebrew (and Syriac and Greek). He also inspired us, especially when he was side-tracked into revealing his own theories and his wide knowledge of biblical and theological studies. It was in such asides that I first heard of his interest in Ugaritic and specifically of his interest in the problem of the Ugaritic and Hebrew Rephaim, which had been the topic of his M.A. thesis. Also in his lectures on the Psalms he was certainly one of the first university teachers to make use of the still incomplete commentary of Mitchell Dahood, whom he had known in Rome. Dahood was, of course, at the forefront of the application of Ugaritic studies to the Bible and he was particularly interested in the importance of the afterlife in the Psalms. Professor Ryan's enthusiasm for these new ideas fixed them in my imagination. When I eventually (having been converted from Philosophy to Semitics) came to choose a subject for my doctoral thesis, the Ugaritic ideology of the dead and the afterlife became the central theme.

I owe a tremendous amount to Dermot Ryan. In subsequent years he took a lively interest in my progress. From his own pocket he helped financially with academic research projects which would otherwise have been a burden upon my young family. My wife Elizabeth too, formerly a U.C.D. student in Archaeology and Greek, was the recipient of much kindness and help from him. In ways which will never be told Dermot Ryan affected our lives, carrying out his priestly role. It is thus with great pleasure that in my contribution to this memorial volume I am able to express my gratitude to him by making his work on the Rephaim known more widely.

Dermot Ryan's M.A. thesis for the National University of Ireland, *Rpum and Rephaim. A Study in the Relationship between the rpum of Ugarit and the Rephaim of the Old Testament*, dated 1954, was written at a time when Ugaritic studies had hardly got off the ground. In the introduction he acknowledged the help of Monsignor Patrick Boylan (another cleric-academic who should have received wider recognition) and Fr. René Follet S.J. of the Pontifical Biblical Institute in Rome. The bibliography (pp. iii-vii) shows the primitive state of Ugaritic studies at that time. Very little had been written on the Rephaim problem, so that Ryan himself had to start virtually from scratch. I remember him telling me that it was only at the very last minute that he was able to add reference to D.J. Wiseman's edition of the Alalakh tablets, published in 1953.

Surprisingly little had been added to the published literature by 1972 when I began to work on the Rephaim problem under the supervision of Professor Wiseman as part of a thesis on the Ugaritic conceptions of the underworld and afterlife. Indeed, when I visited Mitchell Dahood in Rome in 1975 to seek his advice, he could foresee no progress on the subject of the Rephaim until more Ugaritic texts on the subject should appear. Almost immediately thereafter new texts *did* appear, followed by an information explosion in the form of numerous articles on different aspects of the question. It is not my intention here to add yet more opinions to those already expressed. My own views have been incorporated in various publications on matters related to the dead. Rather, the focus of my attention will be Ryan's own thesis, which was unfortunately never published. What follows is in three parts: (a) a summary of the thesis, (b) a brief account of the new evidence which has emerged and (c) comment on Ryan's thesis in the light of the new evidence.

(a) The Problem

The problem of the Rephaim was seen at the time of Ryan's research as essentially a biblical one, upon which some light might be thrown by (relatively) new evidence from Ugarit. This is, of course, an approach which dominated much of Ugaritic studies in its early days. There was less attention than there is now to inner-Ugaritic problems and a more confident attitude to the use of extra-biblical evidence in the illumination of biblical problems. One often detects the belief that God had given us things like Ugaritic specifically to help us to understand the Bible, though I hasten to state that this was not Professor Ryan's attitude. With regard to the Rephaim problem, suffice it to say that from today's perspective it was a little optimistic to hope for light on the biblical Rephaim from a study of the Ugaritic Rephaim/*rp'um*, since the nature of the latter was at that stage almost totally shrouded in obscurity! Ryan's thesis is, however, scrupulously careful not to exaggerate the relevance or clarity of the Ugaritic evidence. Indeed, as we shall see, he was, perhaps, over-cautious in this regard.

The "problem" of the Rephaim in the Hebrew and Phoenician sources centres on the following facts. In Hebrew and Phoenician sources we find reference to the Rephaim (Hebrew *r^epā'īm*, Phoenician *rp'm*) in two entirely different contexts with no apparent connection between the two usages. In the Hebrew Pentateuch and historical books they appear as a pre-Israelite people commonly associated with Jordan (e.g., Deut 2:11; 2:20; 3:11; 3:13; Josh 12:4; 13:12; 17:15; Gen 14:5; 15:20), though sometimes they are specifically located in the area south of Jerusalem.[1] In Hebrew poetic tradition (including prophecy and wisdom; e.g., Ps 88:11; Isa 14:9; 26:14; 26:19) and in Phoenician inscriptions of the sixth and fifth centuries B.C. from Sidon (the Tabnith and Eshmunazar inscriptions[2]) they appear as the dead, the inhabitants of the underworld or Sheol.

The Ugaritic evidence available in 1954 was, as has been implied, rather scanty and very unclear, though an important group of texts, often called the "Rephaim Texts" (*KTU* 1.20-22), had been published.[3] There were also a few references to the Ugaritic *rp'um* in other literary texts, the "legendary" Keret and Aqhat texts (*KTU* 1.15 III 2-4, 13-15 and 1.19 I 37; 1.17 I 18, etc.) and the Baal mythological cycle (*KTU* 1.6 VI 43-53). It was on the basis of these that Ryan tackled the problem, having, it may be noted, very little available in the form of previous work on the subject by other scholars.[4]

The thesis begins with discussion of the etymology of the term Rephaim and of personal names containing the root *rp'*. Four major chapters are then devoted to a detailed study of the Ugaritic Rephaim Texts. These are very fragmentary and although much is tentative Ryan's detailed philological discussion remains valuable. The texts are translated as far as that is possible. While it would not be useful to go through every interpretative comment in detail, we can at least note the general drift of the conclusions. The *rp'um* in these texts are, according to Ryan, of considerable military importance and are connected with the *maryannu* warrior class known from other ancient sources (80ff.). They are in demand and invited to banquets because of the services they could render. Left open is the difficult question of how the texts were to be interpreted on the mythological or ritual level, since it is clear that the references cannot be to a warrior class going about its everyday business.

The following chapters deal with the other apparent references to the *rp'um* in the texts. Again emphasis is placed on the *rp'um* as chariot-warriors like the *maryannu* and king Keret and Dan'il are seen as associated with these. The name would be tribal and associated with Amorite tradition. It is argued, therefore, that the *rp'um* were historical figures who also have a mythological garb. The hymn from the end of the Baal cycle (*KTU* 1.6 VI 43-53) would also associate the *rp'um* warriors with the sun-goddess. Ryan's tenth chapter provides a synthesis according to which the *rp'um* were a distinguished group of chariot-warriors, though the name would be essentially tribal, referring to an Amorite clan. They were real people who were eventually promoted to divine rank.

Again in dealing with the biblical Rephaim Ryan assembles evidence (113-141) to suggest that they may well have been historical, at least in essence, even if there was later exaggeration of their size. Though he connects the historical Rephaim of the Old Testament with the Ugaritic *rp'um*, he cannot find any link between the Ugaritic *rp'um* and the Rephaim of Sheol.

I will turn in due course to the question of the revision of Professor Ryan's conclusions in the light of the newer evidence. He cannot be criticised for not knowing what was only later discovered. There are, however, two points in his argument which are hard to sustain, even on the earlier evidence, though it must be admitted that there is necessarily an element of hindsight in this judgement.

(i) In the hymn in *KTU* 1.6 VI the following terms are found in parallel with each other: *rp'im*/*'ilnym*/*'ilm*/*mtm*. Ryan virtually ignored the possibility that *mtm* might refer to the dead, despite the fact that *rᵉpā'īm* and *mētīm* are found parallel to each other in Hebrew (Ps 88:11; Isa 26:14; 26:19). Again the context is the control of the *rp'um* by Šapšu, the sun-goddess, while the Mesopotamian sun-deity, Šamaš, is variously called *šar eṭimmē*, *muballiṭ mīti* and *bēl mīti*, "lord of the dead", etc.[5] In the light of these considerations the connection with the dead, found not only in the Bible but also in the Phoenician tradition which is the direct successor to the Ugaritic tradition, was very probable on the existing evidence.

(ii) The attempt to connect the *rp'um* with the *maryannu* was always rather doubtful. The interpretation of the title *rp'um* as in effect a class term is in any case weakened greatly by the absence of the term from the lists of terms for social groupings known from the texts.[6] Also, as has been shown more recently through a re-examination of the evidence by H. Reviv,[7] chariot-owning was not really an exclusive characteristic of the *maryannu* in the late 2nd millennium. And in *KTU* 1.22 II 24 there may be evidence of the *rp'um* using asses as well as horses. The situation thus is far more complex than Ryan indicated.

(b) The New Evidence

There is new evidence directly on the subject of the *rp'um* as well as considerable indirect evidence. Many new treatments of the topic have been published as a result of these developments. The new texts which have specific bearing on this topic are the following:

(i) *KTU* 1.161 is a cultic text concerned with a ritual analogous to the Mesopotamian *kispum* ritual, in which the ancient kings of Ugarit are called *rp'um* and invited to a banquet for the dead ancestors.[8] The purpose of the rite is to bring blessing upon the reigning royal family.

This is unequivocal evidence for the term *rp'um* referring to a group of the dead. At the same time it confirms the royal connection and suggests why Keret in *KTU* 1.15 III 2-4, 13-15 is promoted among the *rp'um*: he is in fact being blessed with ancestral apotheosis. This goes a long way to explaining away the misleading impression given by the Keret text that *rp'um*, like the parallel *qbṣ dtn*, is a gentilic term. It is not. It refers to the venerated ancestral spirits, the former kings. To be counted among them is clearly a good thing, a blessing, like being counted among the saints of heaven.

(ii) Hand in hand with this text goes another which was not available to Ryan, *KTU* 1.113:12-26, which contains a list of the kings of the Ugaritic dynasty. Each name is prefixed with the title *'il*, "divine one", used virtually as a determinative. The kings were *rp'um* and *'ilm*. This fits well with the use of the latter in close proximity to the former in other texts. These kings may also have been venerated as the *mlkm* in the so-called Ugaritic pantheon list, and a similar usage in a similar context occurs at Mari.[9]

(iii) Ryan was firmly of the view that there was no deity called *rp'u*. In fact this divine title appeared in a text (*KTU* 1.108:1, 19, 22) published in 1968, where *rp'u mlk 'lm* plays a part in a mythical banquet. The precise interpretation of this as to whether the title refers to Baal or some other deity remains disputed, but in any case it shows that *rp'u* can be read as a divine title and it is consistent with the interpretation of *rp'u* in *KTU* 1.22 I 8 as a divine title. The *rp'um* can thus be seen as associated with this deity.

A number of important articles and sections of books have since appeared which try to integrate all this material. Without going into all the varieties of interpretation, note may be made of two. A. Caquot's article in the *Dictionnaire de la Bible: Supplément*[10] is a masterly survey of the whole subject, while the treatment in K. Spronk's Kampen thesis[11] shows above all the revolution in our knowledge of this aspect of Ugaritic belief during the last fifteen years. There is in these and the many other contributions[12] a large measure of agreement on the essential nature of the Ugaritic *rp'um* seen in the light of the new evidence. My own view is, therefore, not atypical.[13]

The Ugaritic *rp'um* are the ancestral spirits of the royal family (and, perhaps, other associated heroic figures), regularly invoked in rituals analogous to the Mesopotamian *kispum* ritual, in which the text called the "Genealogy of the Hammurapi Dynasty" was used in a recital of names of ancestral spirits.[14] Text *KTU* 1.161 is the ritual text for this cult, while *KTU* 1.20-22, the Rephaim Texts, are mythical and were probably recited in association with the ritual. They remain fairly obscure, but the central element of the invitation of the *rp'um* to a banquet is clear enough.

It is not easy to tell from the evidence what the original meaning of the term *rp'um* was. There is probably a connection with the root *rp'* with a meaning related to "healing", but there is no contextual evidence to prove this. The term might simply associate the dead person with ancestral apotheosis and the saving power of Rapi'u, the head of the *rp'um*, i.e. *rp'um* might mean "associates of Rapi'u". The term is not a gentilic in the normal sense, though, of course, if it meant "followers of Rapi'u", it might have been analogous to our use of Benedictine or Nestorian! In effect, however, it was used as a common noun for the great heroes of the past.

It is noteworthy that in the Phoenician tradition, the heir to the Ugaritic tradition, the term has clearly lost its specific associations with the ancestral cult and has become democratised so as to refer to the dead in general. Only one Ugaritic text can be interpreted as containing this wider notion, the hymn at the end of the Baal cycle (*KTU* 1.6 VI 43ff.), but even there it is possible to argue that the *rp'um* were a rather specific group among the dead. The same text is the only one to make the connection directly with the underworld (if we are correct in assuming that this is implied as part of Šapsŭ's realm). It may be that the connection with the underworld became more explicit as the term was widened to refer to all the dead, this not being a prominent part of the principal usage of the term in the other Ugaritic texts.

(c) Where Does This Leave Dermot Ryan's Work?

In one sense, of course, the new evidence renders irrelevant many of his conclusions on the underworld aspect. Certainly, it would now seem, he was wrong in believing that the Rephaim of Sheol were purely a later development. Even if the simple equation with all the dead and the specific connection with Sheol are late, the seeds of this later development are clearly present in the Late Bronze Age tradition of Ugarit as we now know it. The Ugaritic *rp'um* have far more to do with the underworld than with the *maryannu*!

However, the general burden of Ryan's argument, that the Rephaim of Ugarit and Israel were historical groups connected with the Amorites, remains, at least on the Israelite side, a real issue and there is still much to be said for Ryan's view.

Many authors have doubted that the pre-Israelite Rephaim really existed historically. Thus W.O.E. Oesterley and T.H. Robinson[15] regarded them as legendary like the Anakim, Emim, etc. who are often mentioned with them. There are two pieces of evidence which could be taken to point to this conclusion. Firstly the Rephaim were regarded as giants (Deut 2:10-11; 3:11, etc.). Secondly, their name does not always have the definite article where it would be expected with a gentilic. Rather it seems originally to have been descriptive: the attempt to interpret it as "weak ones" (root *rph*) has a long history.[16] On this view the word might have been secondarily treated as a gentilic. Also some of the gigantic features of the Rephaim might have come to be emphasised because they were connected in popular tradition with the megalithic monuments of the Jordan area (Deut 3:11, where we find Og's bed).

At first glance this sceptical view seems to be confirmed by the Ugaritic evidence, suggesting as it does, that any gentilic aspect to the title *rp'um* is unlikely. However, we cannot dismiss too readily the considerable amount of historical detail in the Hebrew texts in question. Apart from their appearance in Gen 14, which many would regard as of doubtful historical value, we are told that the Rephaim held the territory of the Ammonites and Moabites (Deut 2:20; 2:10-11), while Og, the last of the Rephaim and king of the Amorites, ruled Bashan (Deut 3:8). It is true that J.R. Bartlett[17] has suggested that the link with Jordan is unhistorical, since the term is used as a secondary designation by the Deuteronomic writer in that context, but this only emphasises the authenticity of the connection of the Rephaim with the area south of Jerusalem.[18]

Also it should be noted that the exaggeration of the size of these people can easily be explained as an attempt to magnify the Israelites' victories and the power of their god (Num 13:32). There are, in fact, signs of an underlying awareness in the Old Testament tradition that the Rephaim were of normal size. Thus their size is not always referred to in the texts, and, as Ryan pointed out (128), success against the Rephaim does not seem to give the Israelites confidence in the face of their other enemies (Deut 9:1ff.). The exaggeration was continued in the literary tradition in Pss 135:11; 136:20 and Amos 2:9, probably reinforced by association with monumental structures like the megaliths. But this does not prove that there was no historical kernel to the later elaboration. Indeed one cannot ignore the independent tradition of giants in Palestine reflected in the 13th century Papyrus Anastasi I.[19] But even setting this aside, at the very least it is possible that the Israelites fought or heard of memorably mighty men, some of whom may actually have been called Rephaites or descendants of Rapha.

Finally, the explanation of the term as "weak ones" cannot be upheld. It must be a secondary feature, a false etymology of a later date, since all the evidence points to the spelling with *aleph* and connection with the root *rp'*.

As Caquot notes, the view that the Ugaritic *rp'um* might have a gentilic sense has been almost totally abandonned in view of the Ugaritic evidence now available. M. Heltzer, however, continued to defend it.[20] He finds it in the texts already cited from the Aqhat and Keret legends. The latter needs no discussion, since the Keret blessing can be understood perfectly well in the context of the ancestral *rp'um* and was referred to above. Of Dan'il's title in the Aqhat cycle, *mt hrnmy/mt rp'i* (*KTU* 1.19 I 37, etc.), we need only say here that it is much disputed and need not be interpreted in a gentilic sense. Indeed, *KTU* 1.20 II 7 makes the connection between Dan'il and the *rp'um*, so that it is most natural to take his title as associating him with the same context – which is certainly to do with the ancestral cult.

Heltzer would go further and suggest a connection between these supposedly tribal *rp'um* and the Rabbeans, an Amorite tribe evidenced in the Mari texts.[21] The connection is, however, tenuous and has to overcome numerous difficulties including the rather different form of the name in the Mari texts. Heltzer does not attempt to connect these Rabbeans with the Hebrew Rephaim, though if his main contention were correct, it would be natural to take this next step.

If, finally, we are to look for a way of making sense of the Hebrew and Phoenician evidence, it is obvious that we must start with the Ugaritic situation which is now very clear and can throw light on the Hebrew and Phoenician sources in a more satisfactory way than was possible in 1954.

It seems likely that the term Rephaim came to ancient Israel principally from the context of Canaanite religion, with two different aspects of the original Canaanite concept becoming detached from each other. The religious context of the significance of the Rephaim, the ancestral cult of the heroic dead, would have been lost completely to the Israelites and was, perhaps, never properly understood by them. To the Israelites the Rephaim would be simply legendary heroes of the Canaanite/Amorite past. By this means they came to be associated with other legendary prehistoric inhabitants of the land and perhaps connected with megalithic tombs and other Cyclopean monuments which were left behind by the former inhabitants. On the other hand there is sufficient specific evidence to suggest that the Israelites may well have encountered an actual tribe called Rephaites or the like, perhaps in southern Judah. The Old Testament tradition has (almost inevitably) confused these two, emphasising gigantic features to magnify victories and the power of the Israelite God. At the same time Israelite poets and writers, who drew so much from the Canaanites, found the term Rephaim convenient within the literary tradition as a term for the dead, perhaps at first the royal dead. In the absence of the cult of the royal dead the term Rephaim would have come to refer simply to the dead in general. But this process of democratisation of the term was not confined to Israel: it is also characteristic of the Phoenician tradition so far as we can tell and this trend may have resulted from the general breakdown of the Rephaim cult with the collapse of Late Bronze Age society in the region. Thereafter only vestiges of this important pillar of Canaanite religion remained.

If this paper implies the setting aside of some of Professor Ryan's views on the subject of the Rephaim, this is simply because we are fortunate in having so much more material at our disposal than was available to him. Most of the philological detail in his comments on these very difficult texts remains valid. The works of earlier scholars are always worthy of re-examination and Professor Ryan's on this subject is especially important because of its pioneering nature. In view of the subject of this paper and of the person to whom it is dedicated it is not, perhaps, inappropriate to recall the saying of Bernard of Chartres reported by John of Salisbury:

> Bernard of Chartres used to say that we are like dwarfs on the shoulders of giants, so that we can see more than they, and things at a greater distance, not by virtue of any sharpness of sight on our part, or any physical distinction, but because we are carried high and raised up by their giant size.[22]

Notes

1. As in 2 Sam 21:15-22, where the Rephaim are called "descendants of Rapha"; reference to the Valley of Rephaim south of Jerusalem is common: Josh 15:8; 18:16; 2 Sam 5:18, etc. For a recent survey of the evidence see A. Caquot, *DBS* X, fasc. 55 (Paris 1981) cols. 344-357.

2. J.C.L. Gibson, *Textbook of Syrian Semitic Inscriptions* III (Oxford 1982) 27:8; 28:8; H. Donner, W. Röllig, *Kanaanäische und Aramäische Inschriften* (Wiesbaden ^{3}1971) 13:8, 14:8. Note also the later, first century A.D. Punic inscription from Libya, *ibid.*, 117:1.
3. C. Virolleaud, *Syria* 22 (1941) 1-30. *KTU* = M. Dietrich, O. Loretz, J. Sanmartín, *Die keilalphabetischen Texte aus Ugarit* 1 (Neukirchen-Vluyn 1976).
4. Note C. Virolleaud, *RevEtSém* (1940) 77-83; J. Gray, *PEQ* 81 (1949) 127-139; 84 (1952) 39-41.
5. See J.F. Healey, in *Death in Mesopotamia*, B. Alster (ed.) (Copenhagen 1980) 239-242, especially 240 and footnote 14.
6. See A.F. Rainey, *JAOS* 94 (1974) 188. M.S. Drower, in *Cambridge Ancient History* II, 2 (Cambridge ^{3}1975) 151, was wrong in thinking that the *rp'um* appear in the Ugaritic texts as priests or in any administrative context.
7. *IEJ* 22 (1972) 218-228, especially 219-222. There was a flourishing trade in chariots.
8. See A. Caquot, *Annuaire du Collège de France* 75 (1975) 427-429, for the first publication and P. Bordreuil and D. Pardee, *Syria* 59 (1982) 121-128, for definitive re-publication. Of the many secondary studies note recently B.A. Levine and J.-M. de Tarragon, *JAOS* 104 (1984) 649-659.
9. See J.F. Healey, *UF* 10 (1978) 89-91.
10. X, fasc. 55 (Paris 1981) cols. 344-357.
11. *Beatific Afterlife in Ancient Israel and in the Ancient Near East* (Neukirchen-Vluyn 1986), especially 161-196.
12. Note in addition to those already cited the contribution of Y. Onodera on the *rp'um* to the XXXII ICANAS Orientalist Conference, Hamburg, 1986. This brings to bear special insights on ancestral cult from Japanese tradition.
13. My own views were set out most fully in my London Ph.D. thesis, *Death, Underworld and Afterlife in the Ugaritic texts* (London 1977) 147-197, with a Postscript to incorporate *KTU* 1.161.
14. On this text see J.J. Finkelstein, *JCS* 20 (1966) 95-118.
15. *Hebrew Religion* (London ^{2}1937) 249ff. See also R. de Vaux, *Histoire ancienne d'Israel* (Paris 1971) 130, 209, 524.
16. See Caquot, *DBS* X, 55 cols. 349-350.
17. *VT* 20 (1970) 257-277, especially 265-271.
18. Note especially the Valley of Rephaim, Josh 15:8, etc. and the *y^{e}līdē hārāpā*, 2 Sam 21:15-22.
19. See B. Margulis, *JBL* 89 (1970) 299-300; *ANET* (Princeton ^{3}1969) 477.
20. *OLP* 9 (1978) 5-20, especially 14-18.
21. The same basic material is dealt with in my thesis, *Death, Underworld and Afterlife* 151-152, and was of great interest to Dermot Ryan, since it tended to give weight to his view.
22. *PL* cxcix, 900; translation: *Oxford Dictionary of Quotations* (Oxford ^{3}1979) 41.

THE TREATMENT OF BIBLICAL ANTHROPOMORPHISMS IN PENTATEUCHAL TARGUMS

Carmel McCarthy, R.S.M., *University College Dublin*

The focus in this study will be less on Targums as such and more on how certain translational adjustments in them can help to sensitise us to the climate and context through which the biblical text has been transmitted to us. It was while engaged in trying to identify some of the ways in which the biblical text underwent deliberate emendation on the part of those responsible for its transmission that I became aware of how the official Masoretic Text was indeed subjected to interpretative modifications of varying kinds, and at various points in the history of its transmission. Of these interpretative modifications the most famous are the so-called *Tiqqune Sopherim*, or Emendations of the Scribes. The usual explanation of this phenomenon is as follows: according to Jewish tradition, the received text of the Hebrew Bible has undergone several changes (*tiqqunim*) at the hands of scribes (*sopherim*), who sought to change seemingly inappropriate statements about God into forms more acceptable to a later and more refined theological outlook.

It was while engaged in that research that I found it helpful to distinguish between what I have elsewhere[1] called *original* and *secondary euphemisms*. Original euphemism refers to any form of euphemistic or substitute expression which can be accepted with reasonable certainty as having formed part of the original text, congenital as it were with the rest of the passage. The simplest and best known examples of this kind of primary or spontaneous euphemism are the six biblical instances of *blessing* God, where the real meaning is quite clearly that of *cursing* God. For instance, in Job 1:5, Job wonders whether perhaps his sons may have *blessed* God; in 1:11 and 2:5 Satan taunts the Lord that perhaps if Job is suitably afflicted he will *bless* God to his face, and in 2:9, Job's wife encourages him to *bless* God and die!

By contrast, the term *secondary* euphemism is intended

to cover the various instances whereby a later intervention deliberately altered the original text, so that the resulting emended text becomes a *euphemism* of one kind or another. One example of this kind will suffice: the MT of Ps 84:8 may be translated as follows:

> They go from strength to strength,
> One will appear before God in Zion.

Investigation of the textual situation for this passage shows that beneath this MT reading lies a more original, but less theologically apt, reading:

> *They will see the God of Gods* in Zion.

A study of the use of euphemism in targumic material can surely offer some interesting illustrations of the hermeneutical process whereby interpretative modifications were inevitable, since such modifications represent attempts of later editors, scribes, or, as in the case of the Targums, translators, to have the sacred text conform to more developed and "appropriate" theological views. The dilemma, of whether to render the text quite literally, or whether to interpret and thereby run the risk of modifying it, meets every translator, both ancient and modern.

In a parallel but prior way, this tension was already felt by those responsible for the transmission of the sacred text, as can be demonstrated by the number of theological emendations that the MT contains.[2] A study of the treatment of certain biblical anthropomorphisms in the Targums can give us some interesting insights into what was going on in circles which were certainly contemporary if not also interconnected with those responsible for the transmission of the authoritative Hebrew Scriptures.

For this purpose I have selected only two of the Pentateuchal Targums, namely Neofiti (*Tg. Neof.*) and Onqelos (*Tg. Onq.*), since these are sufficiently distinct from each other to illustrate different ways of using the same hermeneutical presupposition. Because of the widespread endeavour within targumic literature as a whole to eliminate or soften anthropomorphic or other potentially misleading expressions in relation to God, this study of the targumic hermeneutical dynamic will of necessity have to be limited. I have chosen passages typical of the endeavour to render the biblical text in a more appropriate turn of phrase and in keeping with a more sophisticated theology.

Before looking at some specific texts from the Hebrew Pentateuch which could be described as very definitely anthropomorphic in expression and then comparing how these have been interpreted by the two Targums in question, some few preliminary observations on the targumic method in general may be of help. Great advances in targumic studies have been made in the last number of decades.[3] Of particular interest for this present study are the discussions concerning the dating of the targumic traditions for the Pentateuch,[4] and the interrelationship of "targumism" and midrash. Both questions are closely intertwined and interdependent, and the last word concerning either problem has not yet been uttered. The term "targumism" as developed by le Déaut[5] describes a much wider phenomenon than the strict technical idea of a translation of the Hebrew scriptures into Aramaic.[6] Inasmuch as targumism, or the targumic method contains two essential features of midrash,[7] namely, a scriptural context and awareness of the need to make the scriptures relevant and understood by later generations, it can be said to form a type of midrash.[8] Yet if it is midrashic by nature, what is specific to targumism is:

(a) the limits imposed upon it by the fact that it is a translation cum paraphrase[9]
(b) the liturgical synagogal *Sitz im Leben* which required that the formulation be in theologically acceptable terms.[10]

Thus, what distinguishes the targumic method from that of midrash in general is the intention (i.e., a periphrastic translation and not a commentary) and the liturgical setting in which it developed, even if the end result is often similar and at times indistinguishable from that achieved in the *Beth ha-Midrash.*

The problem that arises from the close relationship between targumism and midrash and from the fact that a considerable amount of the midrash found in the Targums is also attested in other Jewish rabbinic sources,[11] gives rise to the question of priority. Are the early Palestinian targumic traditions dependent on these other midrashic sources or vice versa? R. Bloch,[12] followed by le Déaut,[13] considered these early targumic traditions as the "articulation joint" between the scriptural text and its interpretation in subsequent midrashim. This conclusion harmonises with the view that the Palestinian targumic traditions in general had been formed by A.D. 132.[14]

This has been taken as presenting a considerable case for arguing that the earliest Palestinian targumic traditions to the Pentateuch[15] constitute the stepping stone[16] or point of transition from the final stage of the crystallisation of the scriptural text to the creation of a vast store of midrashic literature destined both to protect and to actualise these scriptures for later generations. The different *Sitze im Leben* indicated above, however, would not allow this as a necessary conclusion. In relation to the question of the priority of midrash or targumism the problem might be formulated as follows: there are three *logical* possibilities:

(a) The targumic text is prior and influences the Midrashim.
(b) The Midrashim are prior and influence the targumic translations.
(c) Targums and Midrashim are at least partially contemporary and influence each other and are influenced by already extant tendencies.

None of these possibilities can be excluded purely on the grounds of textual evidence.

However inconclusive the precise nature of the relationship between the targumic method and the more liberated field of midrash may be, an examination of some typical targumic passages which rendered the biblical text in a more acceptable theological form should be of importance in any attempt to unravel and clarify the development of the various forms of euphemisms which are to be found in the biblical text. The choice of passages, of necessity, must be limited. In the following paragraphs, as already indicated, examples will be taken from the *Tg. Neof.*[17] and *Tg. Onq.*[18] Reference to the latter requires some few words on the relationship between the various Palestinian recensions and *Tg. Onq.*, for this too, is another subject of much debate.[19]

Without wishing to over-simplify this question, it seems an attractive solution to see in *Tg. Onq.* a "reduction" of some of the earlier Palestinian traditions.[20] On the one hand, *Tg. Onq.* contains a considerable amount of interpretative material, much of which is parallel to that represented by the Palestinian Targums; yet, on the other hand, it is much closer to the Hebrew text, and as such would appear to reflect a deliberate attempt to make an Aramaic translation. In the opinion of J. Bowker,[21] "the translator(s) who produced Onqelos was well aware of the existing Palestinian Targum-tradition, and he not only based his translation on it, but was also prepared to incorporate its interpretations into his translations as being the proper meaning of the text." It is generally accepted that *Tg. Onq.*, although Palestinian in origin, received its finishing touches in Babylonia and became "our Targum" (*b. Qidd.* 49a).[22]

As already mentioned above, the two chief characteristics of the targumic method are:

(a) the rendering of the Scriptures intelligible for a later generation, and
(b) in theologically acceptable language.[23]

It is the second of these characteristics that will now be taken up in more detail, for it is precisely for this reason that there grew up so many different euphemistic devices.[24] It is necessary to keep the synagogal and liturgical *Sitz im Leben* in mind, for the *meturgeman*[25] could only translate one verse of the Torah at a time.[26] In so doing, if the text was difficult to understand or contained problems of correct theological expression, he could introduce as much interpretation as was deemed necessary.[27] There was no feeling that he was emending or altering the original text, for the text had already been read in Hebrew. In this way, it becomes clear how these euphemisms formed part of the interpretative traditions accompanying the Scriptures, and can be accepted as congenital or original[28] within these traditions. As such, they constituted no threat of contaminating the scriptural text since they were not presented as rival readings.[29] One of the commonest of these euphemistic devices is concerned with some of those biblical passages which speak of God as if he were possessed of a human body, with eyes, ears, hands, etc. and will be illustrated with some examples from *Tg. Neof.* and *Tg. Onq*. These illustrations will be grouped into four main categories in the paragraphs which follow.

§ 1 Euphemistic expressions which soften or eliminate biblical anthropomorphisms which speak of God as though possessed of a body (e.g. *in the eyes of; by the hand of*; *by the mouth of* and *the face of God*).

(i) *In the eyes of the Lord.* When the Hebrew text uses the phrase *b'yny yhwh, "in the eyes of the Lord"*, in the Pentateuch, *Tg. Neof.* and *Tg. Onq.* invariably render this anthropomorphism by *qdm/mn qdm*, "*before/from before* the Lord". For example, when Noah "found favour *in the eyes of* the Lord",[30] both *Tg. Neof.* and *Tg. Onq.* say that he "found favour and mercy" (*Neof.*), "found mercy" (*Onq.*) "*before* the Lord". When Aaron asks Moses: "If I had eaten the sin offering today, would it have been acceptable (*hyyṭb*) *in the eyes of* the Lord?"[31] both *Tg. Neof.* and *Tg. Onq.* ask "would it be proper (*špr, Tg. Neof.*)/correct (*hqyn, Tg. Onq.*) *before* the Lord?" By contrast, when the phrase refers to *in the eyes of* some human person, e.g. Abraham (Gen 21:11), Isaac (Gen 28:8), Pharaoh (Gen 41:37; Exod 3:21), it is rendered invariably in the Pentateuch by *b'pyh d, in the face of*, etc. by *Tg. Neof.*, and quite literally *in the eyes of* by *Tg. Onq.*[32] There is only one passage in the Pentateuch where "*the eyes of* the Lord" is retained in both Targums quite literally, but in this case, the expression is different: "the eyes of the Lord, your God are forever on it" (i.e. on the promised land).[33]

Since the expression *qdm* occurs consistently in both Targums in place of "in the eyes of" (the Lord), but is not found when the expression refers to human beings,[34] it is necessary to mention at this point an article by M.L. Klein,[35] in which he set out to demonstrate that this preposition is a pseudo-anti-anthropomorphism in the Targums. He is accurate in pointing out (503):

(a) the dangers of generalised statements with regard to anti-anthropomorphisms in the Targums,
(b) the inconsistency of the Targums, which at times

retain "some of the crudest biblical anthropomorphisms" alongside circumlocution and paraphrase, and

(c) the need for a full-sized monograph to investigate "when the Targums avoid anthropomorphic expressions" and "whether there is evidence for a consistent theology underlying this targumic activity."

He then undertook to "examine one widespread targumic feature that has traditionally been labelled as a circumlocutionary device for avoiding direct contact or intercourse between God and man, namely, the 'buffer preposition' *qdm* ('before')." He gives some examples from various contexts to illustrate how the preposition is used,[36] but it would seem that he goes beyond the evidence or overstates his case when he maintains: "I believe that there is extensive evidence to show that there is probably no connection at all between the use of the preposition *qdm* and the alleged anti-anthropomorphic theology of the Targums".[37]

The first point he develops to sustain his contention is that, in the Aramaic portions of Daniel, the preposition is used out of deference to high office or nobility, *before* the king as well as *before* God (cf. Dan 6:23), whereas the king speaks *to* commoners, and commoners speak *to* each other. From this he concludes:[38] "that the use of the indirect preposition *qdm* in the Book of Daniel is out of deference to high office or nobility, and not related to the nature of the deity". He then returns to the Targums to make a similar inference: "the use of *qdm* is not confined to the divine context, but is rather an expression of deference that is frequently applied to man and human institutions."[39]

However, it is precisely in distinguishing too radically between the use of the preposition as a "buffer" term in relation to God and its use out of deference in certain human situations, that Klein overstates his case. It has already been pointed out how thin the line of demarcation is in the use of euphemisms referring to God and in those concerned with his especially chosen ones.[40] The examples from Daniel, of the use of both, in reference to God and the king, could be cited as a further instance of this sense of fitness which resulted in the use of euphemism, both in relation to God and to certain men. It is less confusing to use the more general term of "euphemism" for this phenomenon, of which anti-anthropomorphism is but one usage, rather than to distinguish too radically between its use in relation to God and to privileged people. And, as already indicated,[41] there are very definite uses of the preposition which are not only euphemistic, but also anti-anthropomorphic.

In showing that the expression "in the ears of" is rendered by the Targums in a figurative sense, "in the hearing of", both when it refers to God and to human beings, Klein has made a good choice so as to be able to conclude that "there is therefore no connection between this normal translational device and anthropomorphism".[42] However, if he had chosen the phrase "in the eyes of" and compared the translations in *Tg. Neof.* and *Tg. Onq.* both in relation to God and human beings, he might have had to revise his conclusions.[43]

The value of Klein's article is to reinforce a point already made,[44] namely, that the Targums do not appear to be totally consistent in their use of euphemism and anti-anthropomorphism, and that there is need for full-scale systematic investigation of the translational choices made by the different Targums, in order to determine more precisely whatever patterns of usage which may emerge. But Klein's conclusions fall into the very category he sets out to criticise, namely, that of "generalisations". In certain instances, the preposition *qdm* may have a neutral or merely translational role, but it reappears sufficiently often in a euphemistic usage as to still deserve the description of "buffer" term in these instances.

(ii) *The hand of the Lord.* This anthropomorphism undergoes various euphemistic surgery depending on the context. In Exod 9:3 the consequences for Pharaoh of refusing to free the Israelites will be that "*the hand of* the Lord will fall with a very severe plague upon your cattle", etc. The solution of *Tg. Neof.*: "the plague of *my punishment* shall be upon the cattle", etc., differs from that of *Tg. Onq.*: "a plague *from before* the Lord shall be upon your cattle", etc.[45] In Exod 16:3, the grumbling of the Israelites, "(would that we had died) by *the hand of* the Lord in Egypt" is rendered by both as simply "*before* the Lord". The question in Num 11:23, "is the

Lord's *hand* shortened?" is paraphrased by *Tg. Neof.* as: "is there *deficiency before* the Lord?", whereas *Tg. Onq.* asks "is *the memra of* the Lord obstructed?"[46] Again it is helpful to compare these translations with those other pentateuchal passages which use the phrase "the hand of" in reference to a human person, where the sense is figurative ("into the power of" or "in the possession of"). In most cases the phrase is translated literally,[47] with one or two exceptions, in the sense of "under the authority of" in *Tg. Neof.*,[48] but not with the preposition *qdm*.

(iii) *The mouth of the Lord. lpy yhwh* is a very common phrase and is usually translated in the RSV by "according to the command of the Lord". *Tg. Neof.*[49] renders it as "according to *the decree of the memra* of the Lord", while *Tg. Onq.* has a shorter form,[50] "according to *the memra* of the Lord".[51] When this expression is used of ordinary people, such as Moses, etc., it is rendered varyingly, but without much significant difference. For example, in Gen 45:21, *Tg. Neof.* renders it "according to the decree of the mouth of Pharaoh".[52]

(iv) *The face of the Lord.* The "seeing of the face of God" was an expression which caused a certain amount of theological problems and scruples for later generations.[53] There are eight passages in the Pentateuch (MT), which are presently vocalised as a type of *niphal*, "to be seen/appear before the Lord",[54] but which read more smoothly if they were vocalised as *qal*, "to see the face of the Lord". It is not surprising to find that all eight passages in *Tg. Onq.*, and seven in *Tg. Neof.*,[55] are expressed reflexively, "to be seen/to appear before the Lord".[56] *Tg. Onq.* is very close to the MT for all passages, whereas *Tg. Neof.* exhibits some parenetic expansions, as for instance in Exod 23:17: "All your males shall be seen *seeking instruction before* the Lord of all ages, the Lord", or in Exod 34:20: "And they shall not be seen *before me empty of every precept*".[57] Elsewhere, "the face of the Lord" is rendered by both *Tg. Neof.* and *Tg. Onq.* as "*before* the Lord", whereas the phrase, "and they saw the God of Israel" in Exod 24:10 is paraphrased in *Tg. Neof.* as: "and they saw *the glory of the Shekinah of* the

Lord", and as: "And they saw the *glory of the* God of Israel" in *Tg. Onq*. The Codex Vaticanus and recension of Origen for the LXX tradition present an interesting alternative paraphrase tied up with the continuation of v.10: "And they saw *the place in which* the God of Israel *had stood*."[58]

Other similar euphemisms employed to conform with the more refined theological concepts of God of a later generation may be also found in relation to the voice of God/the Lord,[59] his spirit,[60] and his heart.[61] Even a superficial reading of some pages of any of the Targums will produce evidence of how strongly impregnated with this approach were their authors, and presumably also their audience.[62]

§ 2 Euphemistic expressions which change certain verbs from active to passive, where God is the subject, or which use other similar devices, so that God is only indirectly connected with a given action.

(i) *Four typical verbs where God is subject (to go down, to hear, to see, and to know) and which the Targums render in a passive form, so that God is no longer anthropormorphically represented as the agent of a human action.* In Gen 11:5, it is related that "The Lord came down to see the city". In *Tg. Neof.*, the translation is expansive: "and *the glory of the Shekinah of* the Lord *was revealed* to see the city", while *Tg. Onq*. is more concise: "It *was revealed to* the Lord concerning the *work* of the city". A similar difference in paraphrase occurs at Exod 19:11 ("the Lord will come down"): *Tg. Neof.* renders "*the glory of the Shekinah of* the Lord will *be revealed*", and *Tg. Onq*. simply says "The Lord will *be revealed*".[63] The verb "to hear" with God as subject also occasions various euphemistic phrases. In Gen 16:11 ("The Lord has given heed to your affliction") *Tg. Neof.* reads "because your afflictions *have been heard before* the Lord" but *Tg. Onq*. attests "the Lord has *received your supplications*". However, in Gen 29:33; Num 11:1 and 12:2, both *Tg. Neof.* and *Tg. Onq*. render "and it *was heard before* the Lord" in each case. In Num 21:3, *Tg. Neof.* does not use any euphemistic device, but renders the MT[64] while *Tg. Onq*. reads "the Lord has *received* (or *heard*) *your supplication*".[65]

The verb "to see", with God as subject, is paraphrased similarly in the passive in Gen 29:32; Exod 2:25 and Deut 32: 19.[66] In each case, the paraphrase in *Tg. Neof.* and *Tg. Onq.* consists of "*it was revealed before*". The verb "to know" is also rendered as "*it was revealed before*" in Gen 3:5 (*Tg. Neof.* and *Tg. Onq.*) and Deut 34:10 (*Tg. Onq.*), whereas Exod 2:25 ("and God knew") is rendered with an active paraphrase similar in intent to those which will be examined in the next paragraph: "And *he determined in his memra to redeem them*".

(ii) *Expressions which reformulate the meaning of certain verbs, so that God is only indirectly connected with a given action* constitute another very common targumic device to eliminate anthropomorphism. The very simple image in Gen 8:21 ("and when the Lord smelled the pleasing odour") is suitably reworded by both *Tg. Neof.* and *Tg. Onq.* as "and the Lord *received the sacrifice* of Noah *with favour*". The description of the Lord "going his way" after bargaining with Abraham in Gen 18:33 is described in *Tg. Neof.* as "the *glory of the Shekinah of the* Lord went up" and more simply in *Tg. Onq.* as "*the glory of* the Lord went up". In Gen 28:13, at the top of Jacob's ladder, the description in Hebrew "the Lord stood above it/him" is expressed in *Tg. Onq.* as "*the glory of the* Lord was standing . . ." but in *Tg. Neof.* the MT is retained.[67]

In Gen 26:28 ("the Lord is with you") and 39:3 ("the Lord was with him") *Tg. Onq.*[68] speaks of "the *memra* of the Lord"[69] being present as an aid. There have been various interpretations of the significance of the *memra* of God/the Lord.[70] It is beyond the scope of this present examination to enter into details concerning the frequency with which it is used,[71] or the specific connotations it assumes in the different contexts.[72] The observations of L. Sabourin[73] are particularly pertinent to the purpose of the present investigation:

> In fact the Memra speculation can be seen as one of the means used to deanthropologise the language about God (the biblical angelology can be seen as partly responding to the same purpose).

Jacob's exclamation after his dream, "surely the Lord is in this place" (Gen 28:16) is rendered by *Tg. Neof.* as "truly, *the glory of the Shekinah of* the Lord *dwells* in this place", and by *Tg. Onq.* as "truly *the glory of* the Lord *dwells* in this place". Exod 15:18 ("the Lord will reign for ever and ever") is paraphrased extensively by *Tg. Neof.*[74] and rendered more simply by *Tg. Onq.* as "The Lord, *his kingship* is forever and ever". The idea that the Lord should fight for his people[75] was the object of various targumic euphemisms in the Pentateuch. In Exod 14:25 ("the Lord fights for them against the Egyptians") *Tg. Neof.* again paraphrases,[76] while *Tg. Onq.* says "It is *the might of* the Lord which is *making war* against the Egyptians". One final example from this type of verb which was reworded for theological reasons, is taken from Num 23:16 ("the Lord met Balaam"). *Tg. Neof,* renders "and *the memra of* the Lord met Balaam", while *Tg. Onq.* attests "*a memra from before* the Lord encountered Balaam".

§ 3 Transformation of rhetorical questions, etc., into statements (positive or negative), if their original wording is suggestive of doubts or misunderstandings regarding divine omnipotence.

In Gen 50:19, Joseph reassures his brothers that they are forgiven. The rhetorical question: "Fear not, for am I in the place of God?" is rephrased by *Tg. Neof.* and *Tg. Onq.* differently, but in each case, any potential misunderstanding is removed. *Tg. Neof.* paraphrases the verse according to the context ("Do not be afraid, because far be it from me to repay you the evil that you did to me. Are not the thoughts of the sons of man manifest before the Lord?"), while *Tg. Onq.* makes Joseph neatly affirm: "Fear not, for I am one who fears the Lord" (cf. Gen 42:18).

In Exod 14:15, the Lord asks Moses, "Why do you cry to Me?" *Tg. Neof.* retains the question format, but expresses it more suitably, together with an extended paraphrase,[77] while *Tg. Onq.* removes the question altogether, and what remains, "I have received your supplication", could be seen as parallel to part of *Tg. Neof.*'s paraphrase: "Your prayers have been heard before me".[78] In the Song of Moses, the following rhetorical question is asked:

> Who is like thee, O Lord, among the gods?
> Who is like thee in majesty? (Exod 15:11)

This is rephrased negatively by *Tg. Onq.* as follows:

> There is no one apart from you who is God, O Lord,
> There is no one who is majestic in holiness.

Tg. Onq. attests a similar type of rewording in Deut 3:24. The question, "For what god is there in heaven or on earth, who can do such works and mighty acts as thine?" is rendered positively as "For you are God, whose Shekinah is in heaven above and whose dominion is on earth; *there is no one* who does works like your works and mighty acts."[79]

In Gen 4:14, Cain says to the Lord, "and from thy face I shall be hidden". Both *Tg. Neof.* and *Tg. Onq.* correct this statement in accordance with a more sophisticated theology: "and from before you *I will not be able* to hide". In Exod 18:11, Jethro confesses "Now I know that the Lord is greater than all gods" which *Tg. Onq.* duly renders as "I know that the Lord is great and *there is no other god apart from him*", and in Gen 18:25 Abraham pleads for the innocent in Sodom and Gomorrah by asking "Shall not the Judge of all the earth do right?", which *Tg. Onq.* renders more appropriately in the affirmative: "The Judge of all the earth *will surely do justice*."

§4 Protection of Divine Transcendence by various other euphemistic devices.

Finally, two other typical protective measures, euphemistic in character, will be examined briefly here. The first of these concerns the verb, *hthlk*, "walk before or with" in certain passages of Genesis. For instance, of Enoch it is said that "he walked with God" (Gen 5:22, 24). In *Tg. Neof.* this is rendered in both verses as "and Enoch *served in truth before* the Lord", while *Tg. Onq.* has "and Enoch *went in the fear of* the Lord" in both verses. Noah too "walked with God" (Gen 6:9), but in the Targums "he *served before the Lord in truth*" (*Tg. Neof.*), or merely "*went in the fear of the* Lord" (*Tg. Onq.*). Abraham was requested by the Lord "to walk before me" (Gen 17:1). This is reworded in *Tg. Neof.* as "*serve before me in truth*", and simply as "*serve before me*" in *Tg. Onq.*[80]

The image of easy familiarity with God underlying these texts in their original wording was not acceptable to the theology of this later age.

The second typical euphemistic change occurs regarding the names given to false or potentially rival gods. The phrase *'lhym 'ḥrym*, "other gods" occurs sixteen times in Deuteronomy.[81] *Tg. Neof.* renders it as "other idols" consistently, while *Tg. Onq.* attests the formula "the idols of the nations" in all sixteen occurrences.

The above illustrations by no means exhaust the wealth of euphemistic expression in these Targums to the Pentateuch; they merely serve as an indirect witness to the atmosphere in which the sacred text was being handed down in a given era, and to the types of midrashic traditions that were accumulating about it by way of interpretation and actualisation. Apart from illustrating aspects to the so-called targumic method, they also help to show how those responsible for the transmission of the authoritative text of the Hebrew scriptures could be influenced by this kind of sensitivity to anthropomorphic expressions and how they could make attempts, conscious or otherwise, to emend some of the expressions which they considered inappropriate from a more refined theological viewpoint. The periphrastic nature of the targums brings into focus the influence of a systematic orthodoxy in the translation of canonical texts which themselves are theologically naive. This tendency can still be seen at work in contemporary biblical translations such as The New English Bible, the New International Version and the English translation of the Jerusalem Bible.

Notes

1. C. McCarthy, *The Tiqqune Sopherim and Other Theological Corrections in the Masoretic Text of the Old Testament* (OBO 36; Fribourg-Göttingen 1981) 167 ff.
2. *The Tiqqune Sopherim*, 197-240.

3. Evidence of this growth of interest can be had by consulting B. Grossfeld's *A Bibliography of Targumic Literature* (Cincinnati-New York 1972) (Vol. 1 with 1045 entries) and 1977 (Vol. 2 with a further 767 entries, making a total of 1822). Similar and supplementary bibliography may be found in P. Nickels, *Targum and New Testament, A Bibliography together with a New Testament Index* (Rome 1967); J. Bowker, *The Targums and Rabbinic Literature. An Introduction to Jewish Interpretations of Scripture* (Cambridge 1969) 327-348; A. Paul, "Littérature Intertestamentaire: I Les Études Targumiques", *RechSR* 60 (1972) 430-444; M. Klein, Review of B. Grossfeld, *A Bibliography of Targumic Literature*, *Bib* 55 (1974) 281-285; *idem*, *The Fragment-Targums of the Pentateuch according to their Extant Sources* (2 vols.; AnBib 76; Rome 1980); A Díez Macho (ed.), *Neophyti 1, Vol. IV, Numeros* (Madrid 1974) 11*-16*; *Vol. V, Deuteronomio* (Madrid 1978) 13*-25*; M. McNamara, "Targums", *IDBSupp* (Nashville 1976) 861; *idem*, *The New Testament and the Palestinian Targum to the Pentateuch* (Second Printing with Supplement containing Additions and Corrections: AnBib 27a; Rome 1978) xviii-xxiv; 287ff; *idem*, *Palestinian Judaism and the New Testament* (Wilmington, Delaware 1983) 205-252. The existence of an "Association for Targumic Studies" in the United States and the publication since 1974 in Toronto of a "Newsletter for Targumic Studies" are further evidence of this extensive growth in targumic study.
4. Cf. Díez Macho, "Fecha de composicion del Targum palestinense de Neofiti I", *Neophyti 1, Vol, I, Genesis* (Madrid 1968) 57*-95*; *idem*, "La datacion del Neofiti I: Las denominaciones de Dios", *Neophyti 1, Vol. III, Levitico* (Madrid 1971) 70*-83*; *idem*, "Neophyti 1: Textual Crystalization", *Neophyti 1, Vol. V, Deuteronomio* 83*-100*; McNamara, "Some early rabbinic citations and the Palestinian Targum to the Pentateuch", *RSO* 41 (1966) 1-14; *idem*, *The New Testament and the Palestinian Targum* 45-66; 294-295; *idem*, *IDBSupp* 858-861; R. le Déaut, "The Current State of Targumic Studies", *BThB* 4 (1974) 22-26; *idem*, *Targum du Pentateuque, Vol. 1, Genèse* (*SC* 245; Paris 1978) 20ff.; A. York, "The Dating of Targumic Literature", *JTS* 25 (1974) 1-11; S.A. Kaufman, "The Job Targum from Qumran", *JAOS* 93 (1973) 317-327; M. Klein, *The Fragment-Targums of the Pentateuch*, Vol. 1, 23-25.
5. Cf. "Un phénomène spontané de l'herméneutique juive ancienne: 'le targumisme' ", *Bib* 52 (1971) 505-525.
6. He borrows the term "targumism" from R. Harris, "Traces of Targumism in the New Testament", *ET* (1920-21) 373-376, and others; cf. "Un phénomène spontané" 506, *Tg. Neof.* 2.
7. Cf. le Déaut, "A propos d'une définition du midrash" 413: "Le midrash a produit des oeuvres de formes littéraires très diverses et est très hétéroclite quant à son contenu . . . En consérvant les deux notes essentielles du midrash (contexte scriptuaire – adaptation) bien des critères peuvent être envisagés . . ."

8. Cf. le Déaut, "The Current State" 19: "Will it ever be possible to draw a division line between Targum and Midrash, to distinguish them radically? The examination of the targumic methods and of the targumisms has convinced me that the two *genres* are not only parallel but imbricated".
9. Whereas the midrashic writings and Talmud are at liberty to cite various opinions and interpretations of a given scriptural verse, the Targum has to make a choice and confine this choice to a minimum amount of paraphrase. Cf. le Déaut, *Targum du Pentateuque*, Vol. 1, 45.
10. Cf. Bowker, *The Targums and Rabbinic Literature* 13-16. Both he and le Déaut ("Current State" 18) rightly point out, however, the risk of neglecting important elements concerning the nature of the Targums at their origin and during a period of their oral tradition, if one insists too exclusively on this liturgical synagogal *Sitz im Leben*. As Bowker puts it excellently: "There was, therefore, no such thing as *the* Targum, only a Targumic tradition, or perhaps more accurately, Targumic traditions. The Targum texts (or fragments) that have survived are isolated moments extracted from a continuous process: they are, as it were, 'cross-sections' of an evolving tradition, revealing what the tradition was at a particular time" (15). It follows, therefore, that there is equally no such thing as *the* targumic method, but rather the targumic method of each recension, although it is possible to identify common characteristics (cf. le Déaut, *Le Targum du Pentateuque*, Vol. 1, 46f.).
11. Cf. McNamara, "Targums", *IDBSupp* 858.
12. "Midrash", *DBS* V (1957) 1279.
13. "Un phénomène spontané" 525. At the end of this article le Déaut proposes, with some hesitation, the following definition of targumism: "le *targumisme* couvre l'ensemble des phénomènes spontanés inconscients ou conditionnés par des techniques et des règles herméneutiques – qui naissent dès le premier contact du traducteur ancien (et modern) avec le texte biblique, quand il s'agit d'une version liturgique. On appellera *targumismes* les résultats concrets auxquels aboutit cette rencontre du texte avec les tendances en jeu. On constatera que c'est le phénomène midrashique lui-même, mais au niveau de la jonction immédiate avec le texte, celui de la toute première exégèse qui s'impose à tout traducteur."
14. Cf. McNamara, "Targums" 859-861, where he gives a summary of the arguments in favour of this dating as well as some of the main objections from certain circles. He concludes: "The following rule of thumb for the date of the Palestinian Targs. has been proposed: Unless there is specific proof to the contrary, the haggadah of the Palestinian Targs. is likely to be tannaitic and to antedate the outbreak of the Second Jewish Revolt in A.D. 132" (859). See also Bowker, *The Targums and Rabbinic Literature*, 15-27 and n.4 above.
15. Neofiti 1; Fragment Targum, Cairo Geniza Fragments, and Pseudo-Jonathan.

16. Cf. Bloch, "Midrash" 1267-1276: "Les origines bibliques du Midrash".
17. Cf. Díez Macho, *Neophyti 1, Targum Palestinese. MS de la Biblioteca Vaticana* (with translation into Catalan by the editor, into French by R. le Déaut, and into English by M. McNamara and M. Maher) (5 vols.; Madrid-Barcelona 1968-78); le Déaut, *Targum du Pentateuque* (4 vols.; Paris 1978-80) (a translation into French of two Palestinian recensions of the Targum to the Pentateuch: Pseudo-Jonathan and Neofiti I). For a history of Codex Neofiti 1, cf. le Déaut, "Jalons pour une histoire d'un manuscrit du Targum palestinien", *Bib* 48 (1967) 509-533. See also the introduction in *Targum du Pentateuque*, Vol. 1, 38-42 for a description of Neofiti I and its relation to the pentateuchal targumic recensions.
18. Cf. A. Sperber, *The Bible in Aramaic* (5 vols.; Leiden 1959-1973). Vol. 1 contains *The Pentateuch according to Targum Onkelos*. The older edition of A. Berliner (1884) has been reprinted in Jerusalem (1968). Cf. also le Déaut in *Targum du Pentateuque*, Vol. 1, 20-22 for a short description of the nature and age of Onqelos.
19. Cf. Díez Macho, *Neophyti 1, Vol. I, Genesis* (Madrid 1968) 98*-114*; Paul, *RechSR* 60 (1972) 440-442; Bowker, *The Targums and Rabbinic Literature* 24.
20. Cf. le Déaut, "The Current State" 19.
21. *The Targums and Rabbinic Literature* 25.
22. The move towards a more standard translation may have been part of the wider movement in Judaism to provide authoritative texts as a protection against the growing involvement of Christians in the Septuagint. Onqelos, in time, supplanted the earlier Palestinian recensions. Bowker thinks that "Onqelos may have been in existence in Babylonia before the end of the third century A.D., because it was apparently established and worked on in Nehardea and Nehardea was temporarily destroyed in the second half of that century" (*The Targums and Rabbinic Literature* 26).
23. See above 3 ff. In both "Un phénomène spontané" (1971) and Vol. 1 of *Le Targum du Pentateuque* (1978) 42-62, le Déaut further subdivides these basic characteristics into seven and six various aspects, respectively.
24. Cf. S. Maybaum, *Die Anthropomorphien und Anthropopathien bei Onkelos und den spätern Targumim* (Breslau 1870) (in particular, 8-28 and 40-54 for Onqelos); M. Ginsburger, "Die Anthropomorphismen in den Thargumim", *JPTh* 17 (1891) 262-280 and 430-458; L. Ginsberg, "Anthropomorphism", *The Jewish Encyclopedia*, Vol. 1, 621-625; D. Muñoz Leon, "Soluciones de los Targumin del Pentateuco a los antropomorfismos", *EstBib* 28 (1969) 263-281; le Déaut, "Un phénomène spontané (1971) 519-520; *idem*, *Le Targum du Pentateuque*, Vol. 1, 59-62; A.J. Brawer, "Substitution of Anthropomorphisms in Ancient Translations of the Bible", *BetM* 57 (1974) 161-193 (in Hebrew, with an English summary, 304-305); M. Klein, "The Preoposition *qdm* ('Before'): A Pseudo-anti-

anthropomorphism in the Targums", *JTS* 30 (1979) 502-507.

The Targum to the Prophets also contains excellent examples of euphemisms to avoid anthropomorphic and other theologically "inapt" expressions. Cf. in Sperber, *The Bible in Aramaic Vol. IVB, The Targum and the Hebrew Bible* (Leiden 1973) 37-41, where he cites, under the heading, "Changes and Additions for Reasons of Dogma and Belief" sixty-three targumic passages from the Codex Reuchlinianus, ranging from Josh 4:24 to Zech 1:8, together with literal retroversion into Hebrew and the corresponding MT, in order to illustrate how "the Targum aims at the elimination of all phrases, which are reminiscent of anthropomorphism, and to substitute for them other expressions, which were better suited for the more refined ideas concerning God of later generations" (37). Sperber's similar analysis of Onqelos (193-198) will be mentioned further below (nn. 62, 66). Cf. also J. Stenning, *The Targum of Isaiah, edited with a Translation* (Oxford [2]1953) Introduction, xii ff. For similar types of exegetical tendencies in the LXX, see M.H. Goshen-Gottstein, "Theory and Practice of Textual Criticism", *Textus* 3 (1963) 130-158; C. Rabin, "The Translation Process and the Character of the Septuagint", *Textus* 6 (1968) 193-200; C.T. Fritsch, *The Anti-anthropomorphisms in the Greek Pentateuch* (Princeton 1943); J. Wevers, "Exegetical Principles underlying the Septuagint text of 1 Kings ii 12-xxi 43", *OTS* 8 (1950) 300-322 (see 314ff. in particular for theological variations).

25. Cf. McNamara, *The New Testament and the Palestinian Targum* 40 ff., for details concerning the Targums and the liturgical reading of the Scriptures. The person who translated the Scriptures into Aramaic is called a *tergeman*, *turgeman* or more often a *meturgeman*.
26. *j. Meg.* 4:4.
27. But within certain conventions. See Bowker, *The Targums and Rabbinic Literature* 14 n.1.
28. Cf. C. McCarthy, *The Tiqqune Sopherim* 170, where the term "original euphemism" is defined as referring "to any form of euphemistic or substitute expression which can be accepted with reasonable certitude as having formed part of the original text, congenital as it were with the rest of the passage. Such original or spontaneous 'euphemisms' may be either sacred or profane in character or motivation, though it is not always possible or even wise to distinguish too rigidly in many cases. The lines of demarcation between things pertaining to God and things pertaining to his chosen ones or his chosen people are often blurred".
29. It is important to remember that the Targum in its infancy was an oral tradition of translation and interpretation. While there may have been written Targums at an early date (cf. the Job Targum from Qumran, J.P.M. van der Ploeg and A.S. van der Woude, *Le Targum de Job de la grotte XI de Qumrân* [Leiden 1971]; J.A. Fitzmyer, "Some observations on the Targum of Job from Qumran Cave 11", *CBQ* 36 [1974] 503-524) these possibly served for private

study or as texts to prepare for the liturgy. The actual compilation of the Palestinian recensions and later Targums represents a further stage of development. McNamara prefers to speak of "a relatively fixed tradition that would ensure that the different oral renderings would be basically the same" rather than "postulate the existence of a fixed primitive Palestinian Targ." (Cf. *IDBSupp* 860).

30. Gen 6:8. Cf. a similar rendering by both *Tg. Neof.* and *Tg. Onq.* of this same expression in two other passages of Genesis: 38:7, 10.
31. Lev 10:19. The other pentateuchal passages containing the expression "*in the eyes of* the Lord/God" and which are all consistently rendered by *Tg. Neof.* and *Tg. Onq.* as "*before* the Lord", are: Num 23:27; 24:1; 32:13; Deut 4:25; 6:18; 9:18; 12:25, 28; 13:19; 17:2; 21:9; 31:29.
32. The other pentateuchal passages, apart from the four mentioned above (Gen 21:11; 28:8; 41:37 [bis]; Exod 5:21) and which are rendered consistently by *Tg. Neof.* as *in the face of* and by *Tg. Onq.* as *in the eyes of* are: Gen 19:14; 31:35; 33:8, 15; 34:18 [bis]; 39:21; 45:16; 47:25; Exod 3:21; 11:3; 12:36.
33. Deut 11:12. In this context the observation of le Déaut, *Le Targum du Pentateuque*, Vol. 1, 60, is worth recording: "il n'y a ni uniformité ni régularité dans le traitement des anthropomorphismes. Mais la tendance générale à éviter certains mots ou expressions montre qu'il y a ici plus qu'une question de style." See also, L. Ginsberg, "Anthropomorphism" 623, who also draws attention to this lack of consistency.
34. See above, nn. 31-32.
35. "The Preposition *qdm* ('before'): A Pseudo-anti-anthropomorphism in the Targums", *JTS* 30 (1970) 502-507.
36. Cf. Gen 17:18 ("and Abraham said to the Lord"), which is rendered by *Tg. Onq.*, *Tg. Ps.-J.* and *Tg. Neof.* as "and Abraham said *before* the Lord"; Exod 10:8 ("Go serve the Lord your God"), which is rendered by *Tg. Onq.*, *Tg. Ps.-J.* and *Tg. Neof.* as "Go serve *before* the Lord, your God"; Deut 1:41 ("We have sinned against the Lord"), which is rendered by all three Targums as "We have sinned *before* the Lord".
37. Cf. "The Preposition *qdm*" 504.
38. "The Preposition *qdm*" 505.
39. "The Preposition *qdm*" 505.
40. Cf. C. McCarthy, *The Tiqqune Sopherim* 170 and 225-240.
41. See above, 50 ff. and nn. 31 and 32 in particular.
42. "The Preposition *qdm*" 507.
43. See above, nn. 31 and 32. See n. 45 below also, concerning "the hand of the Lord", compared with "human hands".
44. See above, n. 33.
45. Note the use of "from before" in this and the following instances. In Deut 2:15, the MT, "*the hand of* the Lord was against them" is interpreted in both in terms of a plague: "and *plagues* (*Tg. Neof.*)/a *plague* (*Tg. Onq.*) from before the Lord . . ." even though the MT does not speak of a plague in this passage.

46. For further details on the use of the term *memra*, see below, n. 69.
47. Cf. *Tg. Neof.* and *Tg. Onq.* for Gen 30:35; 32:17; Exod 18:10; 35:29; 38:21 etc.
48. Cf. *Tg. Neof.* for Gen 39: 6,22 and 41:35 which renders "under the authority of" and in Exod 9:35 "with" (the gloss in *Tg. Neof.* translates literally). In all these passages *Tg. Onq.* renders the phrase literally.
49. Cf. Exod 17:1; Num 3:16, 39, 51; 4:37, 41, 45, 49; 9:18, 20, 23; 10:13; 13:3; 14:41; 22:18; 24:13; 33:2; Deut 1:26, 43; 9:23; 34:5. The formula is the same in all these references apart from slight variations in orthography.
50. The shortened form consistently appears in *Tg. Onq.* for all the references cited in the previous footnote.
51. It is worth noting in passing that where *Tg. Neof.* and *Tg. Onq.* differ in the passages cited above and subsequently, *Tg. Neof.* is usually more colourful and varied in the choice of euphemism or alternative wording, whereas *Tg. Onq.* is more brief and typical. This would be in keeping with the view expressed above, which sees *Tg. Onq.* as a "reduction". See above, 49.
52. The same is true also in Exod 38:21 (Moses).
53. For a fuller examination of this expression and the textual problems it raises, see C. McCarthy, *The Tiqqune Sopherim* 225-240.
54. Exod 23:15, 17; 34:20, 23, 24; Deut 16:16a, 16b; 31:11.
55. Deut 31:11 is rendered with an active infinite, "to see". Cf. C. McCarthy, *The Tiqqune Sopherim* 199 n. 8 for comment.
56. For other illustrations of the targumic characteristic of changing active verbal forms into passive for theological motives, see below, 54 ff.
57. This latter expansion is also present in *Tg. Neof.* at Deut 16:16b.
58. See Tosephta, Megilla IV, 41 for a discussion attributed to R. Judah ben Ilay as to how this verse should be translated. See also McNamara, *The New Testament and the Palestinian Targum* 41.
59. In Gen 3:8; "the voice of the Lord God" becomes "the voice of the *memra* of the Lord God (*Tg. Neof.* and *Tg. Onq.*); the same is true for Deut 5:26.
60. In Gen 1:2 "the spirit of God" becomes "a spirit *of love from before* the Lord" (*Tg. Neof.*), and "a spirit *from before* the Lord" (*Tg. Onq.*).
61. In Gen 8:21 "the Lord said in his heart" is rendered as "*in the thought of* his heart" (*Tg. Neof.*), "in his *memra*" (*Tg. Onq.*).
62. Cf. Sperber, *The Bible in Aramaic*, Vol. IVB, 197, for a series of illustrations of anti-anthropomorphisms in *Tg. Onq.*
63. The same variation between *Tg. Neof.* and *Tg. Onq.* occurs again in Exod 34:5 and Num 12:5; in each case the verb "to go down" is rendered in the passive, "was revealed".
64. An indication that the targumic terminology was never totally consistent (see above, n. 33). *Tg. Neof.* renders the MT also for Deut 1:34, 45.

65. *Tg. Onq.* repeats this phrase in Deut 1:45; 10:10 and 26:7, but in 1:34 renders the passive, "it was heard". *Tg. Neof.* renders the usual passive for Deut 26:7, but for 10:10 has a longer (active) paraphrase, "and the voice of *the memra of* the Lord listened" which is similar to the devices to be examined in the following paragraphs.
66. For some further examples of this type of euphemism, see Sperber, *The Bible in Aramaic*, Vol. IVB, 194-195.
67. See above, n. 33 and n. 64. However, the gloss in *Tg. Neof.* at Gen 28:13 says that "an angel of mercy from before the Lord stood placed above him".
68. *Tg. Neof.* keeps to the MT for both verses, but *Tg. Neof.* (gloss) for the former carries also "the *memra* of the Lord".
69. A selection of some studies on the *Memra* includes the following: H.L. Strack-P. Billerbeck, *Kommentar zum Neuen Testament* (Munich 1922-28) Vol. 2, 302-333; G.F. Moore, "Intermediaries in Jewish Theology", *HTR* 15 (1922) 41-85; G.H. Box, "The Idea of Intermediation in Jewish Theology", *JQR* 23 (1932-33) 103-119; D. Muñoz Leon, "Apendice sobre el Memra de Yahweh en el MS Neophyti 1", *Neophyti 1, Vol. III, Levitico* *70-*83; R. Hayward, "The Memra of YHWH and the Development of its Use in Targum Neofiti I", *JJS* 24 (1973) 412-18; L. Sabourin, "The Memra of God in the Targums", *BThB* (1976) 79-85. The last cited article is a presentation in brief of a comprehensive study of D. Muñoz Leon, *Dios-Palabra, Memra en los Targumim del Pentateuco* (Granada 1974).
70. For a summary of the different positions regarding Memra as either an hypostasis or as a "buffer-word", see Sabourin, "The Memra of God" 79-80.
71. Sabourin, "The Memra of God" 79, states that "the expression *Memra di Yhwh*, 'the Word of Yahweh' occurs more than 600 times in the different Aramaic Targums of the Pentateuch". Hayward, "The Memra of YHWH", 412, estimates that "*Memra* is found 338 times in N and 628 times in Ngl (= glosses on N)" and that "N to Deuteronomy is curiously richer in occurrences of Memra than the other four books".
72. Cf. the results of a survey carried out by D. Muñoz Leon in "Apendice sobre el Memra de Yahweh" 70* ff.; Hayward, "The Memra of YHWH", 414-418.
73. "The Memra of God" 84-85. The position of Muñoz Leon (*Dios Palabra* 631-632) allows for a certain hypostatization within the monotheistic framework of Judaism; the substitution removes the anthropomorphic representation by saying that God acts and communicates through his *Memra*.
74. "The sons of Israel say: How the crown of kingship becomes you, O Lord! When your sons saw the signs of your wonders in the sea, and the might between the waves, at that hour they opened their mouths together and said: 'Of the Lord is *the kingship* before the world and for all ages'."

75. Exod 14:25; Deut 1:30; cf. Sperber, *The Bible in Aramaic*, Vol. IVB, 38 for other paraphrases à propos of the Lord in battle.
76. "It is the Lord who worked their battle victories for them when they were yet in Egypt and he is about to work their battle victories for them again at the Reed Sea". In Deut 1:30, *Tg. Neof.* renders "he will accomplish your battle victories for you" and *Tg. Onq.* has the more stereotyped "his *memra* will attack for you".
77. "How long will you stand praying before me? Your prayer has been heard before me; besides, the prayer of the sons of Israel has anticipated yours."
78. In four of the five remaining examples chosen to illustrate this device, it is noteworthy that *Tg. Neof.* retains the original MT turn of phrase (with additional paraphrase in most cases, which does not affect the rhetorical question), whereas in all four cases *Tg. Onq.* represents a more developed sensitivity. Does this indicate that *Tg. Onq.* represents a more developed awareness, which is only beginning to emerge in *Tg. Neof.* with regard to these rhetorical questions? A thorough investigation of such questions and statements in the various targumic recensions should be interesting.
79. Apart from having removed the rhetorical question, *Tg. Onq.* represents a milder version of *Tg. Neof.*'s paraphrase.
80. In the two further instances of this "walking before God" (Gen 24:40 and 48:15) *Tg. Neof.* has "to serve before in truth" for the former and "to go before in truth" for the latter, while *Tg. Onq.* has the simpler form, "to serve before", for both passages.
81. Cf. Deut 6:14; 7:4; 8:19; 11:16, 28; 13:3, 7, 14; 17:3; 18:20; 28:14, 36, 64; 29:25; 31:18, 20.

SOME OBSERVATIONS ON THE DATING OF TARGUM JOB

Céline Mangan, O.P., *Dominican Convent, Cabra, Dublin*

Dermot Ryan was a tall man and the room in which I studied Semitic languages with him in the old University College Dublin, was a narrow high room with a long window at one end under which his desk stood. I remember on one occasion as we students entered the room I happened to glance over his head and, noticing the catch broken on the window, said: "Had you a break-in last night?" He looked around the room and blanched – his tape recorder was missing on which he had a tape just acquired from Rome of an Armenian reading some Syriac texts. Dermot Ryan's teaching of Semitic languages was never merely a pursuit of dead languages. He managed to transmit to his students a love of these languages as the living interpretation of the sacred texts.

The Targums, the Aramaic translations of the Hebrew Bible, are part of that great tradition of handing on the living text. The Meturgeman (translator) brought the text of the Hebrew Bible to life for the people of his own time and handed it on renewed to the next generation. This process was going on from the time Aramaic began to replace Hebrew as a spoken language (see Neh 8:5-8) but the writing down of these Aramaic translations did not occur until much later. How much later is the question that has always exercised the minds of those engaged in targumic studies.

I have been working for the past number of years on the translation of the rabbinic Targum of the Book of Job (henceforth *Tg.* Job), for the edition of a translation (with notes) of the Aramaic Bible currently being published by Michael Glazier Inc. of Wilmington, Delaware, and the problem of the dating of *Tg.* Job has been my constant companion in the endeavour. This paper will attempt to throw some light on one or two aspects of that problem but first we will need to consider *Tg.* Job in the context of other Targums of Job.

Early Targums of Job

One would have thought that the discovery of a Targum of Job in Qumran (found in Cave 11, so generally called *11QtgJob*) would have greatly facilitated the understanding of the dating of *Tg.* Job. Unfortunately the two Targums seem to have come from totally different traditions and so have little in common.[1]

Likewise there is a mention of what would appear to be a Targum at the end of the LXX where it says: "this is translated from the Syrian (i.e. Aramaic) book." This is the opinion, for instance, of P. Kahle, in the first edition of his *Cairo Geniza*. He says this "can scarcely mean anything else than the Aramaic Targum."[2] Other scholars, however, would consider that the appendix is referring to a midrashic elaboration rather than to a Targum proper which would point at least to an early association of midrashic content with the Book of Job, unlike the Qumran Targum which is very literal.[3]

Another mention of an early Targum of Job comes from Rabbinic sources. The earliest mention of the tradition about such a Targum is to be found in Tosephta, *Shabbat* 13:2.[4]

> R. Jose said: "R. Ḥalaphta once visited Rabban Gamaliel in Tiberias and found him sitting on the table of Joḥanan b. Nazif, and in his hand was a Targum scroll of Job, and he was reading in it. R. Ḥalaphta said to him: 'I recall that Rabban Gamaliel, your grandfather,[5] was sitting on a step of the Temple mount, and they brought before him a Targum scroll of Job, and he told the mason to secrete it under the course of stones.' "

It is difficult to say whether the Rabbi's suppression of the Targum was due to the stricture about the writing down of oral tradition or because he disapproved of translating a book such as the Book of Job. In either case we have no way of knowing to which Targum he is referring. Some scholars would suggest it was *11QtgJob*.[6]

Witnesses to Tg. Job

One is forced, then, to try to solve the problem of the dating of *Tg.* Job from the internal evidence of the Targum itself and this method, also, is fraught with difficulties. Work on the targum has been hampered until recently by the lack of a critical edition. Judgments on dating were made on the evidence of the printed editions, the earliest of which, Daniel Bomberg's *Biblia Rabbinica*, only dates from the sixteenth century.[7] A critical edition, which takes into account the manuscript traditions behind these printed editions, has at last been produced. It was prepared as a doctoral thesis by F.J. Fernandez Vallina under the late A. Díez Macho at the present great centre of targumic studies in Madrid.[8] Fernandez Vallina takes a fourteenth century MS from Cambridge as his basic text,[9] but his critical apparatus refers to several others, the oldest being a Vatican MS from the thirteenth century which, though having much in common with the Cambridge MS, is not in as good a condition.[10]

Access to the manuscript traditions will necessitate the revision of many statements about the dating of *Tg.* Job which were based on the printed editions and the presence or absence in them of alternative versions of the text.[11] N.N. Glatzer, for example, in his otherwise very valuable article on "The Book of Job and its Interpreters",[12] can make the following statement:

> The original version of the extant Targum, composed in Palestine probably in the fourth or fifth century, reduced the impact of provocative or obscure passages of the text by referring them to events of the Biblical past or by reading into them meanings suggested by rabbinic thought. This version was revised in the eighth or ninth century by a translator who planned to restore the plain meaning of the text, at least in the case of crucial sentences.[13]

A study of the manuscript evidence shows that it is impossible to be this dogmatic. In the Cambridge MS, for example, sometimes the more literal is the text (e.g. 5:7; 9:26; 14:4) and at other times the more midrashic (e.g. 6:6; 7:12; 12:6). Even among the printed editions there can be variety: the Antwerp Polyglot, for example, even though its tendency is to give a literal text, sometimes keeps the version with the midrashic allusions as its text (e.g. 1:6, 15; 2:1; 3:6), sometimes in spite of having a shorter version available (e.g. 7:12; 14:22).

The Dating of Tg. Job

But these MSS themselves are still very late. We can push the witnesses to the text further back into the eleventh century as it was extensively used in the writings of Saadya Gaon[14] and from then on by many of the early medieval commentators with some notable exceptions such as Rashi and Ibn Ezra. Saadya's work is the *terminus ad quem*. How far back can one go for the *terminus a quo*?

Every century from the first to the ninth has been proposed by scholars.[15] Certainly *Tg.* Job has much midrashic material in common with the Babylonian Talmud. To give but a few examples:

> "Dinah" is given as the name of Job's wife (see *Tg.* Job 2:9; *b. BB* 15b); similar meanings are given to the names of Job's three daughters (*Tg.* Job 42:14 [alt.]; *b. BB* 16b); a similar interpretation is given of the way in which the three friends are made aware of Job's misfortune (*Tg.* Job 2:11; *b. BB* 16b).

It is difficult to know, however, whether *Tg.* Job is dependent on the Babylonian Talmud for this midrash, the Talmud on *Tg.* Job or both on common sources.

In fact there is also some material from the earlier Tannaitic period in the targum. W. Bacher, for example,[16] draws attention to interpretations of the text already in the Mishnah. He also lists the many references to the Patriarchs in the Targum (e.g. 3:19; 4:7; 5:17; 14:18; 15:10), a fact which links the Targum with the older midrash which considered Job as belonging to the time of the Patriarchs, whereas the later midrash made of him a pious Jew.[17]

But reading further back still, it is also possible to discern material which *Tg.* Job shares with the New Testament and pseudepigraphal literature, such as:

> the use of: "mammon" (*Tg.* Job 22:3; 27:8; Matt 6:24); "fire of Gehenna" (*Tg.* Job 3:17; Matt 5:22; *Apoc. Abraham* 15:6; *Ascension Isaiah* 1.3); "paraclete" considered as advocate (*Tg.* Job 33:23; 1 John 2:1-2; *Vita Moses* 2.134); "flesh and blood" for human person (*Tg.* Job 37:20 [alt.]; Matt 16:17; John 6:56; *Pseudo Philo* 63:6); "new" wine splitting skins (*Tg.* Job 32:19; Matt 9:17).

Titles for God in Tg. Job

Among such concepts are some titles for God in *Tg.* Job:

(i) "Father who is in heaven":

J. Jeremias thought that this was a late insertion into *Tg.* Job because it is not to be found in the printed editions,[18] but it is in all the MSS. While rare in Jewish literature, its presence in the NT ensures its antiquity (see Matt 6:9).[19] It is also present in some MSS of *Test. Job*, a first century work.[20] While its inclusion in *Test. Job* could conceivably be due to Christian editing of the MSS[21] this cannot possibly be true of the Targum, though perhaps its being edited out of the printed edition could be due to a bias in the opposite direction.

While no claim for an early dating can be made from this single usage in the Targum, therefore, the fact that other early names for God are also to be found there might point towards at least a very early core to the Targum.

(ii) "Powerful One"

Closely linked to "Father in heaven" is the title "Powerful One"[22] which was used in Jewish sources as a proper name for God, at least by the end of the first century A.D. – in a dialogue attributed to Rabbi Eliezer and Rabbi Joshua (see *Pseudo Philo* 18:11; 20:4; etc.).[23] It was already used in the New Testament in Matt 26:64 (see Luke 22:69). There are three passages in which it occurs in *Tg.* Job: 5:8; 14:18 (alt.); 18:4 (alt.). 5:8 reads:

> But, as for me, I would seek out *instruction from the Powerful One* (MT: *'ēl*) and to God I would state my case;

14:18 (alt.) reads:

> And, indeed, *Lot who separated himself from Abraham, who is likened to a tall* mountain, fell away and *the Powerful One* removed the *glory of his Shekinah from Sodom which is* his place.

18:4 (alt.) reads:

> *Is it possible* that, because of you whose life is wearied in

> itself, the earth should be *forgotten from being inhabited* and the *Powerful One* be removed from his place.

Both 14:18 and 18:4 have the same Hebrew phrase: "or the rock be removed from its place." While both include "the Powerful One", 14:18 has a midrashic interpretation while 18:4 does not, again pointing up the lack of consistency in the addition of midrashic elements to the text.[24]

(iii) Shekinah

The *Shekinah* as the representation of God's presence in creation occurs generally very frequently in the Targums.[25] Its use in *Tg.* Job, however, is limited to three instances: 13:24; 14:18 (alt.); 34:29. 13:24 reads:

> Why do you remove your *Shekinah* and count me as an opponent to you?

14:18 (alt.) reads:

> And, indeed, *Lot who separated himself from Abraham, who is likened to a tall* mountain, fell away and *the Powerful One* removed the *glory of his Shekinah from Sodom which is* his place.

34:29 reads:

> When he is quiet who can condemn him and when he removes his *Shekinah* then who can observe him? . . .

In 13:24 and 34:29 *Shekinah* takes the place of "face". While the targumist, as we shall see, does not usually avoid the anthropomorphic "face", he has difficulty with the use of "remove" in relation to the face of God.[26] It is interesting that the LXX also avoids the phrase in 13:24. In the other passage (14:18 [alt.]), *Shekinah* is linked to "glory". This is also common in the targums, though in many instances *Shekinah* can take the place of "glory". The combination of the two terms is thought to have originated in the time of R. Aqiba.[27]

(iv) Memra

Much more frequent is the insertion of *Memra* into the Targum.[28] There are three main ways in which this occurs:

as an addition to the name of God;
as an avoidance of anthropomorphism;
as a pronominal substitution.

Memra is added to the following names for God: *yyy* (1:21 [bis]; 2:9; 42:9, 10 [bis], 12); *'lh'* (4:9); *Shaddai* (29:5). There are many instances of these names, however, before which *Memra* does not appear.

Memra replaces the "breath" of God: of *'lh'* (4:9; 37:10); of *Shaddai* (32:8; 33:4). It takes the place of *rûaḥ* before "mouth" in one instance (15:30 [alt.]). There is also one example of a subtitution for "mouth" itself in the *Miqra'ot Gedolot* (39:27) but the MSS have "the word of your mouth" (see below). While these substitutions can be seen as an obvious avoidance of anthropomorphisms, this avoidance is more honoured in the breach than in the observance in *Tg.* Job as in *Tg.* Pss.[29]

Shunary's detailed analysis of the method of translating parts of the body in relation to God shows that in *Tg.* Pss literal translation is more frequent than avoidance and circumlocutions. Those parts most frequently avoided in *Tg.* Pss are the face, eyes, mouth and feet while the lips, nose, heart, head, arm, are never avoided. There is similar ambivalence in *Tg.* Job: God's "nostrils" (e.g. 4:9), "lips" (e.g. 11:5), "heart" (e.g. 36:5) remain in the text. This is true for the eyes also though sometimes "before" is substituted for them (e.g. 25:5). "Mouth", as we have seen, can be translated by *memra* but it can also be translated literally (e.g. 37:2). "Hand" remains in the text on many occasions (e.g. 5:18) but very often *mḥt*, "plague", is inserted before it (e.g. 1:11; 2:5; 12:9) or substituted for it (e.g. 19:21; 30:24).[30] It has to be pointed out, however, that this can even apply to Job's hand (see 23:2 – though LXX and Syriac refer this to God: see RSV). "Face" can also remain in the Targum (e.g. 13:20) even in a verse where "plague" is added to "hand" and *memra* is inserted (see 1:11; 2:5). But there are instances, as we have seen, of its being translated by *Shekinah*.

"Breath" is the only part of the body, therefore, always avoided in the Targum. Shunary does not actually treat it as a part of the body in his treatment of *Tg.* Pss. It is interesting that in the one passage in *Tg.* Pss where it occurs in relation to God (18:16) it is also translated by *memra.*

The Pronominal Use of *Memra* in Tg. Job

The use of *memra* for dating purposes still remains problematical. R. Hayward, for example, goes to great lengths to prove its antiquity in the Pentateuchal Targums (especially *Tg. Neofiti*) by the theological content of the expression. Apart from a link with the justice of God in 1:21,

> The *memra* of the Lord gave and the *memra* of the Lord *and the house of judgment* has taken away,

the same kind of theological expression is not in evidence in *Tg.* Job. Does this mean, then, that *Tg.* Job is at a later stage of development than the Palestinian Targums if, as Hayward contends:

> ... the *Memra* lost its original theological sense and became a mere replacement for the Tetragram YHWH.[31]

Certainly on this criterion, *Tg.* Job would be very late indeed but, it seems to me, *Tg.* Job's method of using *memra* is more valuable as a means of dating the Targums. This is in the prevalence of its pronominal use. It was to be expected that this pronominal use would be frequent in relation to God in *Tg.* Job and sure enough it is there. It is used as the subject of a verb (1:10), as object (2:3), as nominal suffix (1:11; 2:5; 15:30 [alt.]), or with a preposition (13:9; 21:15). This latter usage has often been seen as another example of the avoidance of anthropomorphism.[32]

In fact, this pronominal use of *memra* also relates to human beings in *Tg.* Job. There are several examples of this usage to be found in the Targum: see 7:8; 19:18; 27:3; 30:20; 34:2.[33] In 19:18 it is used of Job:

> Even young children loathe *my memra* (MT *me*) (see 27:3, 30:20);

in 7:8 it is used of Job and not of God even though both have a pronoun in the same verse:

> ... your eye is upon *my memra* (MT *me*) but I am not there;

and in 34:2 it is used of Elihu:

> Hear my words, O you wise ones, and you who know, listen to *my memra* (MT *me*).[34]

It seems to me that we could have in this pronominal use of *memra* for human beings a pointer to an early core to the text of *Tg.* Job since it seems unlikely that the usage would be introduced once *Memra* became a popular name for the deity. The sequence in timing would seem to be: first of all the pronominal use of *memra* for human beings, then the same use in relation to God, after which its use was extended to becoming a title for God. It seems clear that the pronominal use for human beings was largely edited out of the Pentateuchal and Prophetic Targums at this later stage and left only in those of the Writings (e.g. *Tg.* Ruth 3:8; *Tg.* 2 Chron 16:3; 23:16).[35]

Unfortunately there is no way of checking the dating of the usage from *11QtgJob*, since all the places where it is to be found in *Tg.* Job are missing in the Qumran Targum.[36] One slight indication might be discernable in 39:27: where the MT has *'al-pîkā* (lit. "by your mouth"), the MSS of *Tg.* Job have *'l-mymr pwmk* (lit. "by the word of your mouth"), and *11QtgJob* has *'l m'mrk* (lit. "by your word") which could be "by you",[37] but this is ambiguous since, as we have seen, it may be merely a substitution for "mouth". The Targums in general often substitute *memra* for "mouth" to give the sense of the command of God: e.g. at Deut 1:26; 9:23.[38]

Conclusion

Tg. Job as we have it now is undoubtedly an amalgam of various traditions from different periods. As R. Weiss puts it:

> It is very probable that in its present form the Targum to Job is a collection of various Targums, perhaps even from different periods.[39]

But it seems to me that a very early core can be discerned in the Targum, especially by the presence in it of material with it has in common with New Testament and pseudepigraphal literature and also by the pronominal use of *memra* for human beings. I am aware that one cannot make a total judgment about the targumic use of *memra* from one single Targum but the findings of *Tg.* Job can perhaps add to, and correct if necessary, the theories about *memra* already in existence.

If it is true that the pronominal use of *memra* which has come to light from a study of *Tg.* Job is a very old phenomenon, then the core of our present Targum may be precisely the same as the Targum which Rabbi Gamaliel had in his hand long ago. Whether this is so or not, the handing on of the targumic traditions about Job which he tried to stop has continued on in spite of him to the present day.

Notes

1. For a detailed analysis of *11QtgJob*, see M. Sokoloff, *The Targum to Job from Qumran Cave XI* (Ramat-Gan 1974); see also, J.A. Fitzmyer, "The First-Century Targum of Job from Qumran Cave XI", *A Wandering Aramean* (Missoula, Montana 1979) 161-182.
2. P. Kahle, *The Cairo Geniza* (London 1947) 124. Fitzmyer, "The First-Century Targum of Job" 177 n. 46 points out that this statement is missing in the second edition of the book (Oxford 1959).
3. G. Steinberger's new edition of H.L. Strack's *Einleitung in Talmud und Midrash* (Munchen 1982) draws attention to a *Midrash Job* as the work of a third century Rabbi.
4. It is also to be found in the Palestinian (*j. Shabb.* 16:1) and the Babylonian (*b. Shabb.* 115a) Talmuds and in *Tractate Sopherim* 5:15.
5. See Acts 5:4; 22:3.
6. See Sokoloff, *The Targum to Job*, [4]-[5].
7. The other main printed editions are: the Antwerp Polyglot (*Biblia Regia*, 1569-1572); the *Miqra'ot Gedolot* (based on the *Biblia Rabbinica*) and Walton's Polyglot (London 1654-1657). P. de Lagarde's *Hagiographa Chaldaice* (Leipzig 1873) was used for a long time as a critical edition but it is full of the errors which characterise the original Rabbinic Bible of Bomberg.
8. See F.J. Fernandez Vallina, *El Targum de Job* (Madrid 1982). While I have counted more than thirty orthographic errors in the monograph it was still an invaluable tool to have to hand in the translation of *Tg.* Job.
9. Cambridge MS *Or. Ee. 5.9*; No. 15862 of the Jerusalem Institute of Microfilms.
10. See Fernandez Vallina, *El Targum de Job*, 43-89. His compatriot, L. Díez Merino, has made a special study of the sixteenth century Spanish MSS among them and his book on the subject also provides a valuable introduction to *Tg.* Job: L. Díez Merino, *Targum de Job*

– *Edicion Principe del Ms. Villa-Amil n. 5 de Alfonsa de Zamora* (Madrid 1984). See his "Manuscritos del Targum de Job", *Henoch* 4 (1982) 41-64 and A. Díez Macho, "Le Targum de Job dans la tradition Sefardie", *De la Torah au Messie*, M. Carrez, J. Dore, P. Grelot (eds.) (Paris 1979) 545-556.

11. These alternative translations are a feature of *Tg.* Job, over fifty verses having one or more alternatives. Besides this, in over thirty other verses, there are alternative clauses, phrases or single words.
12. A. Altmann (ed.), *Biblical Motifs* (Cambridge, MA 1966) 203 n. 17.
13. See W. Bacher, "Das Targum zu Hiob", *MGWJ* 20 (1871) 208-223.
14. See E.J. Rosenthal, "Saadya's Exegesis of the Book of Job", *Saadya Studies* (Manchester 1943); G. Vajda, "Quelques remarques en marge de la second redaction du commentaire de Saadia Gaon sur le livre de Job", *REJ* 135 (1976) 157-168.
15. See R. Weiss, *The Aramaic Targum of Job* (Tel-Aviv 1979) [IX]. This work of Weiss is of great importance in the study of *Tg.* Job especially in tracing the language of the Targum and its links with the language of the Yerushalmi Targums to the Pentateuch.
16. Bacher, "Das Targum zu Hiob" 213-216.
17. See L. Ginzberg, *The Legends of the Jews* V (Philadelphia 1968) 381-382.
18. J. Jeremias, *The Prayers of Jesus* (London 1967) 110.
19. For a discussion on texts in the Pentateuchal Targums, see M. McNamara, *Targum and Testament* (Shannon 1968) 115-119.
20. See R.P. Spittler, "Testament of Job", *OTPseudepigrapha* I, 833-834.
21. Spittler, "Testament of Job" 855, note g.
22. See Spittler, "Testament of Job" 855, note g.
23. See E.E. Urbach, *The Sages – Their Concepts and Beliefs* (Jerusalem 1965) 84 ff. and the other texts mentioned there.
24. The *Peshitta* also uses the "Powerful One" as a title for God: e.g. at 5:17 to translate *Shaddai*. There are many links between *Tg.* Job and the other versions to the Hebrew text: see P. Dhorme, *A Commentary on the Book of Job* (trans. H. Knight) (London 1967) clxix ff. This would provide another fruitful field of study for early dating.
25. For a study of the *Shekinah* see M. Kadushin, *The Rabbinic Mind* (New York 1972) 221-261.
26. See R. Weiss, "The Translation of Anthropomorphic Expressions in Targum Job" (Heb), *Tarbiz* 44 (1974) 67.
27. See D. Muñoz, "Apéndice sobre el Memra de Yahweh en el MS Neophyti 1", A. Díez Macho (ed.) *Neophyti 1, Vol. III, Levitico* (Madrid 1971) 81*; L. Díez Merino, *Targum de Job* 252; McNamara, *Targum and Testament* 100-101.
28. For bibliography, see C.T.R. Hayward, *Divine Name and Presence: The Memra* (Totowa, New Jersey 1981) 169-177.
29. See Weiss, *Tarbiz* 44 (1974) 70-71 for a bibliography and a more detailed analysis of these anthropomorphic expressions. For a similar assessment of the LXX of Job, see H.W. Orlinsky, "Studies in the

LXX of Job", *HUCA* 30 (1959) 153-167; 32 (1961) 239-268; for *Tg.* Pss see J. Shunary, "Avoidance of Anthropomorphisms in the Targum of Psalms", *Textus* 5 (1966) 133-144.

30. The same is true of *Tg.* Pss: see Shunary, "Avoidance of Anthropomorphisms" 139-140.
31. Hayward, *Divine Name and Presence* 136.
32. See Hayward, *Divine Name and Presence* 3-4.
33. See D.R.G. Beattie, "Ancient Elements in the Targum to Ruth", *Proceedings of the Ninth World Congress of Jewish Studies* (Jerusalem 1986) 159 165. I am indebted to Derek Beattie for drawing my attention in the first place to the presence of this pronominal usage of *memra* in the Targums of the Writings, for example at *Tg.* Ruth 3:8. E. Levine (*Aramaic Version of Ruth* [AnBib 58; Rome 1973] 32) translates *memra* in this instance as "body" and does not draw attention to the pronominal use at all in his analysis of the text.
34. It is probable also that this pronominal usage is behind the use of *memra* to translate *'imrô* in 20:29.
35. See Beattie, ("Ancient Elements" 163-165) who points to only "a few stray cases . . . in the targums of the Pentateuch", e.g. *Tgs. Onq.* and *Yer. I*, Gen 41:44; *Tg. Yer. I*, Gen 9:17. See also P. Dhorme, *A Commentary on the Book of Job* 278-279. The usage has been discerned in the LXX of Job: see 34:34 where *ly* is translated by *mou to rema*. Is it possible that the beginnings of the usage can be seen in the late Hebrew of the Book of Job where *d^{e}bar g^{e}bûrôt* (41:4) could conceivably mean "his strengths" rather than "the word of . . ."? The Targum translates by "the *memra* of . . .".
36. Though it has to be pointed out that at 42:9 where *Tg.* Job adds *memra* to *yyy*, *11QtgJob* does not do so.
37. Sokoloff translates this as "on your say-so": *The Targum to Job* 93.
38. See Orlinsky, "Studies in the Septuagint of Job" 162 n. 25.
39. Weiss, *The Aramaic Targum of Job* [IX].

PSALMS AS PRAYERS OF THE POOR

James McPolin, S.J., *Milltown Institute of Theology and Philosophy, Dublin*

"The Psalms have regularly been rediscovered in times of oppression"[1] – this forceful insight of a contemporary Scripture scholar affirms that the worldwide voice of the poor and the deprived, which we can hear very clearly today, finds strong echoes in the Psalms. The voice of today's poor can enable us to rediscover, along with themselves, the Psalms and the God of the poor whom they address. The theme of poverty in the Bible is now being re-examined in response to the call of the poor and in the light of our national and international situation of poverty, of the ever-widening gap between the rich and the poor, which is the result of distorted structures in our society. On many levels scholars, spiritual writers and poets[2] are attempting to bridge the gap between texts of Scripture originally composed for life-situations of long ago and their meaning for a new world of diverse cultures, conditions and problems. Some writers show how a renewed and more realistic understanding of the "poor" in the Psalms can further a properly theological reflection in support of the poor and marginalized of today.[3] Our own sensitive listening to human situations of deprivation and injustice and the resulting heightened awareness of human rights, particularly the rights of the poor, and of various forms of oppression at work in society can help us to develop new insights into the Psalms when we read them in the light of the struggles of the poor and social justice.

The Psalms speak of God as the saviour of the poor, their hope, their stronghold and liberator, whether these be prayers of an individual or of the community. In worship, where the Psalms were frequently prayed, the poor seem to regain their rights. There, at least, God's order still prevails:

> Give the king your justice, O God. . . .
> May he defend the cause of the poor of the people,
> Give deliverance to the needy (Ps 72:1, 4).[4]

> The Lord is a stronghold for the oppressed,
> A stronghold in times of trouble.
> He does not forget the cry of the afflicted
> . . . the needy shall not always be forgotten
> And the hope of the poor shall not perish forever (Ps 9:
> 9, 12, 18).

The God of Israel

> . . . executes justice for the oppressed
> . . . gives food to the hungry . . .
> Opens the eyes of the blind
> Lifts up those who are bowed down . . .
> Watches over the sojourners . . .
> Upholds the widow and the fatherless (Ps 146:7-9).

In worship there awakens the awareness that God is present sustaining the poor. The temple itself seems to be the seat of justice for the oppressed. It is even probable that the temple was a sanctuary, a place where they would have a tangible experience of God's care and compassion. The poor, who can feel stigmatized and humiliated, feel rescued by God from these feelings of separateness, inferiority and self-contempt. The Psalms will have nothing to do with the view that the poor are not only unfortunate but also inferior. They have a saviour God. They have God at their side. In their struggle against enemies they can always turn to God. They will always find a hearing with God.

On the other hand, the Psalms do not seem to rank high on the list of Scripture writings most commonly chosen by Christian writers today for their reflections on poverty and justice. Many Christians pray these Psalms about the poor privately or in groups without relating them to the social situation of deprived and marginalized people about them. Generally, the Christian preferential care for the poor does not seem to be linked with the Psalter, the official prayer of the Church. Even with the helps provided by modern scholarship and more suitable translations, the Psalter and particularly those Psalms which refer to the "poor" predominantly serve personal and individual forms of spirituality. They have not become integrated into a social spirituality or theology which focuses rather on those materially, socially poor and deprived people in society and on their relationship to God and to ourselves than on our own personal, individual experience of being "poor", either spiritually or materially.

Certain difficulties and misunderstandings could partially explain this fact. For example, the impression can sometimes be conveyed that the Psalms primarily concern the spiritually "poor" (those who trust in God, recognize God as the source of all life) and have little to say about people who are materially or socially poor and oppressed by injustice. Also, statements and language about the poor can sometimes seem very vague and unrelated to life-situations of today's poor. Yet it is possible to overcome some of these difficulties and to show that some of these Psalms about the "poor" in Israel can be read as prayers of the poor, for the poor, and sung as songs for a very modern world. "The contemporary setting of today's world", says Carroll Stuhlmuller in his recent commentary on the Psalms, "is an essential ingredient for the correct and full appreciation of God's word within the Bible. We emphasize the importance of setting each psalm within our contemporary Church and world, not only for accurate biblical interpretation, but also for indicating how the Bible itself frequently reinterpreted the Psalms".[5]

Language for the Poor

The "poor" (including the state of being "poor" or "afflicted") feature in thirty-three Psalms,[6] in varying degrees of prominence. Besides, in other Psalms there is mention of people who are actually poor, materially or socially, such as the "hungry, sojourners, widows, fatherless", even though the common Hebrew words for "poor" are not used.[7]

Generally in the Old Testament several Hebrew words express the notion of poverty but none of them can be translated exactly by our English term "poor". The most common word is *'ānî* in its singular form.[8] Literally it describes a person who is bowed down, bent over, who occupies a lowly position. The poor person has to look up at others, is bowed down under pressure in a dependent relationship, labours under a weight and is not in possession of his/her whole strength and vigour. The *'ānî* is the humiliated person who can no longer stand upright because of economic and social pressure. It describes a position of inferiority and primarily expresses a relation rather than a state of social distress. When *'ānî* is used alongside *dal* or *'ebyôn* it is more likely to express an economic situation. In a more developed usage *'ānî* implies a state of lowliness or distress and hence a person in a state of reduced competence and lesser worth. The Aramaic and later Hebrew secondary form *'ānāw* (always found in the plural form *'ᵃnāwîm* in the Psalms[9]) is very closely associated with *'ānî*; the terms are used interchangeably.[10] Both words may express material or spiritual poverty. Both are probably connected with *'ānāh*, which means "afflict", "oppress" or "humble another person" and the noun forms *'ᵒnî*[11] and *'ānût*[12] express "poverty", "affliction" or "oppression". Basically *'ānî* (or *'ānāw*) means those who are "bowed down", "afflicted". This fact explains why dictionaries and English versions of the Psalms give a wide variety of translations: "afflicted", "poor", "humble", "oppressed", "downtrodden", "needy", "weak", "lowly" or "meek". The weakness implied in the word makes it possible at times to translate it as "meek", that is, having no will to fight.

'Ebyôn[13] describes the person who asks (from *'ābāh*, "will" or "desire"). Originally the *'ebyôn* is the one who seeks alms, the beggar. The word then comes to be more generally used for the poor person. A person can ask in two senses – from other people as a beggar and from God. The *'ebyôn* is the person who is lacking something and awaits it from another. English translations and dictionaries render it as "needy", "poor", "in want" or "oppressed".

Dal[14] is the "weak, frail or languishing person" (from *dālal*, "hang down", "droop", "dangle", "be weak"). The word is used above all for physical weakness and then applied to the position of the lowest classes, of the peasants as poor, needy, unimportant and therefore it describes people who have been made helpless or reduced in status. Frequently in the Old Testament it expresses material and social deprivation with no other connotations. English versions and dictionaries commonly translate it as "poor", "needy", "weak", "helpless", "low", "thin".

'Ānî, *dal* and *'ebyôn* constitute the predominant language for the poor in the Psalms. Occasionally they are linked with

other words such as *dak*[15] ("downtrodden", from *dākāh*, "crush", "crouch down"), *ḥelkāh* ("hapless", "unfortunate")[16] or *'ašūqîm* ("oppression").[17] They are not neutral descriptions for they all have an emotive connotation. Originally they indicated circumstances which urgently call for change. Towards the end of the Old Testament a neutral term *rûš*[18] appears ("be poor", "be needy"). This word describes an economic, social situation neutrally. It is not surprising, then, that it was never used by the prophets. For them the poverty of their people was an oppressive situation.

This language for the poor in the Psalms gives us some insight into the root meanings of what it was to be poor in Hebrew life. However, there are many, varying traditions about the poor in the Old Testament and therefore this language needs to be listened to attentively not only within its literary setting of the Psalms but also within the historical and social situation of the poor of Israel which they reflect. We cannot conclude merely from the words themselves whether *'ānî*, *'ebyôn* and *dal* express material or spiritual poverty. In fact, they may indicate either or both in different contexts and situations.[19]

Psalms as History of the Poor

Psalms concerning the poor extend over a long period of the history of Israel. They contain old traditions of Israel about the poor and reflect diverse socio-economic conditions from Canaanite to Maccabean times. Despite later changes and additions many Psalms reach back into the pre-exilic period, approaching even the period of David and Solomon. Sometimes they reach back even further. Ps 68, for example, was probably composed initially during the kingship of Saul (1200-1000 B.C.). It tells of God's care for the poor, the fatherless, the homeless, prisoners and widows (vv. 5, 6, 10). Also, Ps 76, a victory song proclaiming God as saviour of all the oppressed (*'anāwîm*, v.9) throughout the world, seems to reflect the initial monarchy either under David or Solomon (1000-922 B.C.) or Hezekiah (715-687 B.C.). Some claim it is one of the earliest Psalms and may have been composed under David.

A tentative dating of these Psalms about the poor, as regards their initial or final composition, shows they are rooted in a long span of Israel's life-story and reflection on the experience of the poor. The composition of these Psalms is to be linked either with the time of the kingship of David, Solomon, even Saul[20] or with the following period before the exile (587 B.C.), especially with the time of the late prophets (e.g. Jeremiah) and the Assyrian and Babylonian invasions,[21] and also with the time during[22] and following the exile,[23] during and after the reconstruction of the temple (520-515 B.C.), even during the period when wisdom literature flourished. These Psalms, then, would reflect a variety of situations and traditions right up to the period of the Second Temple (i.e. the temple of Zerubbabel, rebuilt in 520-515 B.C.) when the Psalter reached its present form. Apart from their long history of composition, these Psalms reflect on traditions about the poor which already existed before they were composed.

Traditions which we find in the books of Exodus and Deuteronomy and in the prophets appear throughout these Psalms. God's care for the underprivileged and the wronged, for the "fatherless and the oppressed" (Ps 10:18) recalls the ancient traditions about the poor as God's special concern.[24] Frequently, the poor are placed under the protection of God's covenant love (*ḥesed*).[25] God's special care of the poor is one of the central themes of Pss 9-10, which constitute a single poem, probably composed in the period of the Assyrian and Babylonian domination. The poor (including the state of being poor, i.e. affliction, poverty) are mentioned frequently. There are several tensions in this prayer: between the nation of Israel and foreign nations, between the suffering of the poor and the success of the wicked, between God as always present in the temple and seemingly absent in time of distress, between God's warm compassion and stern justice in the cause of the poor. The Psalm is to be connected with the covenant which places the poor under the special protection of God's statutes (Exod 20:22-23:33). The needs of the poor, the afflicted, the fatherless, the oppressed and the helpless are linked with God's great "deeds" in history. The poor can be sure of God's help for the traditions about God helping the oppressed in Israel's past are the basis of hope for the poor (9:7-10, 18; 10:14-18). The Lord has always been the help of the "fatherless" (10:14, 18) and does justice for them. The "fatherless" along with widows and sojourners represent, according to an ancient covenant tradition, all oppressed, needy and deprived people (Exod 22:22-24).

The care of the weak and helpless was not unique to Israel. Theoretically it was the duty of Near Eastern kings and the responsibility of at least some of the deities. But in Israel there is a clear and strong tradition that the God of Israel is characterized by justice and care of the defenceless and the poor (Pss 9-10). Ps 82, which gives a prominent place to the poor (called *'ānî*, *'ebyôn*, *dal* and *rāš*), is infiltrated with Canaanite mythology about the assembly of the "gods" (*'elōhîm*). It reflects a long-evolving tradition about pagan gods and arrives at a conclusion about who is really divine through norms of human compassion and social justice. It is practical and condemns pagan "gods" to the same fate as befalls corrupt, self-seeking judges and all those in authority who exploit the poor and the defenceless (vv. 5-6). The Canaanite *'elōhîm* were integrated into Israel's tradition as an assembly of superhuman beings (later angels) and human beings of high position were sometimes called *'elōhîm* (Exod 4:16). By using this tradition the author insists that true divinity, whether in God or in God's representatives, is decided by concern for the weak and the destitute. The credential for the true God in the Mosaic covenant is a God of mercy, compassion and abounding in steadfast love (Exod 34:6-7).

The Psalm integrates a Canaanite element into its theology of the poor. It also manifests the impact of the prophetic preaching in its concern for the poor and the needy. The defence of the destitute and the weak, described in this Psalm (vv. 2-5) was a primary obligation of kings and judges. Failure to practise this important duty was condemned by the classical prophets. In its long, complicated development, the Psalm shows that Israelite religion did not immediately and definitively reject all other gods (especially those who were concerned for the poor). It recognizes that concern for the poor and the destitute was not an exclusively Israelite concern. The essence of the problem, stated in the Psalm, is: why are the defenceless and the poor continually deprived of justice? The reply is: mismanagement by subordinate, "divine" beings who have been entrusted with justice for all humanity, especially for the poor and the destitute.[26]

Within the history of the prayer of the people, the "poor" feature in many forms of prayer in the Psalter, for example, in psalms of praise, in prayers of petition (or "lament") for the individual or for the community, in prayers of thanksgiving for the individual or community, also in the more reflective forms of prayer (wisdom psalms) and in prayers celebrating the king. To what extent these prayers were composed directly for the temple liturgy we cannot be sure. It is possible that fewer psalms were composed directly for the temple liturgy than we often suppose to have been the case. It has been suggested that religious laity played an important role in the formation of the Psalms.

The call of the poor is to be heard within its literary and historical situation. For example, the word "poor" may have a negative or positive meaning according to the situation. It may have a negative meaning if the poor are the afflicted, deprived or oppressed people of society, in order to underline the scandal and evil of poverty. On the other hand, to be poor may mean to stand in need before God, to be open to and welcome God, to direct oneself to God's help. Both meanings may combine to describe those who are deprived and who are open to God.

In reading Scripture about the poor, we also need to ask: who says what, where and to whom? For example, sometimes the authors of the Psalms refer to themselves as poor:

> As for me, I am poor and needy
> But the Lord takes thought for me (Ps 40:17).

More frequently the poor are referred to more objectively:

> God has pity on the weak (*dal*) and the needy (*'ebyôn*)
> And saves the lives of the needy (*'ebyônîm*) (Ps 72:13).

Also, the authors may align themselves with the poor when they call on God for help. They see themselves participate in the special care and protection God offers the poor and the deprived:

> The Lord is a stronghold for the oppressed
> A stronghold in time of trouble. . . .
> Be gracious to me, O God
> Behold what I suffer (Ps 9:9, 13).

Sometimes the literary and historical context enable us to know better who are the poor (all the community or a group within it or the author alone) and how they are poor (materially, socially or spiritually poor). Even with these helps, however, it is sometimes very difficult to determine who are the poor in the Psalms.

The Structures of Society and the Poor

The various traditions about the poor in the Psalms are rooted in the diverse socio-economic conditions of Israel from Canaanite times till the final composition of the Psalter. The socio-economic development of Israel is linked with the pervading motif of the covenant God as the defender of the poor and the needy, a motif found alike in the legal, prophetic, hymnic and wisdom literature.

C. Boerma[27] links the development of poverty with the transition in early Israel from nomadic to agricultural and urban living. In the first books of the Bible, during the first stage of Israel's history (i.e. the patriarchal period: 2000-1300 B.C.) riches and poverty are not a problem. In Genesis the word "poor" is not mentioned because in the nomadic tribal way of life possessions are never a privilege obtained at the expense of others. Possessions are the riches of the tribe or the tribal alliance as a whole. If one person is rich all the members of the tribe are rich. In this context riches are seen as a blessing of God which the whole tribe enjoys together. The land is the Lord's possession to be shared by everybody.

Poverty did not develop of its own accord. After Egypt up to the exile (1200-587 B.C.E.) the structures of society changed and created problems. From being semi-nomads, the Israelites turned into small, independent farmers each of whom owned a small piece of land. The basis of social life was not the tribe but the family. A distinction arose between the poor and those who owned land. The people became rivals in family groups as a result of changing fortunes brought about by better or worse harvests. Anyone who was given a bad piece of land at the outset soon became poor and had to sell himself and his family into slavery. The development of an economy involving dealings with trade and land disrupted the equality of families. Some families became very rich and others slowly became poor. The cause of poverty was the fact that the social and economic situation changed.

The gap between rich and poor widened further with the development of the monarchy and the growth of a large army, which was at the service of the king. The king became increasingly powerful, controlling the army and the economy. This royal monopoly generated a centre of privileged people within the city, in contrast to a poor population settled in the country or on the edge of the city. As these people had to provide goods and services for the court and its circles, they found their existence became increasingly marginal. They became poorer and poorer. In times of crises and war the most cunning or most "fortunate" of the privileged class succeeded in enlarging their possessions considerably. "Woe to you who join house to house, who connect field with field till no room remains and you are to dwell alone in the midst of the land" (Isa 5:8). These rich landowners, criticized by Isaiah, became increasingly remote from the country proletariat which they themselves had created.

Changes in economic and political structures transformed the *social* climate. The frugal atmosphere of communal life gave place to pomp and ceremony associated with palaces and international alliances in which trade, waging war and making treaties played a central role. There came into being a prosperous aristocracy which contrasted with an ever-increasing marginal population. The gulf between rich and poor became deeper. After the exile the basic structure remained the same, though it was aggravated further by wars and their consequences.

Changes in social, economic and political structures influenced the whole fabric of human relationships. The poor were economically and socially poor. They were also made to feel inferior. They were despised, oppressed and all this because of the structures of society. Initially in Israel's history poverty had been a matter of economic inferiority. Then the rich began to treat the poor as if they belonged to an inferior social order. They had fewer rights and less insight: "The wisdom of the poor person is despised and his words go unheeded" (Eccles 9:15). As well as being poor they were trapped, oppressed, exploited. "Poor" became synonymous with "oppressed" – oppressed by people of violence.

The Old Testament responds to this poverty, which was rooted in the injustices of society, with three main approaches: the call to justice which expressed itself in the law, and particularly the covenant law (Exod 20-23) on behalf of the poor and deprived, and also in the message of the prophets, the need for solidarity and a message of hope and self-confidence for the poor. The Psalms take up, in particular, the call to justice and the covenant and also give hope to the poor.

N. Gottwald[28] presents a different analysis of the social context of Israel during the period 1250-1050 B.C. before the rise of the monarchy. He questions the transition from nomadic to agricultural and urban living. The Israelites did not originate outside Canaan, entering the land as nomadic groups bent on conquest or as semi-nomads or pastoral nomads peacefully infiltrating the settled population. Early Israel was an eclectic formation of marginal and depressed Canaanite people, linked with a city-state social structure. Along the social rings surrounding the city-state a pastoralist and agriculturalist peasantry lived. At the outer rings, in the margins, the Hebrews (Apiru) lived. They offered their combat abilities to the feudal landowners who came from the city-state and sometimes aided the village peasantry in defence against opposing lords resident in competing city-states. The story of the patriarchs is set in this background of pre-proto-Israel. The pre-Exodus Israel with its God Elohim consisted of groups that attempted to unite anti-city-state segments of the population. Its enemy were the Canaanites, a social class, an elite who controlled the feudal structure.

A segment of proto-Israelites was subjugated by Egypt and under Moses breaks its Egyptian feudal bonds, enters Palestine under the aegis of its God Yahweh who stood behind and for the liberation from feudalism, from the city-state social structure and for dedication to values and ideals that characterized pre-city-state societal reforms. This group (the "Levi" group) succeeds in bonding proto-Israel. Yahweh takes on some of the attributes of Elohim to whom distinctive Yahwistic traits are added. The social structures of a new confederacy was a retribalization process rather than a carry-over from pastoral, nomadic tribalism. A distinctive feature of this Yahwism, which animated the confederacy, is its concern for social equality.

If this analysis of Gottwald is accepted, then the tradition of Yahweh as the covenant God, who protects the poor and the defenceless, would be seen to be rooted in the quest for liberation and egalitarianism that characterized earliest developments in the growth of Israel.

In later times it becomes clear that the poor are those who suffer injustice. They are poor because others have violated God's law. They turn, therefore, helpless and humble to God in prayer. There is a further development when "poor" takes on a religious meaning. It becomes synonymous with pious and devout in prophetic passages and in the Psalms. The poor and lowly find joy in and hear good news from God (Isa 29:19; 61:1). The terms poor and needy are applied to exiled Israel and to Zion (Isa 49:13, 51:21). In the Psalms the "poor" are synonymous with those who seek God (Ps 69:32). Poverty becomes a word with spiritual connotations.

Justice and the Poor in the Psalms[29]

A first stage in identifying the poor of the Psalms is to examine the connection between justice and the poor. Justice/righteousness (*mišpāṭ/ṣedāqāh*) are often used synonymously in the Psalms.[30] The two root verbs (*špṭ, ṣdq*) are also paired together. *Mišpāṭ* has close legal connections. While the verb (*špṭ*) has clearly a juridical meaning, it is not the verdict of judging as such which is important but rather the elimination of an injury in which the violation of justice consisted. Therefore, it is a suitable word to express the idea of saving the needy and poor from injustice.

The biblical idea of justice means being faithful to the demands of a relationship. It expresses the basic notion of being in right relationship.[31] This is true of God in the Old Testament, including the Psalms. It is not in contrast to other covenant qualities of God, such as steadfast love (*ḥesed*), mercy (*rahᵃmîm*) or faithfulness (*'ᵉmûnāh*), but, in many texts, is virtually equated with them (Ps 36:5-6). Justice is not one of God's ways but affects all of them. It expresses that God is in right relationship, especially towards the poor and deprived (Ps 146:6-9). The just person is in right relationship to God, to others and to the land (Ps 112).

God's justice is a saving justice in so far as God restores harmony to the world, intervenes on behalf of the people, forgives their sin and delivers them from bondage. This justice has also an element of judgment – it restores the afflicted and condemns the wicked. Justice is God's saving power, God's faithfulness to the role of Lord of the covenant. Justice, too, represents a victory over evil powers which threaten the destruction of society. This divine, saving power is particularly active towards those on the margin of society:

The Lord works vindication and justice
For all who are oppressed (Ps 103:6; cf. Pss 140:12; 146:7).

The justice of God receives special emphasis in the enthronement Psalms (Pss 47, 93, 95-100). Several Psalms speak of the poor in relation to divine and interhuman justice. For example, Pss 111-112, probably composed by the same author after the exile, have divine and interhuman justice as a common theme. The just person distributes generously to the poor and the justice of such a person will endure forever. The just person "conducts affairs with justice" and will be rewarded with riches. The double statement about justice enduring forever in the context of both possessing wealth and distributing it captures the biblical notion that the goods of this earth are the sign of the right relationship with God as well as the means to create harmony within the community.

God's justice is the rightness of God, particularly towards those on the margins of society:

God, forever faithful,
Gives justice to those denied it,
Gives food to the hungry,
Gives liberty to prisoners.
God restores sight to the blind,
God straightens the bent,
God protects the stranger,
Keeps the orphan and widow (Ps 146:6-9).

According to Pss 9-10, God is a judge of justice, overcomes the unjust, listens to the cry of the poor and is a stronghold for the oppressed. The fact that God's justice is active towards the poor and the deprived indicates that poverty and oppression are an evil from which deliverance is sought. Ps 72 expresses the hope that the king will "judge" the poor in justice, that is, will achieve justice for them. He is to achieve God's justice. He is the minister of God's justice. This Psalm speaks about God's justice affecting the whole world. Harmony in society and peace come with justice. Biblical justice, as described here, is a human requirement of a religiously binding character. Behind the rule of the earthly leader is God's justice. The justice of the king is a function and mirror image of that justice God promised the people, the poor, and which does not allow the weak to become the prey of the powerful (vv. 1-2). Even the land brings forth plenty because the nation with its leader practises justice (i.e. faithfulness to God, one another and to the land). The Psalm as a whole (cf. vv. 3, 7, 16) shows that the moral realm and the realm of nature form one whole for the Israelites. The king's work of justice for the poor (vv. 12-17) means he is a strong help to those who lack normal supports and defences. They are helpless. The poor are considered blood relatives of the king and he is obliged to come to their rescue out of affectionate loyalty (v. 14). It is clear in this Psalm that the materially and socially poor are the concern of the royal justice.

Ps 76 indicates that God's justice reaches the oppressed throughout the whole world. The criterion for distinguishing Yahweh from other gods is the ability to achieve justice for the weak, the fatherless, the afflicted and the destitute, and to protect them from the injustice of the powerful (Ps 82). This concern for the defenceless in society is not a command designed simply to promote social harmony, but is rooted in the nature of God who is defender of the oppressed.

Who are the Poor in the Psalms?

Some writers underline the religious aspect of poverty in the Psalms, maintaining, for example, that Psalms about the poor come from a distinct group, the *ʿᵃnāwîm*, who constituted a class or community, and not merely an attitude of mind.[32] Thus the "poor" refer to some religious group or "pious association", particularly when they are contrasted with the "wicked".

Others react strongly against an over-spiritualization of the Psalms. J.P. Miranda seeks to understand the poor in many Psalms with reference to injustice, to material and social poverty and oppression.[33] H-J. Kraus warns that we should not move too quickly towards a religious or spiritual designation of the poor. Primarily it is a question of every form of neediness, indigence and hostile threat which finds its expression in the term "poor". The poor, he says, are people whose need drives them to expect all from God and their inner attitude corresponds to this.[34] W.E. Pilgrim also seeks to maintain a balance between the material and religious aspects of poverty in the Psalms: "Even though it is true that we find a spiritualization of the concept of the poor in the Psalter that is not all. The social and political life-settings are still there. The situations of distress are still those of literal poverty, persecution, oppression, affliction and the like. The poor are truly the victims of life and their enemies the powerful and well-to-do". He claims that "the most unique feature about the poor in the Psalms" is "the merging of identity between the socially poor and the religiously pious".[35]

But what is the nature of this "merger"? First of all, certain passages in the Psalms draw more attention to the inner attitudes of the "poor" in relation to God. It is stated that they cry out to God, they are attentive to God's will. They show a spirit of trust in and dependence on God. They stand alongside the "righteous/just" and those who "seek" God. There is a contrast between God's attitude to the "wicked" and God's attitude to the poor, the just and the faithful ("godly"). For example, Ps 25 underlines the inner attitudes of the poor person in relation to God:

> Turn to me and be gracious to me
> For I am lonely and afflicted (*'ānî*) (v. 16).

This individual prayer of petition expresses many inner attitudes. The "poor" person is led by God to do what is right, turns to God in an attitude of dependence, "fears" God (i.e. responds in awe and attraction towards God's word and graciousness) and "waits for" God in the sense of being attuned to God's will in a spirit of trust and expectancy. This "poor" person also experiences the need of forgiveness. Generally in those Psalms where the author speaks of himself as "poor" in the first person, these inner attitudes of poverty before God appear more clearly, particularly in Pss 69 and 109.[36] And yet, at times, the social, material aspect of poverty is not altogether excluded. For example, the "poor and needy" person of Ps 109 expresses a strong spirit of trust in and dependence on God. But an exclusively religious meaning is not demanded in the condemnation of the "wicked" person who

> . . . pursued the poor and the needy
> and the brokenhearted to their death (v. 16).

Some Psalms clearly indicate that the predominant meaning of being "poor" becomes: those who place their total dependence on God, who plead helplessness before God, like the afflicted, poor (*'ānî*) person of Ps 88 (v. 15). Also, the religiously poor of the Psalms may simply be those who are clearly in need of help from God who hears and rescues them, even if their inner attitudes towards God are not described (Pss 12:5; 14:5-6). Sometimes it is difficult to know whether "poor" refers to an attitude of dependence towards God or to a situation of deprivation or injustice. In such cases both senses may be included. For example, Ps 149 (v. 4: *'ᵃnāwîm*), which celebrates a victory, may refer to the poor and deprived whom God cares for or to the people of Israel as a whole. When helpless they place their trust in God. They are delivered not by their own power but by the power of God. In this sense they would be spiritually poor.

Secondly, the economic and social aspect of poverty is very clear in those Psalms which refer to the poor in contexts where the spiritual aspect of poverty is not mentioned implicitly or explicitly. This tendency appears in some of those Psalms which link justice with the poor. Besides, mention of widows, of women who cannot bear children, the fatherless and the sojourner, sometimes alongside the poor, shows that the focus is people who are materially, socially poor:

> Father of the fatherless and protector of widows
> Is God. . . .
> God gives the desolate a home to dwell in. . . .
> In your goodness, O God, you provided for the needy
> (*'ānî*) (Ps 68:5-6, 10).

He raises the poor from the dust,
And lifts the needy from the ash heap,
To make them sit with princes. . . .
He gives the barren woman a home (Ps 113:7-9).

Therefore, the poor are those who have been reduced to poverty and misery by various misfortunes of life. Also the poor are simply those materially needy to whom the "just" person distributes wealth freely (Ps 112:9).

As regards women in the Psalms, widows and women who cannot bear children are to be included among Israel's poor[37] and they are described in that context. In the patriarchal family system of Israel the plight of a widow without sons might be desperate. She was often left without any support or property rights after the death of her husband. Death before old age was often considered a judgment for sin which was extended to the wife who was left. The widow had no voice in Israel – the Hebrew word *'almānāh* which resembles *'ālam* ("be dumb", "be mute") suggests the muteness induced by disgraceful widowhood. No wonder Isaiah speaks of "the reproach of your widowhood" (54:4).

The woman unable to bear children shared with the woman made childless by bereavement the same precarious future. In addition, however, she suffered immediate social and psychological deprivation for her failure to achieve motherhood. Inability to bear children was a reproach. It was interpreted as divine punishment or at least a sign of divine displeasure. It brought derision from other women, especially from co-wives who bore children and it threatened the woman's status as a wife. The woman unable to bear children was deprived of the honour attached to motherhood – the only position of honour generally available to women, representing the highest status a woman might normally achieve. The fatherless are often associated with widows and sojourners – people whose lives were characterized by abject dependence – in biblical pleas that compassion be shown to all those who are on the margins of society (cf. Ps 146).

The poor are also described as those who go hungry for bread, for whom God supplies provisions (Pss 132:15; 146:7). There are sufficient examples to illustrate that sometimes the poor simply are those who are deprived materially, socially and who suffer injustice and oppression. There is no spiritualization of the poor in those texts.

Thirdly, some Psalms describe people who are both materially, socially poor, oppressed, and at the same time religiously poor. Ps 14, a communal prayer of petition, describes oppression of the poor, which involves injustice, in terms similar to those of the prophets (Mic 3). Oppressing the poor is a form of practical atheism in a godless world. It is the work of the "fool" (cf. vv. 1, 4, 6). At the same time God is the refuge of the poor. God hears their cry. Pss 9 and 10 frequently mention the poor in the context of a worldwide struggle for justice in which God supports the oppressed, the poor (9:7-9). God's care for the poor does not depend on race or nationality nor on whether the victims of injustice believe in Yahweh or not. God's justice and equity has a universal outreach. The poor are aligned with the oppressed (*dak* 9:9), the hapless and the fatherless (10:14, 18). They are fiercely pursued and oppressed by wicked people who abuse their power and are greedy for gain. The poor are described as the wronged and underprivileged people of society so that economic and social poverty is implied. At the same time they are spiritually poor, they cry to God for deliverance and they hope (9:12, 18; 10:14, 17). On the other hand, the unjust oppressors of the poor do not believe in the God of justice (10:3-9).

The poverty or affliction of a disabled, handicapped person is vividly described in Ps 88 (*'onî* in v. 9). This prayer is a deeply moving testimony to the difficulty which those who believe in God can experience when they feel that God is silent, that their prayers are of no avail and when they feel stigmatized before society and their friends. The struggling and courageous trust before God of this poor, disabled person is very real. Ps 102 is entitled a prayer of a poor, afflicted (*'ānî*) person who suffers from loneliness, pain and is critically ill. Yet the prayer is dominated by a spirit of hope and trust in God.

Finally, even in the case of those Psalms which express or emphasize the spiritual aspect of poverty, the experience of being spiritually poor is essentially linked with very human, concrete situations. Out of these situations people experience that they need God's help. The spiritual experience of poverty is inseparable from personal poverty-situations, such as hatred, persecution by unspecified enemies with resulting loneliness, even the sense of guilt for sins committed (Ps 25), human aggression, estrangement from family (Ps 69), calumny, desertion by friends (Ps 104), death threats, rejection by "wicked" people and perhaps physical suffering (Ps 34), sickness, imprisonment, loneliness (Ps 22), persecution by arrogant and ruthless people (Ps 86) and disablement (Ps 88).

Certainly the distress of the "poor" in the Psalms refers at times to economic and political hardships with their consequent oppression and suffering. But the circle is wider than these social ills, since the experience of being poor is also sickness and different kinds of moral and religious conflicts, e.g. loneliness, isolation and persecution. But in all these situations, except where people experience themselves as poor because of their sinfulness, where guilt is the person's own responsibility, the poor see themselves essentially as victims who cry out to God for relief and vindication.

The Oppressors of the Poor

Generally the poor are not contrasted with the rich as such but rather with the "wicked" (*rᵉšāʿîm*) or with enemies who put the poor (*ʿānî*) in their lowly position and keep them there. The "wicked" practice violence against the poor and the weak; they exploit the orphan and the widow and they practice deceit and injustice. They constantly oppose the poor (Pss 37:1, 12; 82:3-4; 109:2; 140:1, 12; 146:9).

The poor are the victims of the wicked and seek refuge from them in God. In Ps 82 God is invoked to defend the poor and the needy against the wicked. The "wicked" are described in terms of their aggression towards their neighbours and also as enemies of God (Ps 92:7-8). According to Ps 37 the wicked are those who draw their swords and bend their bows to strike down the poor and the needy, whereas the just/righteous person out of compassion gives generously (vv. 14, 21).

The just and the poor are closely associated. Both are contrasted with the wicked. The poor and the just have much in common: both are harassed by the wicked and both are under the special protection of God. God never forgets the just and the poor. Also, it may be that the poor are seen more and more as righteous or just because the wicked are so unjust towards the poor.

The Poor and the Rich

The Psalms express various attitudes towards the rich. In Ps 49 the poor and the rich are encouraged to listen together to the psalmist's message about riches (v. 2). Here and also in Ps 73 the question of the inequalities of life is addressed. The response is that wealth and every human resource pass away. They cannot give true wisdom and absolute security. It is not argued that wealth is wrong in itself but that its importance can be misunderstood. God cannot be bought off and no wealth, however great, can alter the purposes of God (49:7). The wealthy cannot continue in their riches forever. In this Psalm they are powerful and influential. The psalmist takes a negative stance towards them.

In Ps 73 there is no mention of the poor. Even the "rich" are not mentioned explicitly. But the author describes arrogant, violent and aggressive people with great influence who grow in wealth and prosperity. There is a spine-chilling description of these rich and influential oppressors who successfully impose their demands on those over whom their wealth gives them power. It is not so much the injustice of the rich oppressors which causes the anguished questioning of this Psalm as their complete success, in getting even the oppressed to accept this as inevitable (vv. 8-12). They seem to take over the role of God.[38]

Sometimes the Psalms present a negative view of riches: they can lead people astray, away from trust in God (Pss 49: 6-8; 52:9). Wealth as a blessing raises questions since many "wicked" people are rich and fortunate while many "just/ righteous" people seem to be unlucky and poor. But God will establish a right order of things. Earthly wealth and fortune are impermanent. Faith in God is greater than any wealth (Pss 37; 49; 73).

On the other hand, as in the earlier traditions of the Old Testament, riches can be seen as a gift and blessing from God. The goods of this earth are the sign of the right relationship with God as well as the means to create harmony within society. Besides, the effects of justice are that the land brings forth plenty, and relief of deprivation is a blessing of God to the people (Pss 72; 107; 132).

The God of the Poor

The God of the poor is characterized above all by righteousness in their regard. The poor are entrusted to the righteousness of God, of the king and also of the righteous/just themselves. Not that God's love (*ḥesed*) and mercy (*raḥ^a^mîm*) are separate, contrasting covenant qualities of God. They are all virtually equated at times (Ps 36:5-6). Ps 103 links God's justice, which vindicates the poor and overcomes oppression, with compassion or mercy and love by referring to the revelation of God given to Moses (Exod 34:6-7): "The Lord is merciful (*raḥûm*) and gracious (*ḥannûn*), slow to anger and abounding in steadfast love (*ḥesed*)" (103:6-8). The "poor and needy" person of Ps 86 gives thanks for God's compassion or mercy (*raḥûm*), love and graciousness (cf. vv. 3, 4, 13, 15). God's compassion is specifically to be in solidarity with the needy. Again, in Pss 111 and 112, which deal with divine and interhuman justice, God's compassion (*raḥûm*) is linked with justice (111:3-5; 112:3-9) in relation to the deprived and needy. Justice is related to God's "womb feelings" towards the poor. Compassion, mercy (*reḥem*, *raḥ^a^mîm*, *raḥûm*), in its roots, denotes the love of a mother for the child of her womb and generates a whole range of feelings, including goodness and tenderness.[39] It suggests a feminine aspect of God's justice towards the poor.

God's care for the poor, God's justice, is also linked with covenant love (*ḥesed*). Essential to the covenant were the various commitments to all kinds of people in need of help – slaves, strangers, widows, orphans, the poor (Exod 22-23). In the Psalms the poor are entrusted to this "steadfast love" of God. *Ḥesed* expresses a profound attitude of goodness, faithfulness by virtue of a commitment. Out of this special commitment of love God cares for the hungry and thirsty, and liberates people from oppression and rescues the afflicted. The strength of this love is underlined. It is God's solidarity with the poor and against the oppressors for the sake of justice. It is a volitional attitude orientated to the concept of right and is closely linked with that power through which God reverses the situations of the poor and the wicked:

> The Lord lifts up the downtrodden
> . . . casts the wicked to the ground
> . . . the Lord takes pleasure in those who fear him,
> In those who hope in his steadfast love (Ps 147:6, 11).

Love (*ḥesed*) and compassion (*raḥûm*) are the basis of God's show of strength on behalf of the poor. God's active love towards the poor is imaged as a struggle, as an actual war in this Psalm in which Yahweh is the Warrior[40] who "lifts up the needy and strikes the wicked into the dust" (v. 6 cf. vv. 10-11). Yet this Warrior God is motivated by compassion and love (vv. 1, 11). Ps 74 also characterizes God as a battle hero (vv. 12-14). The war is against oppression so that the "downtrodden may not be put to shame" and that "the poor and needy may praise your name" (v. 21). In contrast to Yahweh, it is the powerful ones who are unjust. They devour and terrorize the people. This is the war of the saviour hero (vv. 3-11).

The Cry of the Poor

In general, the Psalms are sincere expressions of feeling. They are cries of the heart to God expressing fundamental attitudes towards God and human life. The cry of the poor is a calling on God (*qārā'*)[41] and also a cry of deep distress (*ṣā'aq*).[42] The poor and the needy implore God to hear and answer them in their distress and their petition is one of trust.[43] The cry of the poor person in Pss 9 and 10 is that of one whose faith in God is tested by oppression, who has to struggle for the preservation of that trust, who wonders whether God has forgotten and why God is silent. Yet God is never so absent for the poor that God cannot be present to their outcry, so that they can express their belief that there is always hope for the poor. Also, the traditions of faith in Israel that God had always helped the poor and oppressed are a basis of hope. The poor and the righteous sometimes question the justice of God since those who oppress them not only prosper but they also attack, condemn and jeer at them because they suppose God will come to their rescue.

Yet they know that God stands by them, "takes thought of them", hears their cry, their desires. And not only God but also the king hears the cry of the poor. This is expected of the leader of the people:

> For he (i.e. the king) delivers the needy when he calls,
> The poor and him who has no helper (Ps 72:12).

Images for the Poor

Some images from the Psalms convey vividly the human, or rather the dehumanizing experience of being poor. The loneliness, harassment, and abandonment and the feeling of being strangers to society, which are experienced by the poor, are sometimes mentioned.[44] Experiences like these are conveyed in images.[45] For example, it is stated that God

> . . . raises the poor from the dust,
> And lifts the needy from the ash heap,
> To make them sit with princes (Ps 113:7-8).

This vividly conveys the contrast between the poor and the powerful. The image is that of the refuse or rubbish dump outside the town or village which had become the shelter of the poor, the outcasts and diseased. There they begged and ransacked the refuse dump to find some scraps of food and slept there.

The strength and cruelty of oppressors is like a lion waiting for its prey or like a hunter catching animals in a snare, but God is the deliverer who plucks the afflicted, the poor, out of the snare or releases them from the bonds of oppression. The aggression and violence of the wicked towards the poor is described in terms of weapons of war, bows, which, through God's help, are turned against the oppressor. God is the warrior-hero who rescues the poor. The disabled, poor person feels abandoned by friends, "shut in", isolated without God. God "raises", protects, the needy from continued affliction by setting them on high above all trouble. The poor are "despoiled", "robbed", "plundered". They sigh, groan, under the oppression of the wicked who threaten them from every side like prowling animals of prey. Many of these images are taken from aspects of life which were concrete for the people who prayed them – from war and from nature. Recent writers have translated some of these into contemporary images of poverty and oppression.[46]

In conclusion, even if the images may have changed, many of the realities of the Psalms remain contemporary. Although they do not speak of the power of the poor to help one another and to help in the transformation of society, they do offer many insights which can encourage the poor and deprived of today and those who work for them. They echo the afflictions of the poor around us. They remind us that our God is the God of the poor, that the heart of divine and interhuman justice is compassion and that all are called to be spiritually poor, to trust in the strong love of God who wills that the goods of our earth be shared by all.

Notes

1. C. Boerma, *Rich Man, Poor Man – and the Bible* (trans. J. Bowden) (London 1979) 44.
2. E.g. E. Cardenal, *Psalms of Struggle and Liberation* (trans. E.G. McAnany) (New York 1971); *idem*, *Psalms* (trans. T. Blackburn et al.) (London 1981); D. Berrigan, *Uncommon Prayer: A Book of Psalms* (New York 1978).
3. E.g. G. Gutierrez, *A Theology of Liberation* (trans. C. Inda, J. Eagleson) (New York 1973) 288, 296-297.
4. The RSV is followed in this article as regards the numbering of verses of Psalms as well as in translation (with slight modifications).
5. *Psalms* (Old Testament Message; Wilmington, Delaware 1983) Vol. 1, 17-18.
6. Pss 9, 10, 12, 14, 18, 22, 25, 31, 34, 35, 37, 40, 41, 44, 49, 68, 69, 70, 72, 74, 76, 82, 86, 88, 107, 109, 112, 113, 119, 132, 140, 147, 149. In addition, *'ānî* occurs in the title of Ps 102.
7. E.g. Ps 146.
8. In the singular form in 10:2, 9(2x); 14:6; 18:27; 25:16; 34:6; 35:10(2x); 37:14; 40:17; 68:11; 69:29; 70:5; 74:21; 82:3; 86:1; 88:15; 102:1 (in the title of the Psalm); 109:16, 22; 140:12. In the plural form *'aniyyîm* in 9:12; 12:5; 72:2, 4; 74:19.
9. 9:18; 10:17; 22:26; 25:9; 34:2; 37:11; 69:32; 76:9; 147:6; 149:4.
10. Cf. L. Sabourin, *The Psalms: their Origin and Meaning* (New York 1969) Vol. 1, 99.
11. 9:13; 25:18; 31:7; 88:9; 107:10, 41; 119:50, 92, 153.
12. 22:24.

13. 9:18; 12:5; 35:10; 37:14; 40:17; 49:2; 69:33; 70:5; 74:21; 109: 16, 22, 31; 112:9; 113:7; 132:15; 140:12. *'ebyôn* is closely linked with *'ānî* in 35:10; 37:14; 40:17; 70:5; 74:21; 109:16,22 and with *dal* in 72:13 and 82:3-4.
14. 41:1; 72:12, 13; 82:3-4; 113:7.
15. 9:9; 10:18; 74:21.
16. 10:8, 10, 14.
17. E.g. 146:7.
18. 82:3 (with reference to human beings, in 34:10 with reference to animals, i.e. young lions).
19. H-J. Kraus, *Psalmen I* (BKAT 15; Neukirchen-Vluyn [5]1978) 82-83; A.A. Anderson, *The Book of Psalms* (New Century Bible; London 1972) Vol. I, 269-270, 279-280.
20. Pss 18, 68, 76, 132.
21. Pss 9, 10, 12, 31, 35, 44, 72, 109.
22. Pss 22, 40, 74, 82, 149.
23. Pss 14, 25, 34, 37, 41, 49, 69, 86, 88, 107, 112, 113, 119, 140, 147.
24. Cf. Anderson, *The Book of Psalms* 119.
25. Cf. 31-32.
26. Cf. C. Stuhlmueller, *Psalms*, Vol. 2, 41-43.
27. *Rich Man, Poor Man* 7-20.
28. *The Tribes of Yahweh* (New York 1979).
29. Cf. J.R. Donahue, "Biblical Perspectives on Justice", *The Faith that Does Justice*, J.C. Haughey (ed.) (New York 1977) 68-112, esp. 68-78; L.J. Topel, *The Way to Peace* (Dublin 1980) 71-76.
30. V. Herntrich, "krinō", *TWNT* 3:927.
31. J.R. Donahue, "Biblical Perspectives" 68-69.
32. For a description of this viewpoint and a valid criticism of it, cf. H-J. Kraus, *Theologie der Psalmen* (Neukirchen-Vluyn 1979) 188-193.
33. *Marx and the Bible* (London 1977) 101-102.
34. *Theologie der Psalmen* 190.
35. *Good News to the Poor* (Minnesota 1981) 30-31.
36. Cf. also Pss 40:16-17; 70:5; 86:1-7.
37. Cf. P. Bird, "Images of Women in the Old Testament", *Religion and Sexism*, R. Ruether (ed.) (New York 1974) 41-88, esp. 53, 54, 62.
38. Cf. R. Haughton, "Christian Theology of Human Rights", *Understanding Human Rights*, A. Falconer (ed.) (Dublin 1980) 224-236, esp. 225-226.
39. Cf. P. Trible, *God and the Rhetoric of Sexuality* (Philadelphia 1978) 31-56, and Pope John Paul II, *Dives in Misericordia* (trans. London 1980) 21-22.
40. G. von Rad, *Der heilige Krieg im Alten Israel* (Göttingen 1951) 82.
41. Cf. Ps 34:6.
42. Cf. Ps 9:12.
43. Cf. Pss 31:8; 34:7; 40:18; 69:34; 86:1; 109:31; 140:13.
44. Cf. Pss 25; 41; 69.
45. Cf. Pss 10:7-10; 12:5, 8; 25:15-16; 69:33; 74:21; 88:8; 107:41.
46. Cf. note 2.

FAITH CONFIRMED THROUGH CONFLICT – THE MATTHEAN REDACTION OF MARK 2:1-3:6

Peter Briscoe, *Clonliffe College, Dublin*

In the Gospel according to Mark 2:1-3:6 there is a recognised cycle of Galilean controversies which form a clear unit of the Markan composition and structure.[1] In Matthew's Gospel however this neat five-member cycle of stories is split up and used in two very different contexts: Matt 9:1-17 and 12:1-14. It is the purpose of this article to attempt to unravel the Matthean intention behind this rearrangement of the Galilean controversies.[2] Before addressing this issue directly it is necessary to sketch the place and function of the controversy stories in the history of the gospel tradition.

The Development and Function of the Gospel Controversies

In a recent work A. Hultgren has argued that there was a positive trend towards framing aspects of Jesus' teaching in the form of conflict stories.[3] This trend is discernible at the level of pre-Markan as well as the final Matthean stages of the tradition. Teaching of Jesus which could have been transmitted in a non-controversial form, and which actually was so transmitted, was consciously reshaped into the form of a conflict story.

What was the function of this transposition of forms? It is likely that their function was originally apologetic. They arose in a Palestinian Jewish milieu in response to criticism of Christian conduct and belief, especially in cases where these deviated from the faith and practice of the main Jewish groups of the time.

Although addressing issues which arose from criticism from outside of the Christian community itself, these stories were not designed to be instruments of direct debate with opponents nor were they modelled on the form of rabbinic debate stories. They did not set out primarily to present arguments which would be cogent and valid according to rabbinic norms, rather did they appeal to the conduct and teaching of Jesus.

This Christocentric logic means that these stories were intended for use within the Church.[4]

This original Palestinian form of the story was the inspiration for a more complex development of the form which Hultgren links to a Hellenistic milieu.[5] The more developed form of the story made a more direct appeal to Scripture and a more consistent use of scribal methods of exegesis and argumentation. Although this trend indicates an approximation to the norms of rabbinic debate,[6] the basic argument remains Christocentric, so that the *Sitz im Leben* remains that of church catechesis rather than direct debate with opponents.

The thesis here is that even though it was criticism by, and conflict with, Jewish opponents which made this form necessary, once it was developed its use was confined to an inner-church need. It served to confirm the Jewish Christians in their faith and practice while not going so far as to attempt to win over opponents. The development of the form to include more effective scriptural exegesis and scribal argument was not to appeal to those Jews outside the church but to those within. It was the Jewish Christian church itself which developed this unique form of story with its double-sided appeal both to Jesus and to canons of rabbinic argument.

Matthew's Use of the Conflict Story

Before addressing the issues around the significance of Matt 9:1-17 and 12:1-14 in the composition and structure of Matthew, it would be useful to consider overall trends in the way Matthew has adapted the individual conflict story form.

1. Matthew provides much of the evidence for the thesis that there was a positive trend towards the controversialisation of the tradition. Matt 12:38-42; 22:34-40; 22:41-46 all show Matthew reshaping the tradition into a conflict story.[7]
2. Matthew reshapes the tradition by identifying the opponents with the Pharisees or by broadening the gulf between them and Jesus.[8]
3. Matthew introduced scriptural quotations and interpretation into his received tradition: e.g. Hos 6:6 is added at 9:13 and 12:7. He also introduces a more relevant scriptural precedent into the argument at

12:5 and develops a specifically Christian principle of exegesis at 22:40.[9]

4. He makes more use of the rabbinic *Qal wa Homer* argument, e.g. 12:5-7.[10]
5. In some of these stories Matthew presents the pivotal logion of Jesus in the form of a halachic decision for the community e.g. 12:12b, 15:20; 19:9.[11]
6. In one case Matthew's sensitivity to Jewish-Christian faith in, and practice of, the sabbath led him to abandon a too radical logion of the tradition, namely Matt 12:7 where he omits Mark 2:27 ("The sabbath was made for man, not man for the sabbath").[12]

Matthew's catechetical interest in the above tendencies is twofold: to articulate and defend what differentiates Christian faith and practice from that of emergent rabbinic Judaism (cf. nos. 1-2 above); to claim fidelity to and authoritative interpretation of the common ground between Jewish Christianity and Judaism (cf. nos. 3-6 above).

In all of this Matthew presents Jesus as a teacher with authority, an authority in his own right and therefore teaching something "new". He also presents Jesus as a teacher whose authority extends to what is "old", i.e. a command of scriptures, their interpretation and accepted methods of argument. One can perhaps detect in all this a concern to preserve both the old and the new (9:17) for the benefit of the Christian scribe (13:52).

Conflict Stories and the Composition of Matthew

Most of the above analysis of Matthew was concerned with the way he used the conflict stories treated as isolated units or examples of a genre. Our main concern is the question of how Matthew arranged these stories within the sequence and structure of his gospel and particularly with his use of the five stories now occurring at Matt 9:1-7 and 12:1-14. To come to grips with the structural role of these stories in Matthew involves an overview of the Matthean rearrangement of source material, and needs to be seen in the light of the way Matthew's overall sequence relates to that of his sources.

(i) Matt 14-28

It is generally accepted that Matt 14-28 faithfully follows the sequence of Mark 6:14-16:8, never rearranging events but occasionally omitting an episode.[13] His major redactional effort here involves the addition of blocks of teaching or discourse material. These additions have all been made at places in Mark's sequence where an appropriate theme provided a natural point of insertion.[14] The location of the added material was therefore dictated by the pattern of Mark. The situation is otherwise for Matt 1-13//Mark 1:1-6:6.

(ii) Matt 1-13

The following chart compares the sequence of Matt 1-13 with Mark 1-6 and draws attention to the dislocations of the Markan sequence.

Matt 1-13		**Mark 1-6**	
same sequence	material added in (Q or M)	same sequence	Dislocations of Markan sequence
1:1		1:1	
3:1-4:11	1:2-2:23 M	1:2-13	
4:12-22		1:14-20	
	4:23-7:28aQ	1:21	
7:28b-29		1:22	
—		(1:23-28)	
—		(1:35-39)	
8:1-4		1:40-45	
	8:5-13 Q	—	
8:14-17	←		1:29-34
	8:18-22 Q		
8:23-34	←		4:35-5:20
9:1-17		2:1-22	
9:18-26	←		5:21-43
Doublet (Matt 20:29-34)	9:27-31 M		(10:46-52)

Doublet (Matt 12:22-24)	9:32-34		
	9:35-11:1 Q		3:13-19
	11:2-30		
12:1-21		2:23-3:12	
–		(3:20-21)	
12:22-50		3:22-35	
13:1-35		4:1-34	
	13:36-52 M		
13:53-58		6:1-6a	

It can be noted above that for much of the material Matthew follows the same sequence as Mark, simply adding in blocks of discourse at appropriate points,[15] or occasionally omitting material.[16] This then follows the same pattern of relationship between Matthew and Mark's sequence as we found between Matt 14-28 and Mark 6-16.

The chart above does however indicate four dislocations of Markan sequence which are out of harmony with this and which therefore require explanation – namely the relocation of four miracle stories: Mark 1:29-31(34); 4:35-5:20; 5:21-43.

It is clear that the relocation of these miracle stories has brought them into conjunction with other material which Matthew has put together in chs 8-9. Thus we find that he introduces a Q miracle story (8:5-13) and a brief Q dialogue on discipleship (8:18-22). Matthew has concluded this cycle of Jesus' deeds with two miracle stories which he has duplicated from elsewhere in his own gospel, i.e. Matt 9:27-31 (doublet of 20:29-34) and 9:32-34 (doublet of 12:22-24). Finally it has to be pointed out that the three conflict stories (9:1-17), which Matthew has broken off from 12:1-14 to include them here, are located in such a way as to break up the connection between Mark 5:1-20 and 5:21-43.

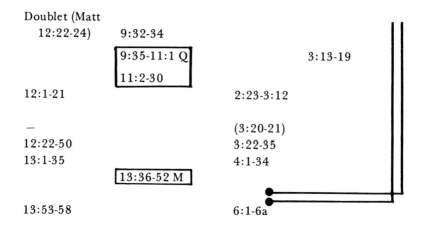

All of this indicates a very considerable activity of rearrangement of sources in order to achieve the precise composition of chs. 8-9. Clearly, any attempt to explain Matthew's reasons for separating 9:1-17 from 12:1-4 involves an explanation of the compositional arrangement of chs. 8-9 and the placing of 9:1-17 within that composition. It would also be necessary to explain why 12:1-14 remains where it is rather than being "moved" along with 9:1-17. We begin with Matthew's placement of the two sabbath conflicts (12:1-14) as the simpler case, given that he had kept them in the same location as Mark.

Matt 12:1-14

As in Mark these stories belong to a section leading up to the parable chapter, a section (Matt 12; Mark 3) which sketches in ever sharper focus the growing alienation of Jesus from his own people, represented by the Pharisees or even his family.[17] This sketching of the alienation of Jesus from those who should have been his own, provides the foil for the identification of those who truly belong to him, i.e. the disciples (cf. Matt 12: 46-50; Mark 3:31-35). All of this sets the scene for the climactic distinction which is made in the parable chapter (and especially in the Matthean redaction), the distinction between the disciples who have faith, who see and understand the message of Jesus, and the others who refuse to believe. At the conclusion of this parable chapter Matthew has omitted the "sea miracles" of Mark 4:35-5:43 and moves straight to the story of Jesus' rejection by his native place. This rounds off the theme of growing alienation and rejection which had developed through chs. 12-13. From this point on Matthew only presents Jesus as giving his teaching to the disciples. He may continue a ministry of preaching and healing and feeding the crowds, but his teaching can only be accepted and understood by those who have become disciples, and so it is reserved for them.[18]

It would seem then that the two Sabbath controversies Matt 12:1-14 are well suited to their context in the Matthean structure. Both their internal Matthean modifications as well as their location in the gospel sequence show them to exercise a consistent redactional function. They present a Jesus in debate with the Pharisees, a Jesus whose teaching becomes increasingly alien to them so that they are led to plot his downfall.[19] This sets the scene for the hostile confrontation of the later part of ch. 12. As noted above in the comments on Matthew's use of the conflict story form, so also here Matthew makes efforts to "improve" the scribal argument in these stories.[20] This is intended to confirm the faith of Jewish Christians who would be amenable to more cogent scriptural argument. At the same time the stories serve to demonstrate the obduracy of the opponents. This fits in with the presentation of an opposition who are also closed to the miracles of Jesus, who see him as an agent of Beelzebul, and who are thereafter accused of the sin against the Holy Spirit (12-31-32). One can conclude that the two sabbath conflicts, like the sequence of Matt 12-13 which they introduce, serve a polemic-apologetic function. They portray an opposition that is blind to the significance of Jesus' teaching as well as his deeds. As such they are designed more for the confirmation of disciples than for the conversion of opponents.

If Matt 12:1-14 fits well into its compositional context in Matthew, what of the first three conflict stories which now find themselves in the midst of the so-called miracle chapters?[21] How are we to explain Matthew's intention in the composition of chs. 8-9 and particularly his inclusion of conflict stories in what appears to be a miracle cycle, and his reasons for including conflict stories in such a way as to break up cycles of tradition in his sources?[22]

The Arrangement of Matt 8-9

The most common presentations of Matt 8-9 concentrate on the miracle stories gathered here. It was sometimes proposed that Matthew's intention in gathering this material together here was to compile a collection of ten miracle stories[23] to correspond to the miracles of the Exodus. Such a parallel is hard to uphold. Alternative numerical patterns have been proposed, perhaps the most useful one being a suggestion that chs. 8-9 consist of three sets of three miracle stories with intervening discipleship dialogues thus:

I 8:1-17 Three miracle stories
8:18-22 Two dialogues on discipleship
II 8:23-9:8 Three miracle stories
9:9-17 Two dialogues on discipleship
III 9:18-34 Three miracle stories.[24]

Allied to such patterns are common efforts to perceive a

precise thematic arrangement and development within these chapters. The most commonly held view corresponds with the numerical arrangement outlined above, i.e. 8:1-17 focusses on the theme of Christology, 8:18-9:17 focusses on the theme of discipleship, and 9:18-34 focusses on the theme of faith.[25]

While the cogency of the arguments for most of this tends to be widely accepted there must be some hesitation regarding the watertight divisions between sections. It is very evident for example that there is strong correspondence between the first and last group of miracles, i.e. 8:1-17 and 9:18-34. This is particularly so of 8:1-13 and 9:18-31. In both sets of stories there is some Christological interest but the predominant motif is that of the power of faith.[26]

While there is a fair consensus then regarding the first and last groups of miracles, there remains some hesitation concerning Matthew's purpose in the arrangement of the central section 8:18-9:17.[27] It is certainly true that much of this material deals directly with the theme of discipleship (8:18-22; 9:9-13) or has been redacted by Matthew to bring out a dimension of discipleship (8:23-27)[28] – the same cannot be said so easily for 8:28-32; 9:1-8. A further complicating factor in discerning Matthew's intention here is the fact that 9:1-8 should be considered as a conflict story rather than a healing and that the final two discipleship dialogues of the section, namely 9:9-17, are also in the form of conflict stories.

Not enough attention has been devoted to the motif of conflict in these stories and its relationship to the Matthean intention in chs. 8-9. Even Hultgren took it that Matt 9:1-8 was incorporated here as a miracle story rather than a conflict.[29] He then goes on to assume that Matt 9:9-17 simply followed on because they were attached to 9:1-8 in the tradition.[30] If that were the case why do the other two conflict stories of the tradition (i.e. Mark 2:23-3:6) not also tag along?

The fact is that Matt 9:9-17 is not here by accident but because it was required here by Matthew just as much as 9:1-8 and he used all three stories precisely as conflict stories. This can be borne out by a consideration of Matthew's redaction of these stories.

Matthew's Version of the First Three Conflict Stories

Matt 9:1-8

Matthew abbreviates the story of the paralytic, much in the same way as he does the other healing stories in these chapters, in order to focus attention on the dialogue and encounter with Jesus.[31] The difference here is that this story does not primarily recount an encounter in faith which leads to salvation but a conflict aiming to demonstrate Jesus' authority to forgive sins. Matthew has further reshaped the conclusion of the story so that the amazement of the crowds is focussed on the authority (*exousia*) that God gives to men. This seems to imply that the authority just exercised by Jesus might be shared with others. This is precisely what happens at Matt 10:1 when Jesus commissions the disciples with the authority (*exousia*) to heal and exorcise which he himself had been exercising. It would appear then that Matthew has included this conflict story at a point in his sequence where it can anticipate 10:1 – a sharing of the *exousia* of Jesus with his disciples.[32] The story further serves to bring out what one might see as an aspect of realised eschatology. The Son of Man already exercises his authority on earth.[33] It may be this motif which explains why this conflict story comes after the exorcism of the Gadarene demoniacs and thereby displaces Mark 5:21-43 from its place in the traditional sequence of Mark 4:35-5:43.

Both of the preceding stories, Matt 8:23-27 and 8:28-34, contain motifs related to the arrival of the *eschaton* and its attendant conflict.[34] Just as the following of Jesus (8:23ff), involves entering into eschatological trial, and just as the eschatological overthrow of evil powers (8:28-34) before the time involves resistance and rejection, so the forgiveness of sins on earth involves a conflict, but in all these situations Jesus proves victorious.

Matt 9:9-13

The history of tradition of this pericope indicates that it too is composed of originally separate narratives: (a) a call narrative (9:9) (b) controversy over eating with tax collectors and sinners (9:10-13). These two elements were already combined in the source used by Matthew in a form in which the controversy story predominates.[35]

However, Matthew has not passively taken it over from the tradition simply because it had followed the controversy about forgiveness. Matthew has devoted enough redactional attention to this story to indicate that this is precisely where he needed to have it in his sequence. Firstly he changed the name of the tax collector from Levi to Matthew. This may have been motivated by some special status of the figure of Matthew for the community where this gospel was written, but it also serves a function in the sequence and composition of Matthew. It prepares the way for the occurrence of Matthew's name among the list of the Twelve (cf. 10:3). The redactional link between 9:9 and 10:3 is confirmed by the identification of Matthew as *ho telōnēs* at 10:3, an identification which is particular to Matthew. Then at 9:11 Matthew omits the reference to the scribes which occurs in the parallel texts. This may have been intended as a means of focussing on the Pharisees as the opponents of Jesus.[36] Lastly he adds a scriptural argument to support the Christocentric and proverbial arguments already in the tradition. He introduces the scripture quotation with a scribal or rabbinic exegetical formula,[37] a procedure closely analogous to his redactional adaptations (cf. 12:1-8, the first sabbath conflict story).

All of this would seem to indicate that Matthew was happy to have this story at just this point in his sequence and that he very much intended it to function in the same way as the other conflict stories. This particular controversy is not only linked to Matthew (who will appear in ch. 10 as one of those who share in the authority and ministry of Jesus), but also to those outsiders who will shortly be described as the lost sheep of the house of Israel (10:6) or sheep without a shepherd (9:35-36). It will be the needs of such people which will provide the context and object for the missionary mandate of the disciples.

It is perhaps significant that one of this group of outcasts, called by Jesus (9:9), will also be one of those who continues that ministry (10:3, 6). Those who are sent out to give freely are those who have freely received (10:8). Just as it is often said that the healing stories of chs. 8-9 illustrate the ministry and authority of Jesus which the disciples are to imitate (10:1, 8),[38] so his ministry of freely giving his compassion to the lost sheep is also to be imitated by those who were themselves its beneficiaries.

The mission of these lost sheep is to be sent out as sheep among wolves 10:16. This makes it clear that the conflict story at 9:9-13 is not simply a model of vocation or the ministry of compassion. It is precisely a story about the conflict that arises around that ministry. It is as such a conflict story that Matthew intends it to prepare the way for the linking themes in the mission of the twelve that we have outlined above.

Matt 9:14-17

Once again it is to be argued that Matthew has not passively handed on what he received from the tradition. Firstly, in 9:14 as distinct from the parallels (Mark 2:18; Luke 5:33) Jesus is addressed in direct speech by the followers of the Baptist. It is possible to argue that this stylistic change has the effect of sharpening the element of confrontation in the dialogue, almost making it into an accusation. This is the first time in Matthew's conflict stories that Jesus is so directly confronted by his opponents and it may have been intended to heighten tension in the development of Matthew's plot. Secondly, as part of Jesus' reply (9:15) Matthew has changed "they don't fast" into "they don't mourn" (*penthein*).[39] Thirdly, part of the difficulty in this pericope is that it contains a number of levels of tradition which reflect a changed Christian practice.[40] The original controversy reflected a time when Christians did not fast, but the final form of the story reflects a time after the death of Jesus when Christians have begun to practice fasting, probably as a way of commemorating the Passion and Death of Jesus. Even though Christians were now fasting they did not do so on the same days or for the same reasons as the Jews, so the fasting issue remained a subject of contention, and the old conflict story was considered relevant for the new situation.

The different layers of tradition mean that within this one story there are two very different apologetics: (a) a defence of the original Christian practice of non-fasting, a defence which must have been considered to be still relevant despite the changed situation; (b) a specific defence of the new fast.

One needs to ask why a defence of non-fasting was maintained at a time when that had actually given way to fasting? There must have been something in the "non-fasting regime" which was considered still relevant. If we turn to Matthew's redactional change at 9:15 (cf. above) we may get some light. Matthew has attempted to circumvent any appearance of inconsistency in Christian practice by describing the original Christian practice as "not mourning". He defends that attitude by adverting to the Christian faith in Jesus as the Messiah. In the presence of the Messiah there can only be messianic joy, and mourning would be out of place.

This apologia for the original Christian practice still has relevance even when Christians do fast. Their appropriate disposition must remain a fundamental "non-mourning", because they still believe that the messianic times have come. The changed situation is that the Messiah has been taken away in death and an appropriate response to this is to fast. This fast however does not express a mourning that signifies a loss of messianic faith or joy, it is perhaps a recognition that the coming of the kingdom, inaugurated by the Messiah Jesus, involves the dimension of struggle and suffering in which they are called to share. But none of this signifies a mourning that would contradict the "non-mourning" evoked by the earthly ministry of Jesus.

It does seem then that Matthew's redactional "improvement" at 9:15 has had the intention of expressing an underlying consistency to Christian behaviour that on the surface appeared to have been inconsistent. This then may be cited as a further example of the Matthean tendency to improve the logic and cogency of the conflict stories which he received in his tradition.[41]

Finally, we need to ask why Matthew has included this story at just this point in his sequence rather than elsewhere (e.g. why did he not keep it in its Markan location before the two sabbath conflicts?) The most obvious reason for its present location is that it was needed here as an anticipation of the material on the Baptist at Matt 11:2-19. In 11:2-6 there is a clear declaration, to followers of the Baptist, that Jesus' ministry fulfills the messianic expectations. After such a declaration it would not have made sense to have the followers of the Baptist come along again and ask a question that also led to a messianic statement but one of a more indirect and allusive kind. *After* 11:2-6 and especially after 11:16-19 (where Jesus is precisely differentiated from the Baptist on the basis that he's a glutton compared to the ascetic John) there would have been no need to ask why Jesus' disciples do not fast. It would have been obvious. Consequently Matthew has placed the conflict over fasting before 11:2-6 and 11:16-17. In this antecedent position it prepares the way for the more explicit messianic statement about Jesus (11:2-6) and the differentiation between Jesus and John in relation to fasting and mourning.

The Unit of the Three Conflict Stories (9:1-17) Within the Composition of Matt 8-9

Reviewing these conflict stories we have seen reasons why each story taken on its own should have come at a point in Matthew's sequence where it could anticipate the Q material in chs. 10-11:

9:1-8	the establishment of the Son of Man's final authority to forgive sins, already now on earth, an authority to be shared with the disciples;
9:9-13	the call of Matthew and the ministry to the lost sheep that leads to hostility;
9:14-17	the distinction between the followers of the Baptist and the disciples of Jesus based on recognition by the latter that the joyful messianic times had come.

All of this belonged in Matthew's sequence before both chs. 10 and 11. Once it was deemed appropriate to use the Q material now in chs. 10 and 11 as the preparation for the rejection themes of ch. 12 then it was necessary that 9:1-17 should be separated from 12:1-14 with which they had been connected in the tradition.

Having seen then that the three conflict stories of 9:1-17 were required to come before chs. 10 and 11 in Matthew's sequence, how do we explain their present location within chs. 8-9, a composition which is usually taken to be centred on miracle stories? It was noted above that 9:1-17 forms part of what is commonly seen as a "discipleship section" within chs. 8-9, i.e. 8:18-9:17. In this consensus approach 9:1-17 is treated as dealing with different aspects of discipleship. However it is sometimes noticed that 8:28-34 and 9:1-8 do not mention the disciples directly (at most their presence is assumed).[42]

Thus we might depict the section as follows:

8:18-22	the demands of discipleship
8:23-27	calming the storm(s) of discipleship
8:28-34	defeat of the demons even before the *kairos*
9:1-8	authority to forgive sins even on earth
9:9-13	the call to discipleship, given to outcasts
9:14-17	the messianic joy of the disciples

One can see from this that discipleship does not provide the link theme between all these episodes; such a link is disrupted by 8:28-9:8. The reason for focussing on this thematic inconsistency (in what is commonly alleged to be a consistent thematic unit) is that part of Matthew's composition of chs. 8-9 was achieved by deliberately rearranging his sources in order to juxtapose 8:28-34 and 9:1-8. Given that these two episodes do not deal with the theme of discipleship we need to look for another thematic link to explain Matthew's redactional intention in bringing them together. Before attempting to address the question of what is the Matthean theme here, we must first establish that it was a deliberate act of Matthew to rearrange his sources in order to make 9:1-8 follow 8:29-34.

From the chart above (p.107) it can be seen that Matthew had available in his sources two different narrative sequences:

A. Matt 8:23-27 (from Mark 4:35-5:43)
8:28-34
9:18-26

and

B. Matt 9:1-8 (from Mark 2:1-22)
9:9-13
9:14-17

In order to "compose them" into the one collection he could have simply added them together in the sequence A +

B or B + A, in order to follow on the material of 8:1-22. What he has done is to take the A sequence and attach its first narrative (8:23-27) to the logion on discipleship. If he had intended to slavishly follow the sequence of his sources thereafter then he would have produced an A + B sequence, i.e. 8:18-22 + A (8:23-34; 9:18-26) + B (9:1-17). In fact Matthew has not slavishly followed the sequence of his source but has "moved" 9:18-26 out of its place at the end of the A sequence to come in after the B sequence. Why has Matthew thus disrupted the A sequence? There are different possibilities.

(i) Matthew wanted 9:18-26 to follow 9:1-17 so he "moved" it there, thus necessitating the 8:28-34 + 9:1-17 sequence. There are some possible thematic links between 9:18-26 and 9:1-17 which might have motivated Matthew to do this, namely the ministry of Jesus to the outcasts of his society, his exercise of "mercy not sacrifice", and his willingness to break taboos and incur various forms of defilement as a consequence.[43] While this is indeed a possible link between 9:1-17 and 9: 18-26 it does not serve to explain why 9:18-26 should not have remained in place immediately before 9:1-17 rather than coming after it.

(ii) Matthew wished 9:18-26 to be part of a concluding triad of miracles focussing on the theme of faith.[44] It is well recognised that Matthew specially composed a doublet at 9:27-31 to illustrate the theme of "faith and miracle" and to combine with 9:18-26 for that very reason. It is also pointed out that this final Matthew sequence of miracles 9:18-34 has been composed to correspond to the catalogue of messianic deeds at 11:5. All in all it does look as if Matthew wanted to have 9:18-26 as part of this concluding set of miracle stories.

However it has to be pointed out that Matthew could have still achieved this concluding sequence without separating 9:18-26 from its original location after 8:28-34. Thus;

	8:18-22 discipleship	
"A" sequence maintained	8:23-27 discipleship	
		8:28-34 an exorcism concluding with a rejection of Jesus
Triad of faith stories	9:18-26 faith and miracles	
	9:27-31	9:32-34 an exorcism concluding with a rejection of Jesus

In such a hypothetical reconstruction one can even see that there is a pattern with discipleship stories corresponding to faith stories, and two exorcism stories also corresponding in that both of them conclude on a note of the rejection of Jesus.

Furthermore it would have made sense to simply use the "B" sequence as an introduction to 8:18-22 given that it supposedly focusses on aspects of discipleship – thus:

"B" sequence	9:1-17	conflicts on aspects of discipleship/the benefits of discipleship
	8:18-22	the demands of discipleship
"A" sequence	8:23-27	the storm of discipleship
	8:28-34	etc.
concluding faith miracles	9:18-26	
	9:27-34	

In such a reconstruction Matthew could have kept his focus on the themes of discipleship and faith without going to the trouble of rearranging either the "A" or the "B" sequences which he found in his source.

So we come back to the fact that Matthew wanted 9:18-26 as part of the concluding set of "miracles of faith" – why then did he "remove" 8:23-34 from their location before 9:18-26 to a new location before 9:1-17? We have already seen that this was not motivated by any obvious need to place 9:1-17 before 9:18-26. The remaining solution is that Matthew made this transposition in order to establish a continuity between 8:28-34 and 9:1-8. Establishing this continuity meant that he removed 9:18-26 from its inappropriate location after 8:28-34 (they had no thematic link) and placed it with a group of stories of similar theme at the end of the collection.

Why would Matthew have wished to establish a continuity between 8:28-34 and 9:1-8 such that he did all this rearranging of sources? We note the common observation that Matthew has a tendency to redact miracle stories so as to focus on the essential elements of the faith-encounter and its resultant salvation. This is part of a general stylistic characteristic of Matthew to abbreviate story-telling details in order to focus on what he saw as the essential features of a narrative. In the case of 8:28-34 Matthew has once again practised his abbreviating style but on this occasion the effect is to focus attention on the encounter and conflict between Jesus and the demons (apart from brief allusions to them in the introductory and concluding verses the demoniacs themselves do not figure in the story – the entire focus is on Jesus versus the demons). It is a conflict in which Jesus is victorious, even though it is before the expected time (*kairos*) of the final affliction and defeat of the evil powers. Jesus is here presented as Son of God who is already here and now inaugurates the defeat of evil.

When we turn to 9:1-8 once again we find a miracle story that has been turned into a conflict story. Admittedly that transformation had already occurred in the pre-Matthean tradition, but it is recognised that Matthew accentuated this transformation by once again abbreviating the story-telling features of the miracle story in order to focus precisely on the issue in controversy. That issue is the authority of the Son of Man to forgive sins on earth. Like the preceding story this also involves a theme of the anticipation of the *eschaton* in the overthrow of evil.

It appears then that there is a warrant both in continuity of theme and in common transformation from miracle to conflict story, for arguing that Matthew has deliberately rearranged the sequence of his source in order to juxtapose 9:1-8 with 8:28-34. Further to this it can be pointed out that the preceding story of the calming of the storm, 8:23-27, also shares the thematic connection just noted.[45] Although it begins with reference to discipleship, the main theme of the story is given a particularly apocalyptic and eschatological colouring by Matthew and thereby focusses on the eschatological tribulation into which the disciples are led. The miracle demonstrates

Jesus' divine control over the demonic forces of chaos which afflict the disciples.

What emerges from the sequence (cf. 8:23-9:17) which Matthew has striven to achieve, is that he has composed a thematic sequence in which Jesus enters into conflict with the forces of evil and overcomes them. These forces may be cosmic (8:23-27) or demonic (8:26; 8:28-34) or persons opposed to his ministry (9:1-17), but over them all his authority is victorious. His authority throughout the sequence is an authority in word, whether word of command, or authoritative word of reply to his opponents. It is the authority of the one who inaugurates the kingdom of heaven, despite the conflict that must be endured in its coming. It does not seem an exaggeration then to claim that what Matthew has composed at 8:18-9:17 is not so much a discipleship as a conflict sequence. While it must be admitted that discipleship is the focus of 8:18-22 and partly of 8:23-27 it must also be pointed out that after 8:23-27 the disciples are never the direct focus of attention in any of the stories of this sequence. In all the encounters and dialogues of 8:28-9:17 Jesus' primary interlocutors are always opponents. If the disciples are mentioned it is only as background to the central conflict dialogue. It does therefore seem more appropriate to designate this as primarily a conflict rather than a discipleship sequence.

If all of this helps to explain the Matthean "arrangement" of the three conflict stories within the sequence of miracle stories in chs. 8-9, we still need to comment on the implications of all this for an understanding of chs. 8-9 as a whole, and within the wider sequence of Matt 4:23-13:58, that wider segment of Matthew where the sequence diverges from that of Mark.

Matt 8-9 in Relation to its Matthean Context

It is most usual to simply designate these as the "miracle chapters" and to claim that Matthew composed them to illustrate the saving deeds of Jesus. Such an illustration was required at precisely this point in Matthew's sequence: (a) to provide a model for the mission of the twelve at 10:1, 6, 8; (b) to provide examples of the deeds of the Messiah (*ta erga tou christou* 11:2) (cf. the catalogue at 11:5), which are cited to confirm that Jesus is the one John expected (*ho erchomenos* 11:3; cf. 3:11); (c) it is further argued by some commentators on Matthew's structure that the miracle material of chs. 8-9 presents the authority of Jesus in deeds (his *exousia*), corresponding to his authority in word primarily illustrated in chs. 5-7 (cf. 7:29). Along with this point goes the observation that Matthew has repeated 4:23 at 9:35 thus creating an *inclusio* to frame the entire section 5-9 on the authority of Jesus in word and deed. This total Christological presentation would then be intended to prepare for the mission of the twelve and the response to the Baptist, both of which include the dimension of the ministry of the word as well as that of deeds (cf. 10:7; 11:5).[46]

All of this consensus on the structural relation of chs. 8-9 to the surrounding context of Matthew is based mainly on the analysis of these chapters as a miracle composition. In the light of our analysis above it now seems appropriate to take account not only of the miraculous but also of the conflict element of these chapters in their relationship to the surrounding context. It cannot be an accident that the very last narrative of the composition under review (9:32-34) is used to present the hostile reaction of the Pharisees to Jesus' ministry. Matthew has deliberately concluded his composition of chs. 8-9 with a doublet (cf. 12:22-24) in which Jesus is accused of being in league with the ruler of demons, so the whole sequence ends on a note of conflict which is intended to anticipate the heightened conflict which will emerge later (12:22ff.) and lead to the estrangement of Jesus from his own people.

What Matthew has composed in chs. 8-9 is a tripartite structure: I – 8:1-17; II – 8:18-9:17; III – 9:18-31 with a conclusion 9:32-34. The miracle stories in I and III, which are closely related to one another in form and in theme, recount those aspects of Jesus' ministry which were required as models for the twelve (10:1,6,8) and examples for the Baptist (11:5). The central conflict section (II) was intended to explain how it could be that despite his messianic works (cf. 11:2 and 5) there were people who would be scandalized at Jesus (11:6). This conflict section portrays specific issues which caused opposition to Jesus (9:1-17) and it also puts that opposition in the context of the conflict that belongs to the messianic times

(8:23-34). It thereby serves to prepare for the theme of persecution of the twelve (10:16ff.) as they go about the mission of continuing the eschatalogical ministry of Jesus.

This central conflict section of chs. 8-9 may be compared in its function to that of the conflict story form itself. It is neither designed for direct debate with opponents nor for their persuasion or conversion. It is rather designed for use by disciples, those of "little faith" (8:26) who are harassed not only by the winds of persecution but also by the waves of detailed criticism of their faith and practice. It confirms their faith not only by demonstrating the saving power of Jesus in time of trial, but also his authoritative answers to external criticism. Further it puts the trials and conflicts to be endured within the design of the messianic times. These trials are necessary before the gospel is proclaimed to all the nations and the end comes (24:14). This conflict sequence and the stories of faith with which it is framed may have been Matthew's way of helping his fellow disciples not to be anxious about what to say when dragged before governors and kings (10:18-20). The whole complex is his way of confirming the faith of those disciples of little faith, who are fearful (8:26) and hesitant (19:31; 28:17) yet are sent on mission to Israel (10:6) and all the nations (28:19).

Notes

1. A.J. Hultgren, *Jesus and His Adversaries: The Form and Function of the Conflict Stories in the Synoptic Tradition* (Minneapolis 1979) 151 ff. and authors cited on 166 ff. Mark 2:1-3:6 has frequently been recognised as a special compositional unit within Mark's Gospel. It is seen as a special collection of five conflict stories with a Galilean as distinct from a Jerusalem setting (cf. Mark 11:27-33; 12:13-37). It is argued that already in the pre-Gospel tradition these stories were made into a collection on the basis of similarity of form, much as there were collections of parables and miracle stories. The purpose of this cycle in Mark's structure was to develop the theme of conflict between Jesus and the Jewish leaders so that already at Mark 3:6 they are plotting his destruction. This functions as an anticipation of the passion theme which is the key to Markan structure.
2. It is accepted here that Matthew was familiar with the five-member cycle of conflict stories in the sequence and collective unity which

they portray in Mark. Given Matthew's penchant for neatly arranged material in numerical patterns (W.G. Thompson, "Reflections on the Composition of Mt. 8:1-9:34", *CBQ* 33 [1971] 368), it is rather surprising that he breaks up the five-member conflict cycle and places its elements in apparently divergent contexts. It is hoped that addressing reasons for this may throw some light on the composition of Matthew.

3. Hultgren, *Jesus and His Adversaries* 50-52.
4. Hultgren, *Jesus and His Adversaries* 176 ff. If Hultgren is correct that the conflict story form was not designed for use in actual debates with Jewish opponents but only for use within the Church then this may explain the unfinished appearance that the form presents in comparison with some rabbinic debate. Gospel controversies rarely portray a real exchange of argument, or a conclusion acceptable to all sides of the debate. It rather appears that the dialogue elements that do occur act simply as a foil for the final pronouncement of Jesus whose vindication is expressed by (a) positive reaction of bystanders/crowds: Matt 9:8; 22:33 (b) silencing of opponents: Mark 3:4; Luke 20:26; Matt 22:46 (c) malicious reaction of opponents: Matt 12:14 (and parallels); 22:22. It would appear then that the form of the Gospel conflict story is an instrument of polemic and apologetic. It presumes an opposition which is beyond persuasion and which is therefore reduced to dumb hostility.
5. Hultgren, *Jesus and His Adversaries* 178 ff.
6. Hultgren, *Jesus and His Adversaries* 32 f.
7. Hultgren, *Jesus and His Adversaries* 45-50, 185-186.
8. Matthew drops reference to the scribes to focus on Pharisees as opponents; e.g. 9:11; 22:35,41; 22:15 adds references to the Parisees. Cf. Hultgren, *Jesus and His Adversaries* 189.
9. Hultgren, *Jesus and His Adversaries* 188.
10. Hultgren, *Jesus and His Adversaries* 188. For explanation and references see 37 n. 33 and 96 n. 74.
11. Hultgren, *Jesus and His Adversaries* 187.
12. Hultgren, *Jesus and His Adversaries* 188.
13. E. Schweizer, *The Good News according to Matthew* (Trans. D.E. Green) (London 1976) 12. The omissions are Mark 8:22-26; 9: 38-41; 12:41-44. This means that the Matthean conflict dialogues on defilement, divorce, Jesus' authority, payment of tax to Caesar, resurrection, the great commandment and David's Son, all occur in the same sequence and location as in Mark.
14. E.g. Mark 9:35-36, 42-50 provided a suitable thematic jumping-off ground for Matthew's development of the community discourse (Matt 18). Mark 12:38-40 was the natural place to insert the woes against the Scribes and Pharisees (Matt 23); and Mark 13 naturally favoured the elaboration of the eschatological discourse (Matt 24-25). As well as this discourse material Matthew also inserts some narrative into the Markan sequence: e.g. Matt 17:24-27; 27:3-10; 27:62-66; 28:11-20. Cf. the comment of P.F. Ellis, *Matthew, His Mind and His*

Message (Collegeville, Minn. 1974) 17: "This has all the earmarks of an author who wishes to expound further what is already familiar to his audience from a well-known earlier gospel".

15. Matt 1:1-7:29 follows the sequence of Mark 1:1-22 while inserting the Infancy Narratives and the Sermon on the Mount. For the insertion of the Sermon on the Mount at a point in the sequence corresponding to Mark 1:22 cf. J.D. Kingsbury, "Observations on the 'Miracle Chapters' of Matthew 8-9", *CBQ* 40 (1978) 560. Ellis, *Matthew, His Mind and His Message* 33 and W.G. Kümmel, *Introduction to the New Testament* (London 1975) 59 takes it that the Sermon was inserted at Mark 1:39. Matt 12:1-13:35 (58) follows the sequence of Mark 2:23-4:34 with the only modification of sequence being the relocation of Mark 3:13-19. Matthew required this choosing of the twelve as an introduction to the mission discourse (ch. 10). It can also be argued in this connection that the blocks of discourse material, mostly from Q, which are inserted at Matt 10 and 11 were added in here as a good lead in to the themes of rejection and conflict which are found in ch. 12 and reach their turning point at 13:53-58, Jesus' rejection by his home town. One can note that the twelve who are sent only to the lost sheep of the house of Israel (10:6) would sometimes not be listened to (10:14), they would be potential victims (10:16) and subjected to hostility and trials of all kinds (10:17-22). These words of warning to the twelve anticipate the note of rejection of Jesus which occurs in 11:20-24 and which prepares for the heightening conflict, hostility and rejection of 12:1-14; 12:22-45; 13:53-58.
16. The main omissions are Mark 1:23-28; 1:35-39; 3:20-21.
17. There are redactional variations between Matthew and Mark in the way they present this. Mark sharpens the rift between Jesus and his family (3:21), an element which is omitted by Matthew. Mark also described the opponents as Jerusalem scribes (3:22) whereas for Matthew they are Pharisees (12:24) (cf. 9:34).

    For the development of the theme of "opposition" in chs. 11-13 cf. Ellis, *Matthew, His Mind and His Message* 53 ff. and J.D. Kingsbury, "The Developing Conflict between Jesus and the Jewish Leaders in Matthew's Gospel: A Literary-Critical Study", *CBQ* 49 (1987) 57-73 and esp. 69 ff. where he shows a heightening of the conflict theme from ch. 11 onwards. Cf. also W.G. Thompson, "Reflections on the Composition of Mt. 8:1-9:34", *CBQ* 33 (1971) 386.
18. Cf. Ellis, *Matthew, His Mind and His Message* 60. The mandate to the disciples to hand on the teaching of Jesus only comes at the end of the gospel (28:20). They are to first make disciples, then baptise and finally teach. This order may not be fortuitous but may reflect the lesson portrayed in ch. 13 – only disciples can be taught to observe Jesus' teaching.
19. Cf. Kingsbury, "The Developing Conflict" 62-70.
20. In 12:5 Matthew introduces a more relevant scriptural allusion intro-

duced by a scribal exegetical formula: *ouk anegnōte en tō nomō* (D. Daube, *The New Testament and Rabbinic Judaism* (London 1956) 67-71 and 433). He makes use of the argument from major to minor, adds the citation of Hos 6:6 and omits Mark 2:27 as perhaps too radical for his Jewish Christian community. Cf. Hultgren, *Jesus and His Adversaries* 111 ff.

21. For this designation of these chapters cf. Kingsbury, "Observations" 559-573. For treatment of the compositional issues in Matt 8-9 cf. H.J. Held, "Matthew as Interpreter of the Miracle Stories", *Tradition and Interpretation in Matthew*, G. Bornkamm, G. Barth, H.J. Held (eds.) (London 1963) esp. 246 ff.; P. Benoit and M.-E. Boismard, *Synopse des Quatre Evangiles* (Paris 1972) 158; Thompson, "Reflections" 365-368; Schweizer, *The Good News According to Matthew* 69 ff.; K. Gatzweiler, "Les récits de miracles dans l'Evangile selon saint Matthieu", *L'Evangile selon Matthieu*, M. Didier (ed.) (BETL 29; Duculot 1972) 209-220; J.P. Heil, "Significant Aspects of the Healing Miracles in Matthew", *CBQ* 41 (1979) 274-287; W.R.G. Loader, "Son of David, Blindness, Possession, and Duality in Matthew", *CBQ* 44 (1982) 570-585.
22. The present relocation of 9:1-17 involved the splitting off of Mark 5:21-43 from 4:35-5:20.
23. Cf. Ellis, *Matthew, His Mind and His Message* 40. This goes back to the theory of B.W. Bacon, "The Five Books of Matthew against the Jews", *Expositor* 8 (1918) 56-66 and *Studies in Matthew* (London 1930) that Matthew's Gospel was given a Pentateuchal structure of alternating narrative and discourse. In the application of the theory chs. 8-9 are seen to present Jesus as a new Moses bringing about ten wonders. This corresponds to seeing the Sermon on the Mount as portraying Jesus as a new Moses promulgating a new Torah on the mountain. Although still maintained by some (e.g. Hultgren, *Jesus and His Adversaries* 185), such typologies have been generally criticized. Cf. Kingsbury,"Observations" 559ff.
24. A slight variation on the proposal of Ellis, *Matthew, His Mind and His Message* 42.
25. Cf. Held, "Matthew as Interpreter" 246 ff.; Thompson, "Reflections" 368 agreeing with Held; Kingsbury, "Observations" 559ff. for a good summary of the Matthean rearrangement of sources in chs. 8-9 and survey of opinions on the inner structure of the chapters where he goes with the main proposals of Held but makes a division between 8:18-34 and 9:1-17 (more on this below).
26. The close similarities in theme and "verbal linking technique" between 8:1-17 and 9:18-31 are given in detail by Thompson, "Reflections" 383-385. The faith theme is just as dominant in 8:1-13 as in 9:18-31 and it seems arbitrary to suggest that the focal theme of 8:1-13 is Christology while that of 9:18-31 is faith. Both sets of stories contain Christological titles (*kurios*, 8:2,6,8; 9:28; *huios David*, 9:27) as well as a stress on faith. Rather than distinguish 8:1-13 (17) from 9:18-31 (34) as focussing on different themes it

is more appropriate to see them as corresponding to one another, and probably acting as a "frame" for the central section 8:18-9:17.

27. Held, "Matthew as Interpreter" 248, notes the difficulty of finding a unifying theme in 8:18-9:17; cf. Kingsbury, "Observations" 560-562 for different opinions.
28. Bornkamm, "The Stilling of the Storm in Matthew", *Tradition and Interpretation in Matthew*, Bornkamm, Barth, Held (eds.) 54 ff.
29. Hultgren, *Jesus and His Adversaries* 185. This seems to be the implication of claiming that 9:1-8 was added here by Matthew to make up a collection of ten miracles. This presentation of 9:1-8 as a miracle story rather than a conflict story does not sit too easily with Hultgren's own observations that Matthew had a tendency to turn non-controversy stories into controversy stories. If Matthew only wanted a healing story at 9:1-8 he could have easily abbreviated it to omit the "conflict" element. Matthew, after all, is a well-known abbreviator of miracle stories. Instead of doing this Matthew has redacted 9:1-8 to focus on the conflict rather than the healing element of the story. This is hardly the action of someone who just wanted another miracle to make up a collection of ten.
30. Hultgren is not alone in this assumption; cf. Kümmel, *Introduction* 60.
31. Cf. Held, "Matthew as Interpreter" 175 ff. It should be noted that in the history of the tradition an original healing story has been adapted so as to become a controversy story. Matthew's abbreviation has the effect of highlighting the controversy aspect of the story and making the miracle element completely subservient to the controversy. This is especially so because the new Matthean conclusion focusses on the controversy rather than the miracle. In this respect Matthew's conclusion differs from the Markan tradition, cf. Held, "Matthew as Interpreter" 176 f.; Benoit and Boismard, *Synopse des Quatre Evangiles* 108-109; Hultgren, *Jesus and His Adversaries* 106-109.
32. Cf. Thompson, "Reflections" 376-376.
33. Cf. J.P. Meier, *The Vision of Matthew: Christ, Church, and Morality in the First Gospel* (New York 1979) 71: "(Jesus) dares to designate himself, even during his public ministry, as the transcendent Son of Man who possesses God's own power to forgive sins. The judicial function of the Son of Man on the last day is anticipated in the now of the public ministry".
34. Cf. Schweizer, *The Good News according to Matthew* 221. In 8:23-27 the word *seismos* (usually = "earthquake") is inserted by the Matthean redactor to describe the storm, precisely because it is a word with apocalyptic and eschatological overtones; it is one of the catastrophes to come at the *eschaton* (cf. Matthew's redactional use of it in Passion and Resurrection Narratives, 27:54; 28:2). In 8:28-34 Matthew adds the note that Jesus as Son of God has come to afflict the demons *pro kairou*, i.e. before the appointed time; he has anticipated the *eschaton* in his overthrow of evil. Cf. Thompson, "Reflections" 375.

35. Cf. Boismard, *Synopse des Quatre Evangiles* 110 f.
36. Cf. Hultgren, *Jesus and His Adversaries* 189, who admits as equally possible Hümmel's thesis that the reference to the scribes as opponents is omitted because "Christian scribes" were important in Matthew's church.
37. Cf. note 20 above.
38. Ellis, *Matthew, His Mind and His Message* 40 ff.; Held, "Matthew as Interpreter" 249-250.
39. It may be possible to argue for some connection between this and Matt 6:16-18 where the practice of Christian fasting is also addressed. At 6:16-18 the attention is turned away from the observable practice of fasting: it is not to be done for show. Here at 9:15 Matthew also diverts attention from the observable practice to the motivation behind it.
40. Cf. Hultgren, *Jesus and His Adversaries* 78 ff.; Boismard, *Synopse des quatre Evangiles* 113-115.
41. There may be some connection between all this and the inclusion of the prarables on "the new and the old" at this point. Originally these were intended to stress the distinction between the practice of Jesus' disciples and that of the followers of the Baptist. Matthew has introduced a modification of the conclusion, 9:17, in which he adds "and both are preserved". Now it is true that (within 9:17 taken on its own) this refers to the preservation of both new wine and new wineskins, but it is hard not to see the phrase having a wider resonance, namely the preservation of the old as well as the new – cf. Matt 13:52. If this is not "reading into" the text one might suggest that the "both" which Matthew wishes to preserve are: (a) the original messianic joyfulness of the ministry of Jesus combined with (b) the new practice of fasting in memory of the death of Jesus. A further redactional change by Matt 9:15//Mark 2:20//Luke 5:35 is the omission of Mark's *en ekeinē tē hēmera* or Luke's *en ekeinais tais hēmerais*. These phrases are usually taken to refer to: (a) a specific fast day, probably Friday in Mark; (b) a number of fast days, possibly Wednesday and Friday in Luke – respectively the days of Jesus' betrayal and crucifixion and the days of the week on which Christians fasted as distinct from the Tuesday and Thursday fasts of Judaism. Matthew's omission of reference to specifics like this may be part of his overall intention to get the discussion away from the observable surface of things to the underlying reality.
42. Cf. Thompson, "Reflections" 371 f., 374f.
43. Cf. L. Cope, *Matthew: A Scribe Trained for the Kingdom of Heaven* (CBQMS 5; Washington 1976) 68 ff.
44. Thompson, "Reflections" 379 ff.
45. Cf. above the comments and notes on 9:1-8.
46. For all this cf. Ellis, *Matthew, His Mind and His Message* 40 ff.; Thompson, "Reflections" 367-368, 386 ff.

THE BIBLICAL AND OTHER EARLY CHRISTIAN MANUSCRIPTS OF THE CHESTER BEATTY LIBRARY

Kevin J. Cathcart, *University College Dublin*

From 1978 to 1984 the late Archbishop Dermot Ryan was chairman of the Board of Trustees of the Chester Beatty Library, so perhaps it is appropriate that a contribution in a volume dedicated to his memory deals with some of the collections in that library and in particular with those manuscripts that are of special importance for the study of the text of the Bible and the history of early Christianity. As it was my privilege to succeed Dr. Ryan as Professor of Semitic Languages at University College Dublin and subsequently as chairman of the Board of Trustees of the Chester Beatty Library, it gives me considerable satisfaction to have the opportunity to offer these pages in memory of him.

The Chester Beatty Library has been famous since the early 1930's when the world of biblical scholarship received the extraordinary news of the discovery of the biblical papyri and saw the rapid publication of them in F.G. Kenyon, *The Chester Beatty Biblical Papyri: Descriptions and Texts of Twelve Manuscripts on Papyrus of the Greek Bible* (Fascicles I-VIII [16 vols.]; London-Dublin 1933-38; 1941; 1958).[1] But A. Chester Beatty was still acquiring important early biblical and non-biblical manuscripts as late as 1956 and many of them have been edited, as the following pages will show. Most of the Chester Beatty Greek papyri are listed in the fundamental catalogues by K. Aland, *Repertorium der griechischen christlichen Papyri. I. Biblische Papyri: Altes Testament, Neues Testament, Varia, Apokryphen* (Berlin-New York 1976), and J. van Haelst, *Catalogues des Papyrus littéraires juifs et chrétiens* (Paris 1976). Despite the title of van Haelst's work, however, Coptic papyri are not listed there.[2] The sheer magnitude of the task of making such catalogues means that perfection in detail is very difficult. Therefore it is most useful to have, for example, T.C. Skeat's detailed review of the publications by Aland and van Haelst.[3]

In the following pages we give a list of all important biblical and early Christian manuscripts. Each entry has a brief description of the manuscript and includes a short bibliography (fuller bibliographies for the Greek papyri can be found in Aland and van Haelst). With the obvious exception of the Samaritan manuscripts, all the manuscripts listed are Christian and are in Greek, Syriac or Coptic. Again, with the exception of Syriac Ms 703 of the Harclean Gospels (12th century) and the Samaritan manuscripts (13th-16th centuries), all manuscripts are early: 2nd-7th centuries. The omission of Armenian and Ethiopic manuscripts is deliberate. The Armenian version of the New Testament was not made directly from the Greek but probably from a Syriac version. Consequently the evidence of these late manuscripts is not of "immediate critical and historical significance for the text of the New Testament".[4] The Ethiopic version too is of limited value and the Ethiopic manuscripts of the Chester Beatty Library are not important for our purposes.

Finally we may note three sources which are invaluable and stimulating for the student of the transmission of the Biblical text in the early Christian world: K. Aland and B. Aland, *The Text of the New Testament* (Grand Rapids-Leiden 1987); B. Metzger, *The Early Versions of the New Testament* (Oxford 1977); C.H. Roberts, *Manuscript, Society and Belief in Early Christian Egypt* (The Schweich Lectures 1977; London 1979).

OLD TESTAMENT

GREEK

Papyrus Chester Beatty IV (Rahlfs 961) (Aland, *Repertorium* AT 5; van Haelst 8)

Date 4th century.
From an original codex of 66 leaves there are 50 leaves containing much of Gen 9:1-15:14; 17:7-44:22. This manuscript and Papyrus Chester Beatty V (see next entry) are important because they contain large portions of Genesis. The two oldest vellum manuscripts of the Greek Bible, that is the Vaticanus and the Sinaiticus, lack all but a few verses of Genesis.
Bibliography: Kenyon IV (Plates).

A. Pietersma, *Chester Beatty Biblical Papyri IV and V. A New Edition with Text-Critical Analysis* (American Studies in Papyrology 16; Toronto 1977).
Aland, *Repertorium* 76.

Papyrus Chester Beatty V (Rahlfs 962) (Aland, *Repertorium* AT 4; van Haelst 7).

Date: Second half of the 3rd century
27 leaves, of which 17 are nearly perfect, plus a considerable number of fragments, containing Gen 8:13-9:2; 24:13-25:21; 30:20-46:33. The codex probably had 84 leaves. This manuscript is remarkable for its writing which is quite different from that of other Greek papyri in the Chester Beatty collection.[5]
Bibliography: Kenyon IV (plates).
Pietersma, *Chester Beatty Biblical Papyri IV and V.* (This important volume also includes photographs of a number of new fragments of Gen 31-35 and 39-40 published for the first time).
Aland, *Repertorium* 73-74.

Papyrus Chester Beatty VI (Rahlfs 963) (Aland, *Repertorium* O5 [= AT 24 and AT 25] ; van Haelst 52).

Date: 2nd century.
50 leaves, of which 28 are substantially preserved, containing Num 5:12 ff. especially chapters 25-36; Deut 1:20-7:20; 9:26-12:17; 18:22-19:16; 27:6-33:27. Some fragments of Deuteronomy are in the library of the University of Michigan, Ann Arbor. The original codex probably had 108 leaves and is another example of a substantial codex (216 pages!) at the end of the 2nd century and compares with the Chester Beatty New Testament Papyrus II (P^{46}), from an original codex of 104 leaves.
Bibliography: Kenyon V.
Aland, *Repertorium* 21-22.
Roberts, "The date of P. Chester Beatty vi (Numbers and Deuteronomy)", *Manuscript, Society and Belief* 78-81.

Papyrus Chester Beatty VII (Rahlfs 965) (Aland, *Repertorium* AT 129; van Haelst 293)

Date: First half of the 3rd century.
There are 29 fragments of a codex of Isaiah, containing Isa 8:18-19:11; 38:14-45:5; 54:1-60:22. Two of these fragments came to Dublin in the Merton collection, and one fragment of the manuscript is in the Bibliotheca Laurenziana in Florence. The manuscript is written in a beautiful hand and there are also marginal notes in the Fayyumic dialect of Coptic.[6]
Bibliography: Kenyon VI.
Aland, *Repertorium* 192.

Papyrus Chester Beatty VIII (Rahlfs 966) (Aland, *Repertorium* AT 139; van Haelst 304)

Date: End of the 2nd century/3rd century.
2 fragments containing Jer 4:30-5:1; 5:9-13; 5:14; 5:23.
Bibliography: Kenyon VI.
Aland, *Repertorium* 199.

Papyri Chester Beatty IX and X (Rahlfs 967) (Aland, *Repertorium* 010, AT 146, AT 148, AT 40; van Haelst 315)

Date: about A.D. 200.[7]
29 leaves containing parts of Ezek 11:25-18:12; Dan 3:72-8:27 (though in this manuscript chapters 7 and 8 precede 5 and 6!); Esth 2:20-8:6). The original codex had 118 leaves. A substantial number of other leaves of the manuscript are in various locations including Princeton (John H. Scheide collection) (substantial parts of Ezekiel), Cologne University (parts of Ezekiel, Daniel, Bel, Susanna, Esther), Barcelona (fragment of Daniel), Madrid (fragments of Ezekiel). The Chester Beatty manuscript has the distinction of containing the Septuagint text of Daniel, for the text of Daniel usually found in Greek manuscripts is that attributed to Theodotion. Roberts has observed that in the Chester Beatty Ezekiel, the beginning of a new section is marked by the enlargement of an initial letter which also protrudes into the margin.[8]

Bibliography: Kenyon, VII.
L.G. Jahn (ed.), *Der Griechische Text des Buches Ezechiel, nach dem Kölner Teil des Papyrus 967* (PTA 15; Bonn 1972).
W. Hamm (ed.), *Der Septuaginta-Text des Buches Daniel Kap. 1-2, nach dem Kölner Teil des Papyrus 967* (PTA 10; Bonn 1969).
——, *Der Septuaginta-Text des Buches Daniel Kap. 3-4, nach dem Kölner Teil des Papyrus 967* (PTA 21; Bonn 1977).
A. Geissen (ed.), *Der Septuaginta-Text des Buches Daniel Kap. 5-12, zusammen mit Susanna, Bel et Draco, sowie Esther Kap. 1, 1a-2, 15 nach dem Kölner Teil des Papyrus 967* (PTA 5; Bonn 1968).
Aland, *Repertorium* 32-33.

Papyrus Chester Beatty XI (Rahlfs 964) (Aland, *Repertorium* AT 105; van Haelst 282)

Date: late 4th century.
2 leaves, 1 complete, containing Sir 36:28-37:22; 46:6-11, 16-47:2. The original codex probably had 54 leaves.
Bibliography: Kenyon VI.
Aland, *Repertorium* 178.

Papyrus Chester Beatty XIII (Rahlfs 2149)

Date: 4th century.
The manuscript contains Pss 72:6-23,25-76:1; 77:1-18,20-81:7; 82:2-84:14; 85:2-88:2.
Bibliography: A. Pietersma, *Two Manuscripts of the Greek Psalter in the Chester Beatty Library Dublin* (AnBib 77; Rome 1978).

Papyrus Chester Beatty XIV (Rahlfs 2150)

Date: 4th century.
The manuscript contains Pss 31:8-11; 26:1-6,8-14; 2:1-8.
Bibliography: Pietersma, *Two Manuscripts of the Greek Psalter.*

Papyrus Chester Beatty XV (Rahlfs 2151)

Date: 4th century.
(See the entry for the *Acts of Phileas*) 3 leaves of this manuscript contain Pss 1-4:2.

SAMARITAN HEBREW AND ARABIC

The only good description of these manuscripts is that by R. Pummer, "The Samaritan Manuscripts of the Chester Beatty Library", *PIBA* 6 (1982) 103-115 (reprinted with corrections from *Studies* 68 [1979] 66-72). See also R. Pummer, *The Samaritans* (Iconography of Religions 23, 5; Leiden 1987) 28-30 + Plates V and VI.

Ms 751

Date: 13th century.
This vellum manuscript is the fiftieth copy of the Torah written by the famous Samaritan calligraphist Abi Barakatah. It is one of the best copies of the Samaritan Pentateuch from the 13th century.

Ms 752

Date: A.D. 1339/40.
Also a vellum manuscript of the Torah written by a well-known copyist, Abisha ben Pinhas ben Joseph ben Uzzi ben Eleazar ben Aaron.

Ms 753

Date: 14th-16th centuries (?)
This manuscipt number covers in fact 5 Torah fragments. The most interesting is one of Num 3:36-9:15 in Arabic and Hebrew (though in Samaritan characters).

COPTIC

Ms Ac. 1389

Date: 4th century.
A manuscript in the Sahidic dialect containing Josh 1:1-6:16;

6:25-7:6; 22:2-19; 23:7-15; 24:23-33b, and the final verses (14:13-15) of Tobit. It is published in A.F. Shore, *Joshua I-VI and Other Passages in Coptic* (Chester Beatty Monographs 9; Dublin 1963). Substantial parts of the same manuscript are in the Bodmer collection and have been edited by R. Kasser, *Papyrus Bodmer XXI. Josué VI, 16-25, VII, 6-XI, 23, XXII, 1-2, 19-XXIII, 7, 15-XXIV, 23* (Cologny-Geneva 1963).

Ms 815

Date: about A.D. 600.
A codex containing Pss 1-50 and Matt 1:1-2:1.

NEW TESTAMENT

GREEK

Papyrus Chester Beatty I (P^{45}) (Aland, *Repertorium* NT 45; van Haelst 371)

Date: 3rd century.
Fragments of 30 leaves of a codex which originally had 110 leaves. There are fragments of Matt, Mark, Luke, John and Acts. The Osterreichische Nationalbibliothek in Vienna possesses one fragment containing part of Matt, 25:41-26:39.[9] The alignment of this fragment with its page in the Chester Beatty Library is shown in plate 27 of Aland-Aland, *The Text of the New Testament*. This is the oldest manuscript containing the Gospels and Acts.
Bibliography: Kenyon II.
Aland, *Repertorium* 270-272.

Papyrus Chester Beatty II (P^{46}) (Aland, *Repertorium* NT 46; van Haelst 497)

Date: about A.D. 200.
This codex originally had 104 leaves of which 86 have survived.[10] 56 are in the Chester Beatty Library and 30 are in the University of Michigan, Ann Arbor. They comprise a nearly complete manuscript of the earliest known copy of the Pauline epistles. The order of the epistles is interesting: Rom, Heb, 1 Cor, 2 Cor, Eph, Gal, Phil, Col and 1 Thess. The seven leaves

missing from the end of the codex may have contained 2 Thess. In Metzger's opinion, the order of the epistles is according to the decreasing lengths of them.[11] It is noteworthy that this earliest manuscript of the epistles includes the epistle to the Hebrews, for the early Church assumed Hebrews to be Pauline.

Bibliography: Kenyon III (note *Supplement*).
Aland, *Repertorium* 275-276.
S. Giversen, "The Pauline Epistles on Papyrus", *Die Paulinische Literatur und Theologie*, S. Pedersen (ed.) (Göttingen 1980) 201-212.
Y.K. Kim, "Palaeographical Dating of P^{46} to the Later First Century", *Bib* 69 (1988) 248-257.

Papyrus Chester Beatty III (P^{47}) (Aland, *Repertorium* NT 47; van Haelst 565)

Date: 3rd century.
Fragments of 10 leaves from the middle of a codex of Revelation, which originally had 32 leaves. This manuscript is the earliest extant witness to the book of Revelation, yet it should be noted that the text of Revelation in Codex Alexandrinus is considered superior to that of both P^{47} and Codex Sinaiticus.[12]

Bibliography: Kenyon III.
Aland, *Repertorium* 277.

Papyrus Bodmer II (P^{66}) (Aland, *Repertorium* NT 66; van Haelst 426)

Date: about A.D. 200. H. Hunger dates this papyrus not later than A.D. 150.[13] Turner, however, proposes a date about A.D. 200-250.[14]
The bulk of this manuscript of St. John's Gospel is in the Bodmer Library in Cologny-Geneva, but the Chester Beatty Library possesses a fragment of it containing John 19:25-28, 31-32.

Bibliography: Aland, *Repertorium* 297-298.

SYRIAC

Ms 703

Date: A.D. 1177.
This fine vellum manuscript contains on 229 leaves the Har-

clean version of the four gospels and was written in the church of Mar Thomas the Apostle.[15]

Bibliography: W.H.P. Hatch, "The Subscription in the Chester Beatty Manuscript of the Harclean Gospels", *HTR* 30 (1937) 149-151.
P.E. Kahle, "The Chester Beatty Manuscript of the Harklean Gospels", *Miscellanea Giovanni Mercati 6* (Studi e Testi 126; Vatican City 1946) 208-213.

Ms 709 St. Ephrem's Commentary on Tatian's Diatessaron

Some preliminary remarks.
In a letter to Wilfred Merton, dated 7 January, 1956, A. Chester Beatty informs him that he is about to acquire "... a very interesting thing: There is apparently a complete Syriac Ms, which is normal book size – about 4 to 5 inches wide, 8 or 9 inches high and 1 inches thick. The binding is missing, but it is in beautiful condition, and it does not look as if there is any particular beginning or ending, but that is very common in these Oriental books, unless there is a title page."[16] It is clear from this and subsequent letters by Chester Beatty that he was very excited about his acquisition, which Cyril Moss of the British Museum was soon to identify as a large part of the original text of St. Ephrem's commentary on Tatian's Diatessaron that was believed to be irreparably lost. In September 1957 the Benedictine monk and scholar, Dom Louis Leloir, who had published an excellent edition and Latin translation of the Armenian version of St. Ephrem's commentary some years earlier,[17] was invited by Chester Beatty to prepare an edition and translation of the newly discovered Syriac text. Leloir published his edition with a Latin translation in 1963,[18] and a French translation in 1966.[19] The present writer was delighted to inform an astonished Dom Leloir in 1984 and 1986 that 5 and 36 more leaves respectively had been acquired by the Chester Beatty Library. These new leaves will be published by Leloir in the near future. In the meantime the text and translation of some of them have appeared in recent articles by the same scholar.[20]

Date: Late 5th or early 6th century.
The vellum manuscript acquired by Chester Beatty in 1956 consists of 75 leaves. The first 10 leaves contain an exchange of letters between Severus of Antioch and Julian of Halicarnassus on the corruptibility or incorruptibility of the body of Christ. Leloir is of the opinion that these leaves are from a later period than the manuscript of Ephrem's commentary on the Diatessaron and dates them in the 8th century.[21] The 65 leaves containing Ephrem's commentary are those published by Leloir in 1963 (see note 18). In 1966 P. Ortiz Valdivieso published a stray leaf from the same manuscript.[22] Any doubts about the association of this leaf, which is in Barcelona, with the Chester Beatty manuscript have been dispelled by the fact that it fits exactly between the last leaf of a part of the manuscript acquired in 1956 and the first of the 5 leaves obtained in 1984. The addition of the 41 leaves purchased by the Trustees of the Chester Beatty Library since 1984 means that most of the original codex has now been assembled and probably less than 30 leaves remain to be discovered.

Bibliography: L. Leloir, "L'original syriaque du commentaire de S. Ephrem sur le Diatessaron", *Bib* 40 (1959) 964.

——, *Doctrines et Méthodes de S. Ephrem d'après son Commentaire de l'Evangile Concordant (original syriaque et version arménenne)* (CSCO 220/Subsidia 18; Louvain 1961). (This includes 4 plates of Chester Beatty Ms 709, showing fol. 1r, fol. 5v, fol. 9v, fol. 10r.)

——, "Le Diatessaron de Tatien et son Commentaire par Ephrem", *La Venue du Messie: Messianisme et Eschatologie*, E. Massaux (ed.) (RechBib 6; Bruges 1962).

——, *Le Témoignage d'Ephrem sur le Diatessaron* (CSCO 227/Subsidia 19; Louvain 1962).

——, *Saint Ephrem: Commentaire de l'Evangile concordant texte syriaque (Manuscrit Chester Beatty 709)* (Chester Beatty Monographs 8; Dublin 1963).

——, "Divergences entre l'original syriaque et la version arménienne du commentaire

d'Ephrem sur le Diatessaron", *Mélanges Eugène Tisserant* 2 (Studi e Testi 232; Vatican City 1964) 303-331.
——, *Ephrem de Nisibe. Commentaire de l'Evangile Concordant ou Diatessaron traduit du syriaque et l'arménien* (SC 121; Paris 1966).
——, "Le commentaire d'Ephrem sur le Diatessaron. Quarante et un folios retrouvés", *RB* 94 (1987) 481-518.
——, "S. Ephrem: Le texte de son commentaire du Sermon sur la Montagne", *Mémorial Dom Jean Gribomont (1920-1986)* (Studia Ephemeridis Augustinianum 27; Rome 1988) 361-391.
R. Murray, "Reconstructing the Diatessaron", *HeyJ* 10 (1969) 43-49 (An important cautionary review of the following work).
I. Ortiz de Urbina (ed.), *Vetus Evangelium Syrorum, et exinde excerptum Diatessaron Tatiani* (Biblia Polyglotta Matritensia 6; Madrid 1967).
——, "Una nueva reconstrucción del Diatessaron de Taciano", *Estudios Eclesiásticos* 44 (1969) 519-526.
P. Ortiz Valdivieso, "Un nuevo fragmento siríaco del Comentario de san Efrén al Diatésaron", *SPap* 5 (1966) 7-17 (with 2 plates).

COPTIC

Three vellum manuscripts in Sahidic and some coins found with them were acquired by A. Chester Beatty in 1924-5. They are in very fine condition and seem not to have been used before they were buried (probably for safekeeping) in the first quarter of the 7th century. They were copied at the monastery of Apa Jeremias at Saqqara.

Ms 813 (H. Thompson's Ms A)

Date: about A.D. 600.
A manuscript of 201 leaves (197 with written text) containing the Epistles of St. Paul (in the following order: Rom, 1

and 2 Cor, Heb, Gal, Eph, Phil, Col, 1 and 2 Thess, 1 and 2 Tim, Tit, Philem) and St. John's Gospel complete with subscription and colophon.[23] The Epistles together with the Acts from Ms 814 (see next entry) were edited by H. Thompson, *The Coptic Version of the Acts of the Apostles and the Pauline Epistles in the Sahidic Dialect* (Cambridge 1932).

Ms 814 (H. Thompson's Ms B)

Date: early 7th century.
A manuscript of 167 leaves. After the initial leaf which contains Matt 5:28-42, there is a complete text of Acts with subscription and the Gospel of St. John with subscription and colophon. As mentioned already (see on Ms 813), the Acts were edited by Thompson. The same scholar, in an appendix to his edition (251-256) published a collation of the Gospel of St. John based on G.W. Horner's Sahidic text in his *The Coptic Version of the New Testament... III* (Oxford 1911) and listed what he considered to be all the important variants from Mss 813 and 814. We are now better served by the recent edition of H. Quecke, *Das Johannesevangelium saïdisch. Text der Handschrift P Palau Rib. Inv.-Nr. 183 mit den Varianten der Handschriften 813 and 814 der Chester Beatty Library und der Handschrift M 569* (Barcelona 1984).

Ms 815 has been listed in the Old Testament section, but it can be noted again here that in addition to Pss 1-50 it also contains the text of Matt 1:1-2:2.

Ms Ac 1390

Date: 4th century.
According to the Chester Beatty Library's records this manuscript was found in a jar in a cemetery at the village of Dishna not far from Nag Hamadi. It consists of 8 leaves. The first 2 leaves contain a Greek text – mathematical exercises, but on the second of these leaves there begins a Subachmimic version of John 10:8-18:38 found in the remaining leaves. It is probably from the 4th century.[24]

OTHER EARLY CHRISTIAN MANUSCRIPTS

GREEK AND COPTIC

Papyrus Chester Beatty XII (Aland, *Repertorium* Ap 2, Ap 3; van Haelst 578, 579, 677).

Date: 4th century.
8 leaves and 3 fragments of a codex containing the Greek text of (a) the apocalyptic work known as 1 Enoch, (b) the Apocryphon of Ezekiel, and (c) the *Homily on the Passion* of Melito of Sardis. 8 leaves of the same codex are at the University of Michigan, Ann Arbor and contain parts of 1 Enoch and the *Homily on the Passion.*

(a) 1 Enoch. 4 Chester Beatty leaves and 2 Michigan leaves together contain chapters 97:6-107:3 (minus 105 because 104 and 106 are continuous). With M. Black it should be noted that this Greek version of an original Aramaic or Hebrew composition was made by Christian scribes for Christians.[25]

Bibliography: C. Bonner, *The Last Chapters of Enoch in Greek* (SD 8; London 1937).
Kenyon VIII (Plates).
M. Black, *Apocalypsis Henochi Graece* (PVTG 3; Leiden 1970).

(b) The Apocryphon of Ezekiel. The Chester Beatty fragments constitute the only part of the apocryphon that has survived. It is quoted by Clement of Alexandria[26] and there is a variant of it in Origen.[27] But the occurrence of a version of it in the Coptic Manichaean Psalm 239:5-6[28] is of particular interest because the manuscript of this text is also in the Chester Beatty Library.[29]

Bibliography: C. Bonner, *The Homily on the Passion by Melito Bishop of Sardis, with some Fragments of the Apocryphal Ezekiel* (SD 12; London 1940) 183-202.
J.R. Mueller and S.E. Robinson, "Apocryphon of Ezekiel: A New Translation and Introduction", *OTPseudepigrapha* I 487-495. Note however that their translation (495) is of the text in Clement of Alexandria.

(c) *The Homily on the Passion* of Melito of Sardis. The Chester Beatty Library possesses 4 leaves and part of a fifth leaf of Melito's treatise, and another 4 leaves of the same manuscript are in Michigan. In addition to the fine publication of the text by C. Bonner mentioned above in the bibliography for the Apocryphon of Ezekiel, there is now B. Lohse (ed.), *Die Passa-homilie des Bischofs Meliton von Sardes* (Textus Minores in Usum Academicum 24; Leiden 1958).[30] In a review of this work, F.L. Cross writes: "Melito's treatise on the Pasch might justly claim to be the most interesting and important Patristic text that has so far come to light in the present century"[31] and "It is evidently a fundamental text for the history of the pre-Nicene Easter".[32] Roberts has identified an interesting example of what he terms "documentary practice" in this part of the manuscript.[33] He comments on the remarkable way in which *chairein* ("to rejoice") is written. The scribe, apparently, was thinking of its familiar usage "greeting" at the beginning of letters and left a space for the name of an addressee.

Papyrus Chester Beatty XV

Date: early 4th century.
The library possesses 17 frames of fragments from a codex of 14 leaves written in Greek. The fragments show that 7 leaves contained the *Acts of Phileas*, bishop of Thmuis, and 3 leaves Pss 1-4:2, though the remaining leaves may have contained more of the Psalms. This information is based on the excellent work of Pietersma (see bibliography) who makes the observation that this Greek text was written "within living memory of the death of Phileas bishop of Thmuis".
Bibliography: A. Pietersma, *The Acts of Phileas Bishop of Thmuis (Including fragments of the Greek Psalter) P. Chester Beatty XV (With a New Edition of P. Bodmer XX and Halkin's Latin* Acta (Geneva 1984) (See the bibliography on 115).

Papyrus Chester Beatty XVI

Date: 4th century (?).
Fragments of a Greek text of a *Book of Jannes and Jambres.*

Bibliography: A. Pietersma and R.T. Lutz, "Jannes and Jambres: A New Translation and Introduction", *OTPseudepigrapha* II, 427-442.

Ms Ac. 1499 (van Haelst 511)

Date: 4th century.
This manuscript of 16 leaves or 32 pages contains a Greek-Latin lexicon (10 pages) and a Greek Grammatical tractate (12 pages). Many of the entries in the lexicon are from St. Paul's epistles (Rom, 2 Cor, Gal, Eph) and the recent publication of an edition of the text by A. Wouters will be of interest to New Testament text critics.
Bibliography: A. Wouters, "An Unedited Grammatical and Lexicographical Papyrus Codex in Dublin", *Ancient Society* 3 (1972) 259-262.
——, *The Chester Beatty Codex Ac 1499. A Graeco-Latin Lexicon on the Pauline Epistles and a Greek Grammar* (Chester Beatty Monographs 12; Leuven-Paris 1988).

Ms Ac. 1493

Date: 4th/5th century.
This manuscript has 10 leaves in Sahidic, containing most of the Apocalypse of Elijah. It is of fundamental importance for the study of this apocryphal work for it is more extensive than the 4th century manuscript in Akhmimic and the 5th century manuscript in Sahidic which were edited by G. Steindorff in his superb work, published at the end of the last century: *Die Apokalypse des Elias, eine unbekannte Apokalypse und Bruchstücke des Sophonias-Apokalypse* (Texte und Untersuchungen 17; Leipzig 1899). The Chester Beatty manuscript has been published in recent years by A. Pietersma and S.T. Comstock with H.W. Attridge, *The Apocalypse of Elijah: Based on Pap. Chester Beatty 2018* (Texts and Translations 19; Chico, California 1981).
Bibliography: O.S. Wintermute, "The Apocalypse of Elijah: A New Translation and Introduction", *OTPseudepigrapha* I, 721-753.
K.H. Kuhn, "The Apocalypse of Elijah", *The*

Apocryphal Old Testament, H.F.D. Sparks (ed.) (Oxford 1984) 753-773.

Mss W145, Ac. 2556, Ac. 1486

These 3 manuscripts are letters of St. Pachomius and one of his followers. Ms W145 is part of a vellum roll in Greek and should probably be dated in the late 4th or 5th century.[34] Ms Ac. 2556 consists of 4 fragmentary leaves of a papyrus codex. It is in Sahidic and can be dated to the 6th century. Ms Ac. 1496 is a vellum fragment also in Sahidic and from the 6th century. It is a letter of Theodore one of the followers of Pachomius.

Bibliography: H. Quecke, *Die Briefe Pachoms. Griechisher Text der Handschrift W. 145 der Chester Beatty Library* (Textus Patristici et Liturgici 11; Regensburg 1975) (3 photographs). Note the important addendum (111-118): "Die koptischen Fragmente und Zitate der Pachombriefe."

——, "Ein neues Fragment der Pachombriefe in koptischer Sprache", *Or* 43 (1974) 66-82 (+ 1 photograph [Tab. II]) (Papyrus fragment No. 54).

——, "Ein Brief von einem Nachfolger Pachoms (Chester Beatty Library Ms. Ac. 1486)", *Or* 44 (1975) 426-433 (+ 1 photograph [Tab. XLII]).

Postscript

It has not been considered appropriate to include here a description of the Chester Beatty Library's Manichaean Coptic papyri. There are 530 folios (= 1060 pages!) which have now been published in facsimile by Søren Giversen of the University of Aarhus.

Bibliography: S. Giversen, *The Manichaean Coptic Papyri in the Chester Beatty Library* (4 vols: Cahiers d'Orientalisme 14-17; Geneva 1986-88). Vol. I *Kephalaia* (1986); Vol. II *Homilies & Varia* (1986); Vol. III *Psalm-book Part I* (1988);

Vol. IV *Psalm-book Part II* (1988).
——, "The Manichaean Papyri of the Chester Beatty Library", *PIBA* 11 (1988) 1-22 (a translation from the Danish of "Chester Beatty-bibliotekets manikaeiske papyri", *Fund og Forskning* 27 [1984-85] [The Royal Library; Copenhagen 1985] 7-28).

Notes

1. The fascicles appeared as follows: I. *General Introduction, with twelve plates* (1933); II. *The Gospels and Acts: Text* (1933); *Plates* (1934), III. *Pauline Epistles and Revelation: Text* (1934); *Revelation: Plates* (1936); *Supplement: Pauline Epistles: Text* (1936); *Plates* (1937); IV. *Genesis: Text* (1934); (Papyrus IV) *Plates* (1935); (Papyrus V) *Plates* (1936); V. *Numbers, Deuteronomy: Text* (1935); *Plates* (Dublin 1958); VI. *Isaiah, Jeremiah, Ecclesiasticus: Text* (1937); *Plates* (Dublin 1958); VII. *Ezekiel, Daniel, Esther: Text* (1937); *Plates* (1938); VIII. *Enoch and Melito: Plates* (1941).
2. For a list of Sahidic manuscripts of the Gospels, see F.-J. Schmitz and G. Mink, *Liste der Koptischen Handschriften des Neuen Testaments. I. Die Sahidischen Handschriften der Evangelien* (Arbeiten zur Neutestamentlichen Textforschung 8; Berlin 1986). There is a list of Chester Beatty Coptic manuscripts in T. Orlandi, "Les manuscrits coptes de Dublin, du British Museum et de Vienne", *Le Muséon* 89 (1976) 323-327.
3. *JTS* 29 (1978) 175-186.
4. K. Aland and B. Aland, *The Text of the New Testament* (Grand Rapids-Leiden 1987) 200.
5. According to Roberts (*Manuscript, Society and Belief* 16 n. 1) "P. Chester Beatty V recalls the official Chancery style of the period".
6. See W.E. Crum, "The Coptic Glosses", Kenyon VI *Text* ix-xii.
7. See Roberts, *Manuscript, Society and Belief* 13 n. 1.
8. *Manuscript, Society and Belief* 17.
9. H. Gerstinger, "Ein Fragment des Chester Beatty-Evangelienkodex in der Papyrussamlung der Nationalbibliothek in Wien", *Aegyptus* 13 (1933) 67-72; G. Zuntz, "Reconstruction of one leaf of the Chester Beatty Papyrus of the Gospels and Acts (Mt 25:41-26:39)", *Chronique d'Egypte* 26 (1951) 191-211.
10. The notable length of this codex is remarked on by Roberts, "Books in the Graeco-Roman World and in the New Testament", *CHB* 1, 62.
11. *Manuscripts of the Greek Bible* (Oxford-New York 1981) 64.
12. Aland-Aland, *The Text of the New Testament* 50, 242-243.

13. *Anzeiger des phil.-hist. Klasse der Ostereichischen Akademie der Wissenschaften* (1960) No. 4, 12-23.
14. *Greek Manuscripts of the Ancient World* (London ^{2}1987) 108.
15. For a list of manuscripts containing this version, see now J.D. Thomas, "A List of Manuscripts Containing the Harclean Syriac Version of the New Testament", *The Near East School of Theology Theological Review* 2/II (1979) 26-32. There is also the shorter list of important Harclean manuscripts and editions in Metzger, *The Early Versions of the New Testament* (Oxford 1977) 71-75. Cf. also P. Harb, "Die harklenische Übersetzung des Neuen Testaments: Neue Handschriftenfunde", *OrChr* 64 (1980) 36-47.

    On the Harclean version the following literature is noteworthy: G.H. Bernstein, *De Charklensi Novi Testamenti translatione syriaca commentatio* (Leipzig 1837); G. Zuntz, *The Ancestry of the Harklean New Testament* (London 1945); *idem*, "Die Subscriptionen der Syra Harclensis", *ZDMG* 101 (1951) 174-196; M. Black, "The Syriac Versional Tradition", *Die alten Übersetzungen des Neuen Testaments, die Kirchenväterzitate und Lektionare*, K. Aland (ed.) (Berlin-New York 1972) 139-141; J.D. Thomas, "The Gospel Colophon of the Harclean Syriac Version", *The Near East School of Theology Theological Review* 3/I (1980) 16-26; B. Aland, "Die philoxenisch-harklenische Übersetzungtradition; Ergebnisse einer Untersuchung der neutestamentlichen Zitate in der Syrischen Literatur", *Le Muséon* 94 (1981) 321-383; Aland-Aland, *The Text of the New Testament* 193-195.

    It is now clear that in A.D. 616 Thomas of Harkel, monk and Bishop of Mabbug in Syria, made a thorough revision of the Syriac Philoxenian version, so called because it was produced by Polycarp in A.D. 507/508 for Philoxenus who was also Bishop of Mabbug. See most recently S. Brock, "The Resolution of the Philoxenian Harclean Problem", *New Testament Textual Criticism. Essays in Honour of Bruce M. Metzger*, E.J. Epp and G.D. Fee (eds.) (Oxford 1981) 325-343.
16. The letter is among several items of W. Merton's correspondence recently donated to the Chester Beatty Library.
17. *Saint Ephrem: Commentaire de l'Evangile concordant, version arménienne* (CSCO 137; Louvain 1953); Latin translation: CSCO 145 (Louvain 1954).
18. *Saint Ephrem: Commentaire de l'Evangile concordant texte syriaque (Manuscrit Chester Beatty 709)* (Chester Beatty Monographs 8; Dublin 1963).
19. *Ephrem de Nisibe. Commentaire de l'Evangile Concordant ou Diatessaron traduit du syriaque et l'arménien* (SC 121; Paris 1966).
20. "Le commentaire d'Ephrem sur le Diatessaron. Quarante et un folios retrouvés", *RB* 94 (1987) 481-518; "S. Ephrem: Le texte de son commentaire du Sermon sur la Montagne", *Mémorial Dom Jean Gribomont (1920-1986)* (Studia Ephemeridis Augustinianum 27; Rome 1988) 361-391.

21. "L'original syriaque du commentaire de S. Ephrem sur le Diatessaron", *Bib* 40 (1959) 964.
22. "Un nuevo fragmento siríaco del Comentario de san Efrén al Diatésaron", *SPap* 5 (1966) 7-17 (with 2 plates).
23. For the Coptic versions of the New Testament, cf. Metzger, *The Early Versions of the New Testament* 99-152; Aland/Aland, *The Text of the New Testament* 196-200.
24. It is being edited with a view to publication by J.M. Robinson.
25. M. Black, *The Book of Enoch or I Enoch. A New English Edition* (SVTP 7; Leiden 1985) 4.
26. *Paed.* I.9.84 *Clemens Alexandrinus*, O. Stählin (ed.) (GCS12; Leipzig 1936) 139.
27. *Homilies on Jeremiah* 18.9 *Origenes Werke* III, E. Klostermann (ed.) (GCS 6; Leipzig 1901) 163.
28. See W.D. Stroker, "The Source of an Agraphon in the Manichaean Psalm-Book", *JTS* 28 (1977) 114-118.
29. C.R.C. Allberry, *A Manichaean Psalm-Book* (Stuttgart 1938) II, 31.
30. For reservations concerning the edition of O. Perler, *Méliton de Sardes, Sur la Pâque et fragments* (SC 123; Paris 1966) see the article by S.H. Hall, "The Melito Papyri", *JTS* 19 (1968) 476-508.
31. *JTS* 11 (1960) 162.
32. *JTS* 11 (1960) 163.
33. *Manuscript, Society and Belief* 15-16. Reference: Kenyon VIII plate II. The Greek sentence, which occurs a few times in this manuscript, is *ouk estin humin chairein*, "There is no joy for you".
34. Cf. Roberts, *Manuscript, Society and Belief* 89.

Plate 1 Chester Beatty Biblical Papyrus V (3rd cent) Gen 24:13-21 (Greek)

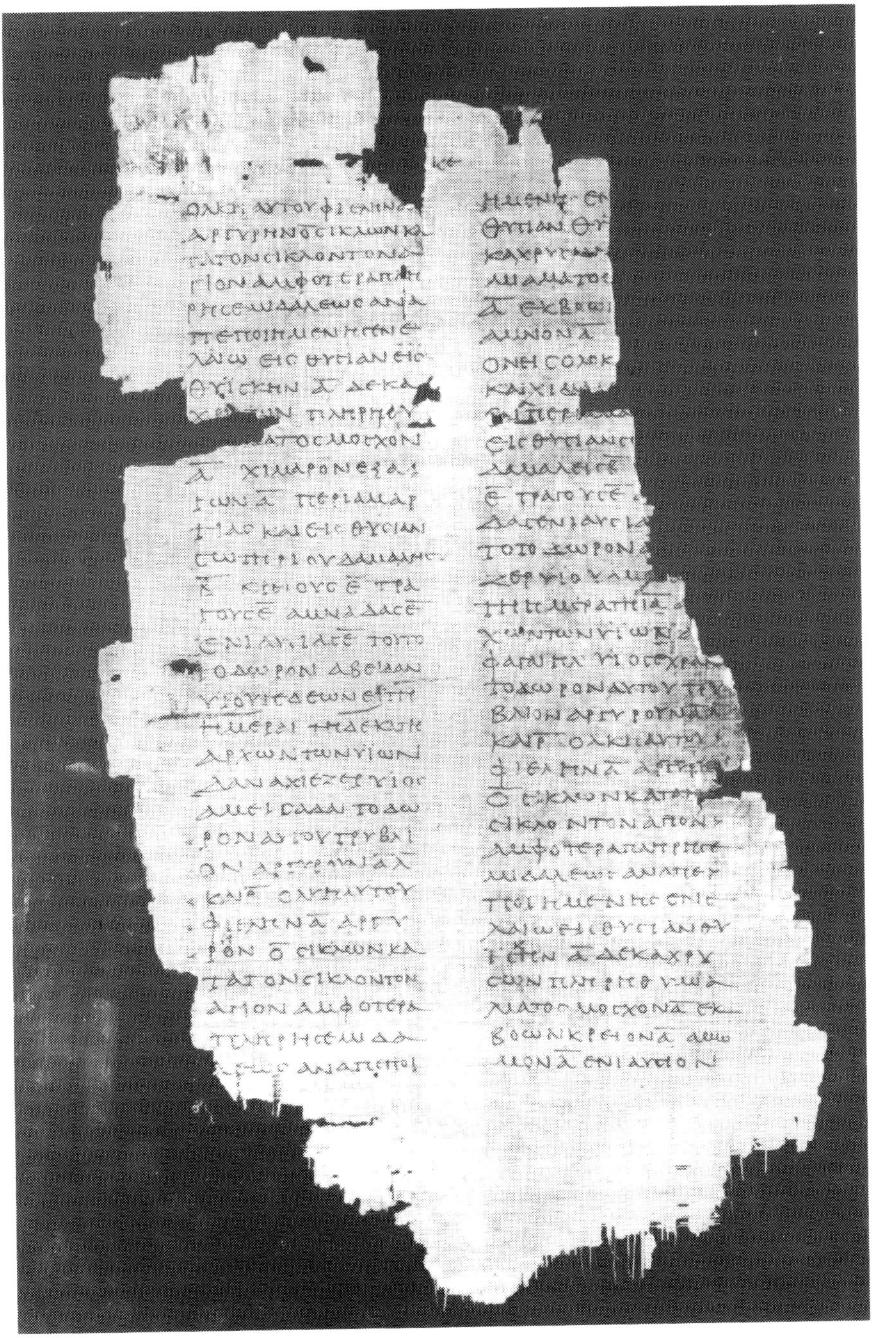

Plate II Chester Beatty Biblical Papyrus VI (2nd cent) Num 7:61-75 (Greek)

Plate III Chester Beatty Biblical Papyrus VII (3rd cent) Isa 15:8-16:4 (Greek with marginal notes in Coptic)

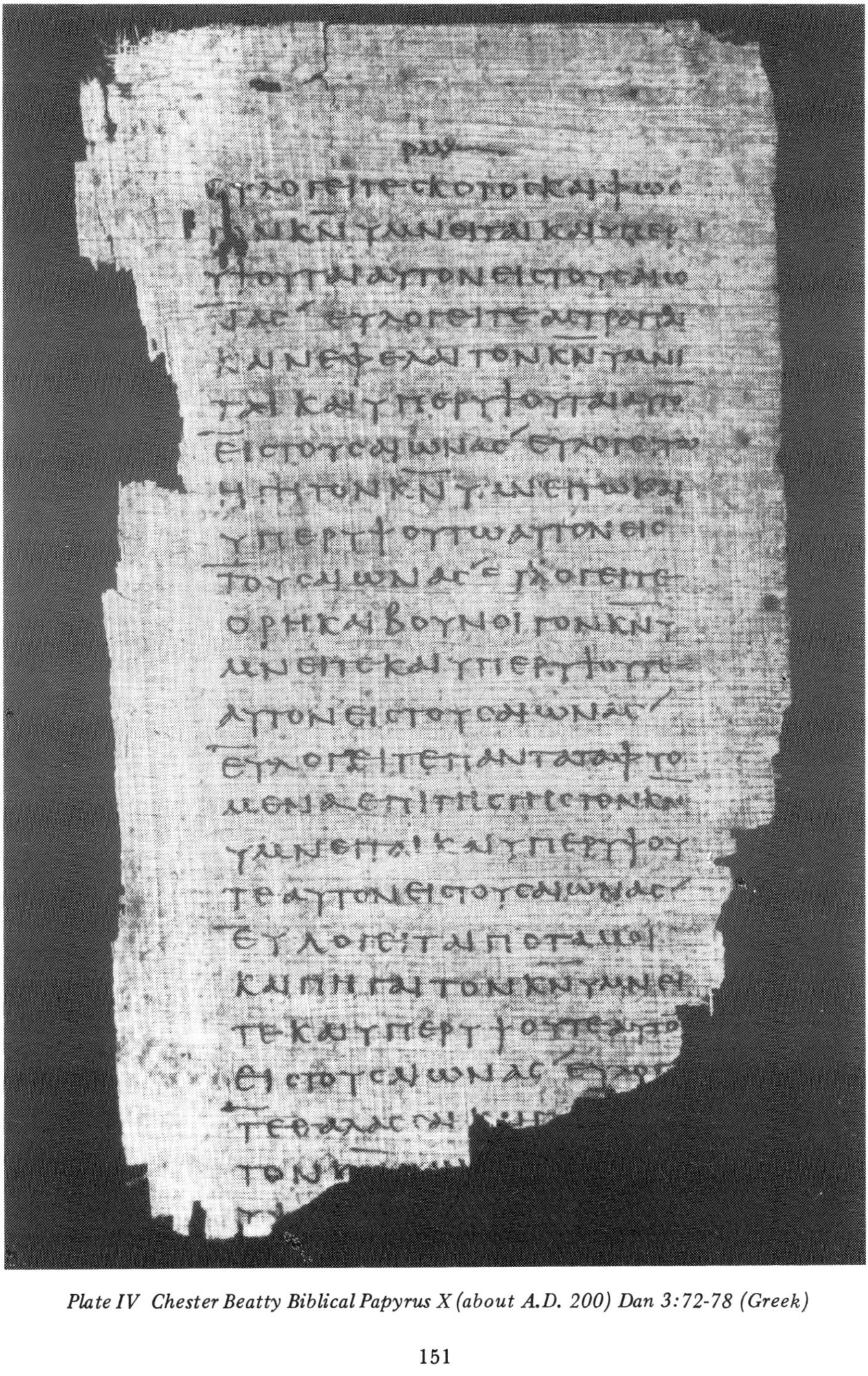

Plate IV Chester Beatty Biblical Papyrus X (about A.D. 200) Dan 3:72-78 (Greek)

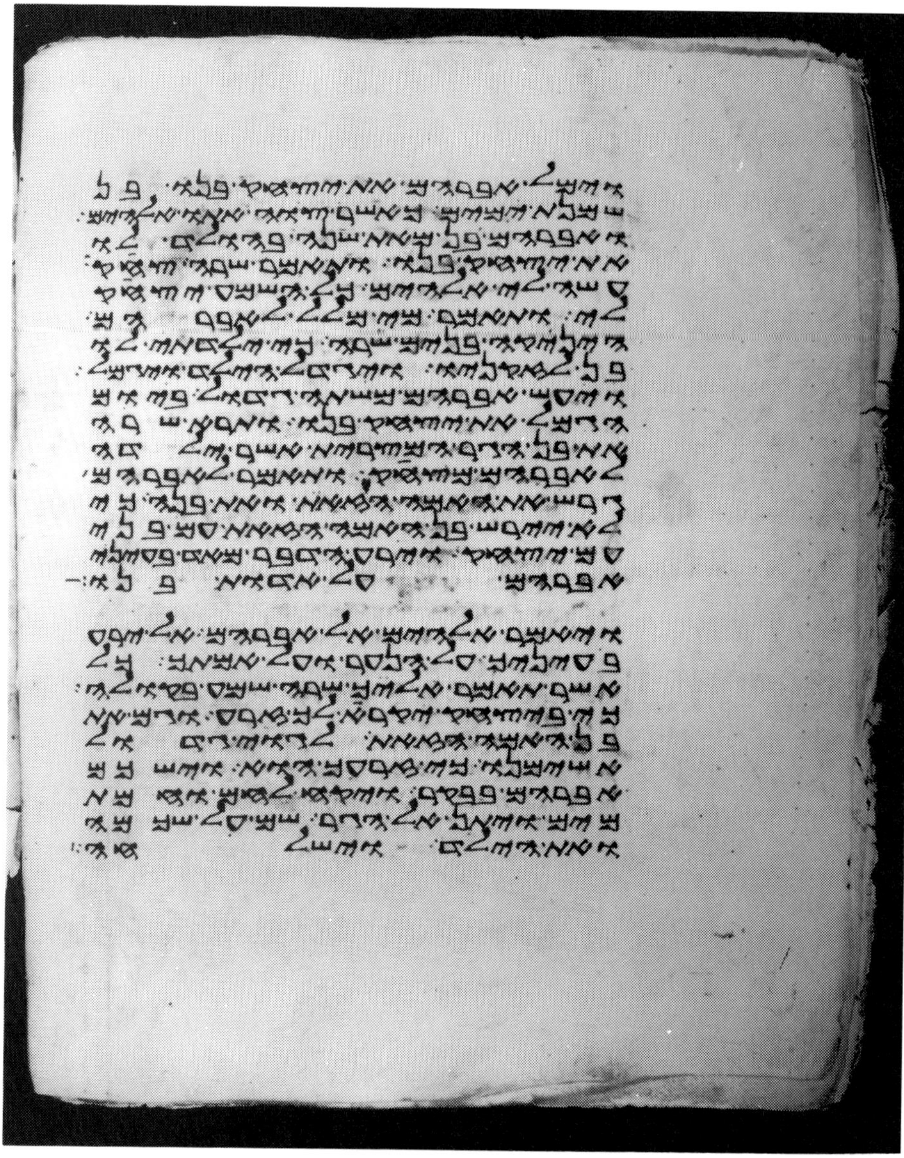

Plate V Chester Beatty Samaritan Ms 751 (13th cent) Gen 21:4-11, 12-14

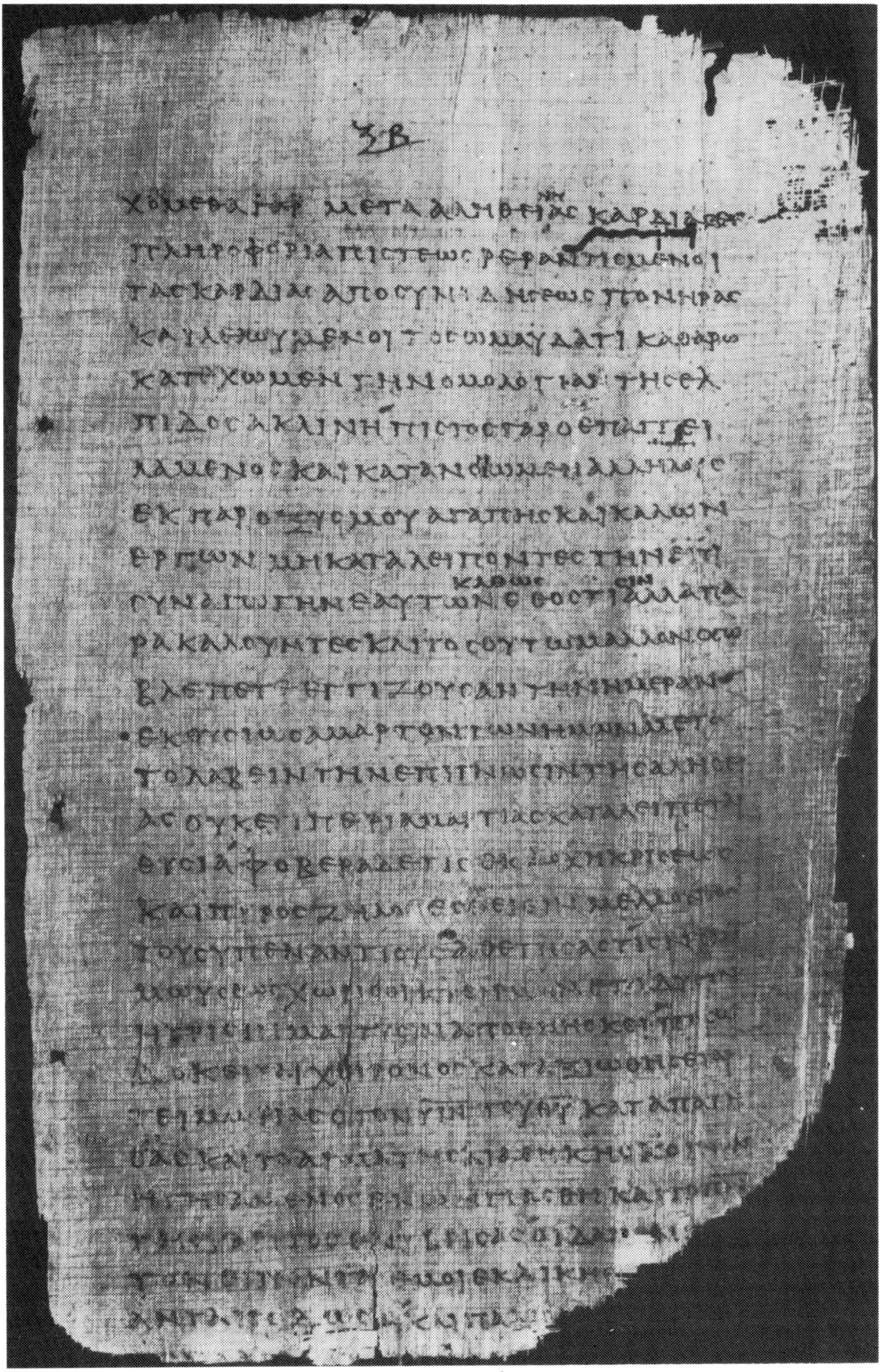

Plate VI Chester Beatty Biblical Papyrus II (P^{46}) (about A.D. 200) Heb 10:22-30 (Greek)

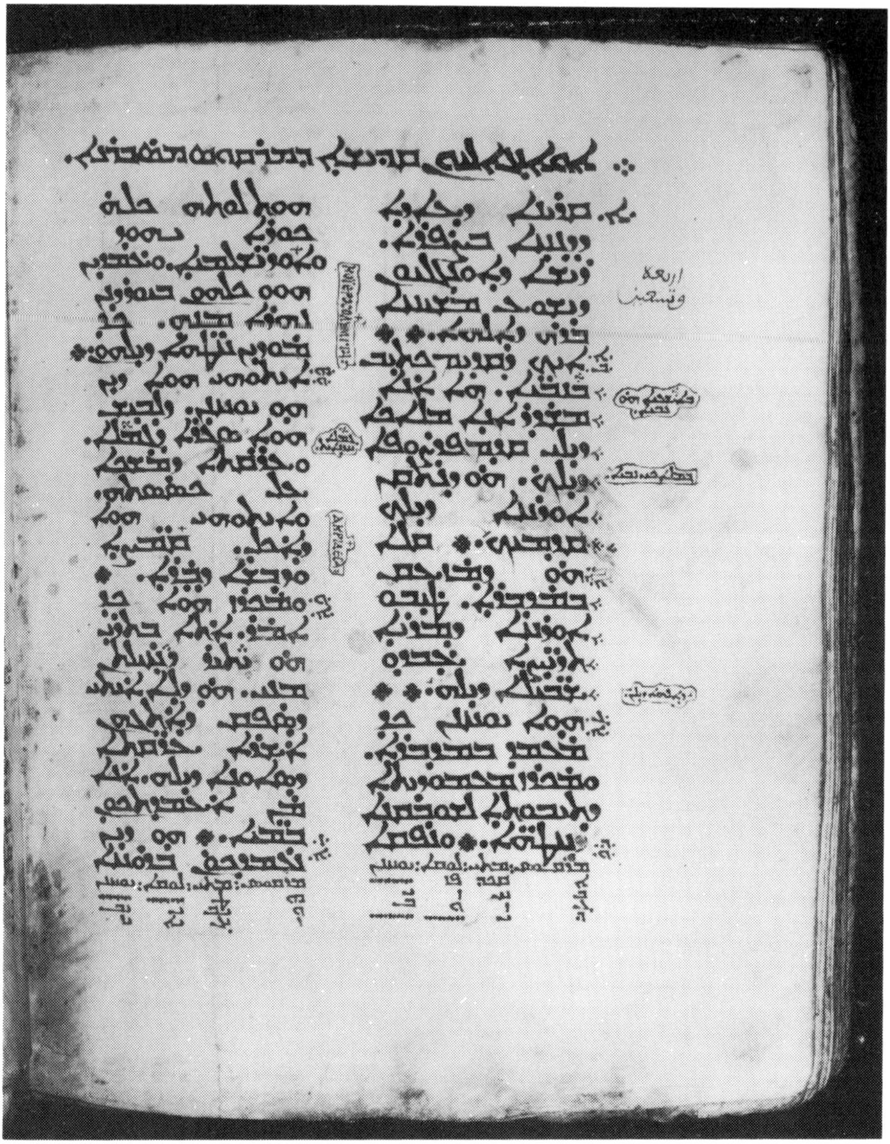

Plate VII Chester Beatty Syriac Ms 703 (A.D. 1177) Harclean version of Mark 1:1-8

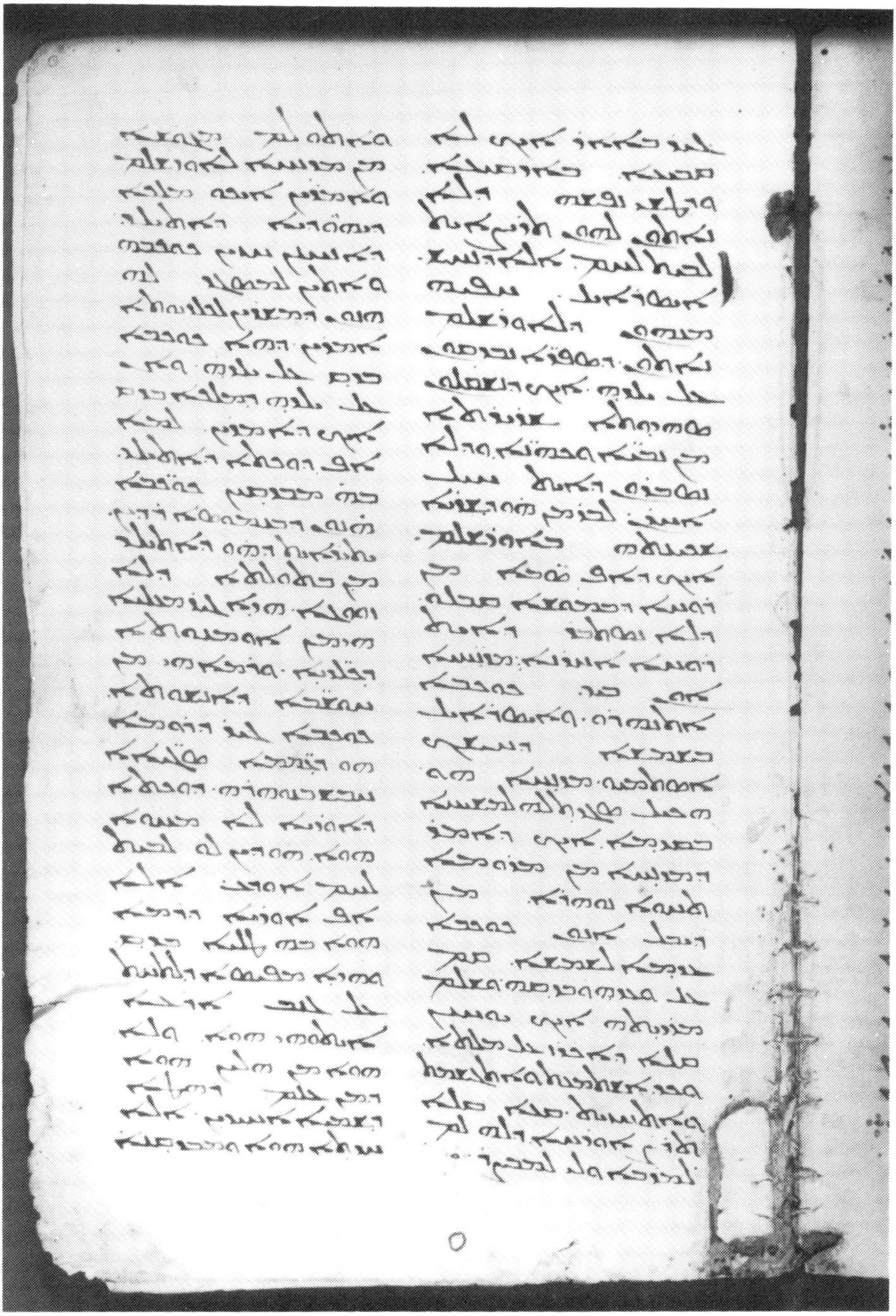

Plate VIII Chester Beatty Syriac Ms 709 (5th/6th cent) St. Ephrem's Commentary on Tatian's Diatessaron (Matt 2:1-2)

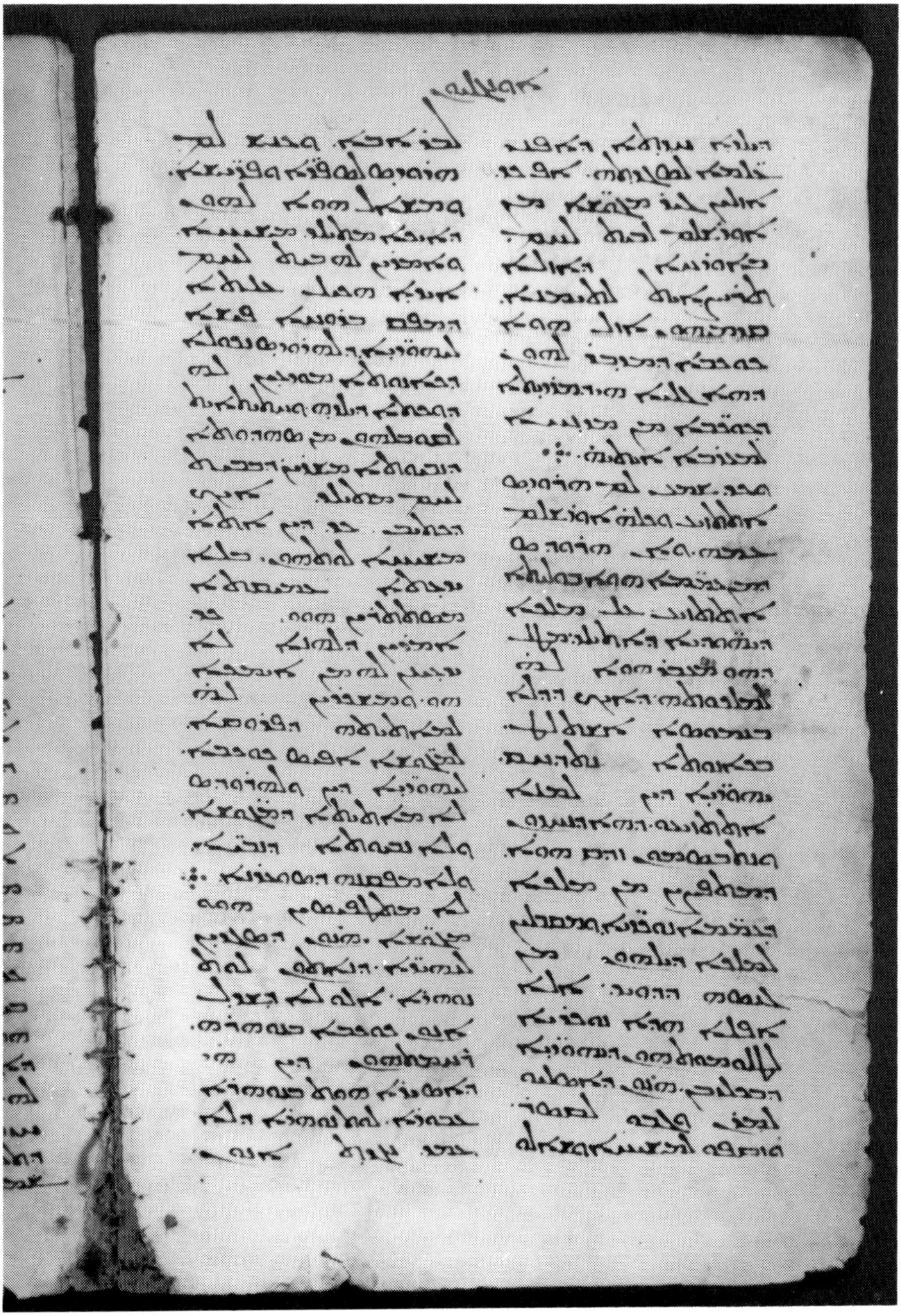

Plate IX Chester Beatty Syriac Ms 709 (5th/6th cent) St. Ephrem's Commentary on Tatian's Diatessaron (Matt 2:3-5)

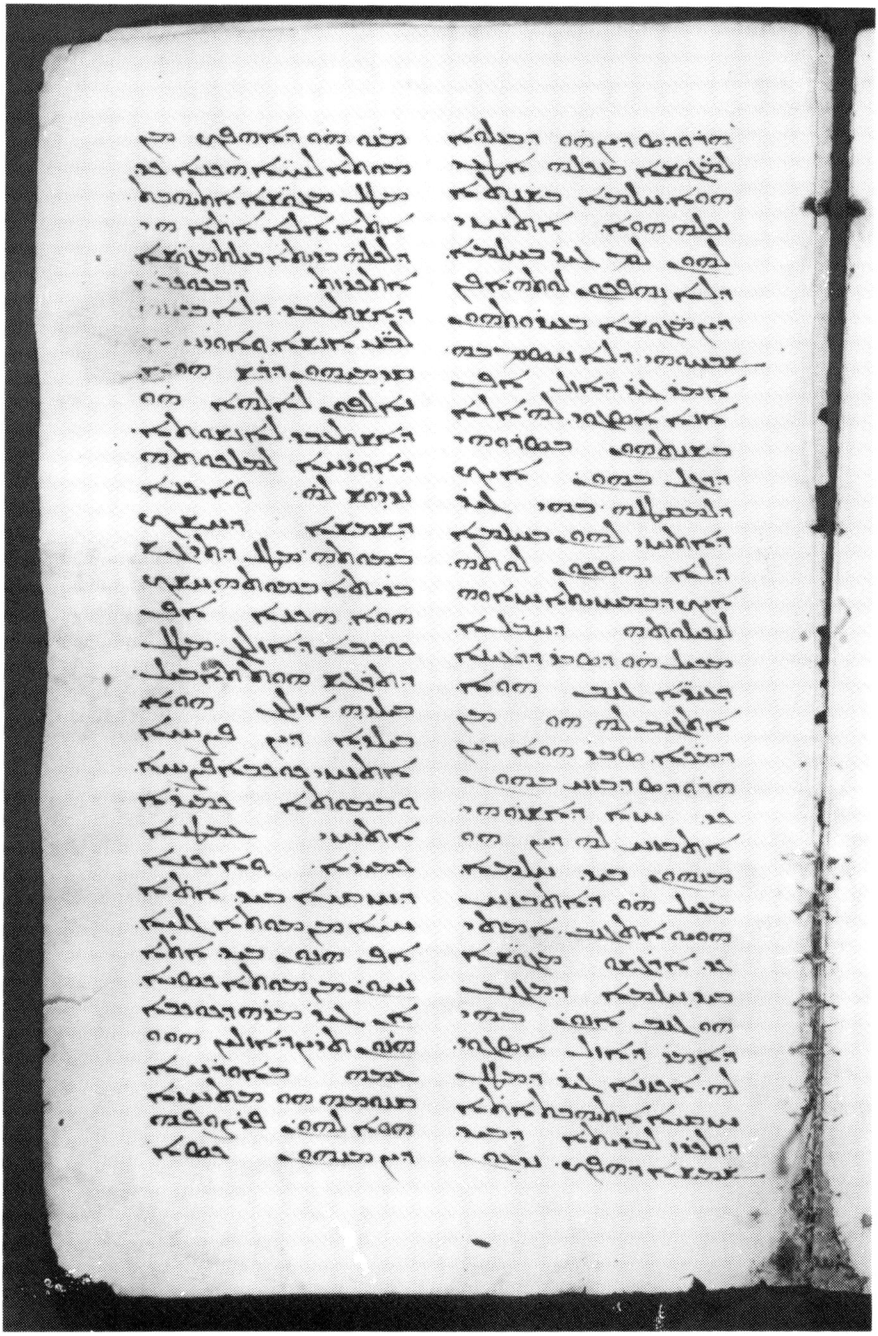

Plate X Chester Beatty Syriac Ms 709 (5th/6th cent) St. Ephrem's Commentary on Tatian's Diatessaron (Matt 2:8, 12)

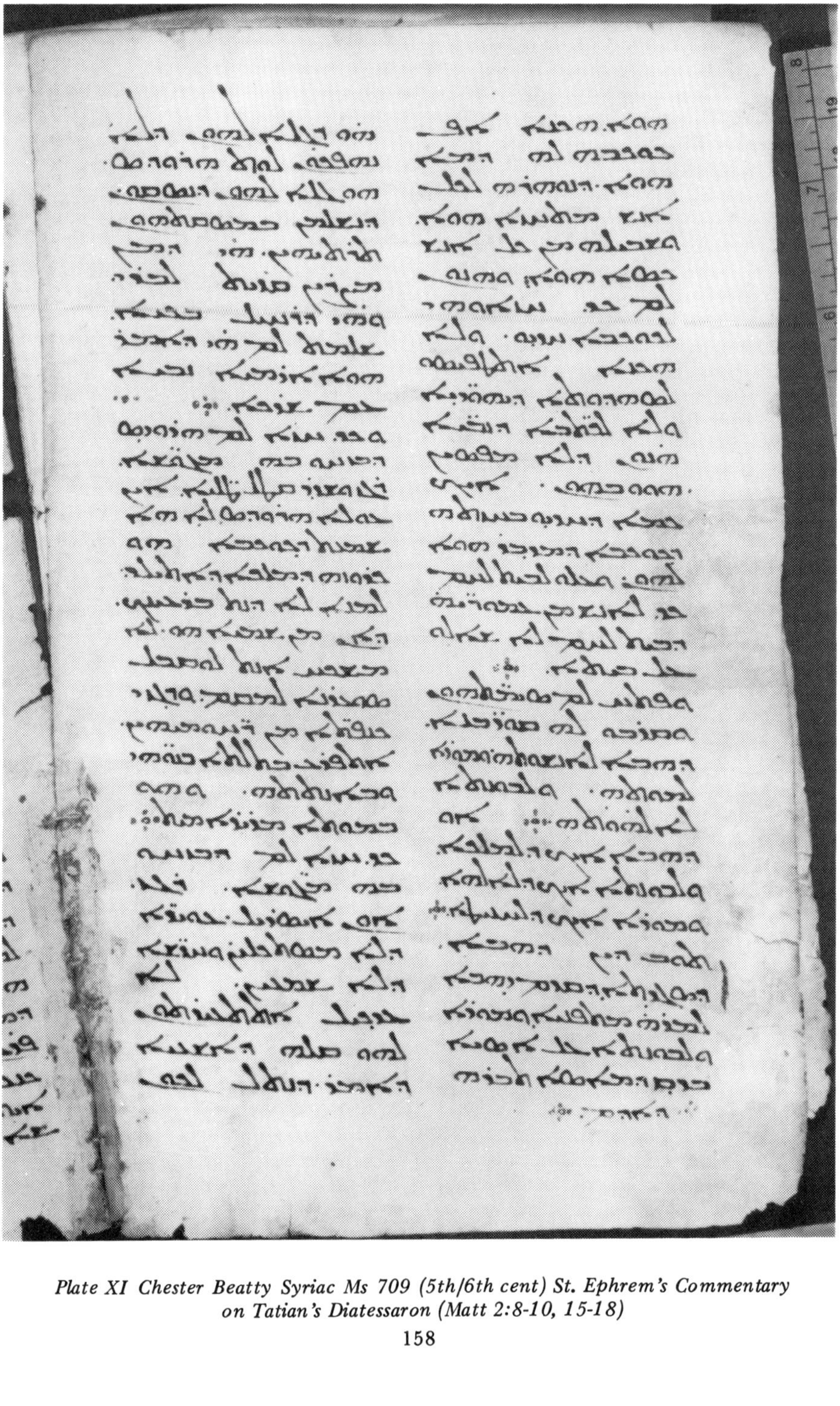

Plate XI Chester Beatty Syriac Ms 709 (5th/6th cent) St. Ephrem's Commentary on Tatian's Diatessaron (Matt 2:8-10, 15-18)

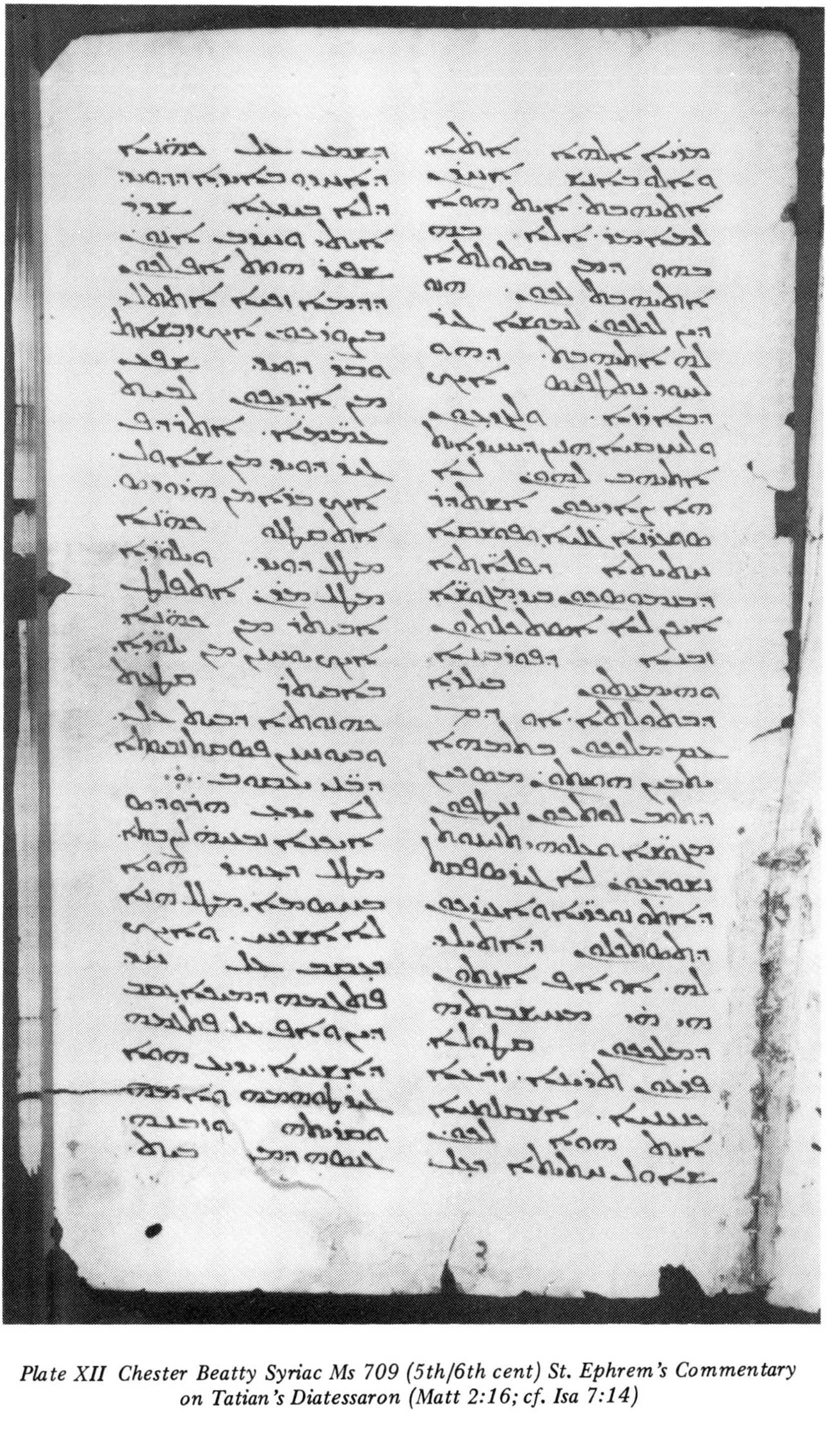

Plate XII Chester Beatty Syriac Ms 709 (5th/6th cent) St. Ephrem's Commentary on Tatian's Diatessaron (Matt 2:16; cf. Isa 7:14)

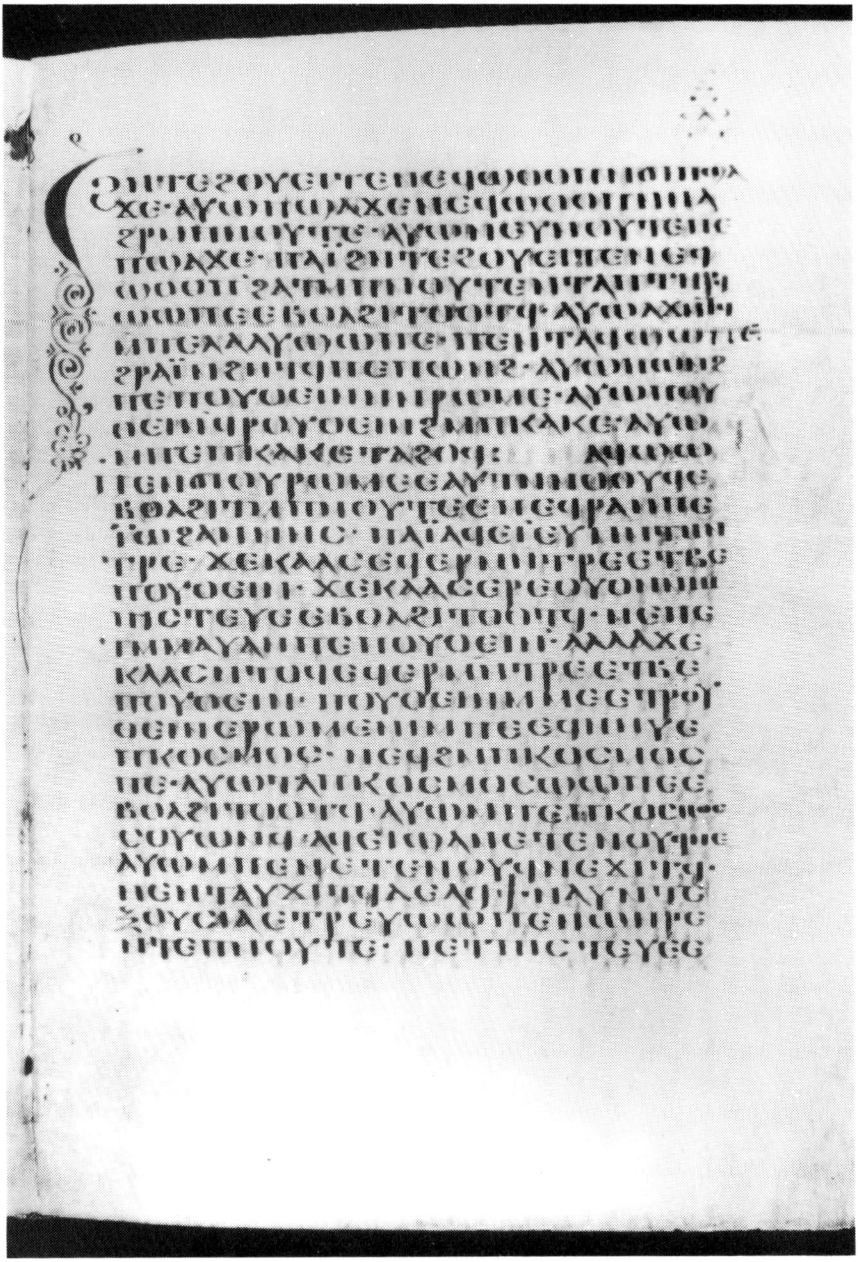

Plate XIII Chester Beatty Coptic Ms 813 (about A.D. 600) Beginning of St. John's Gospel

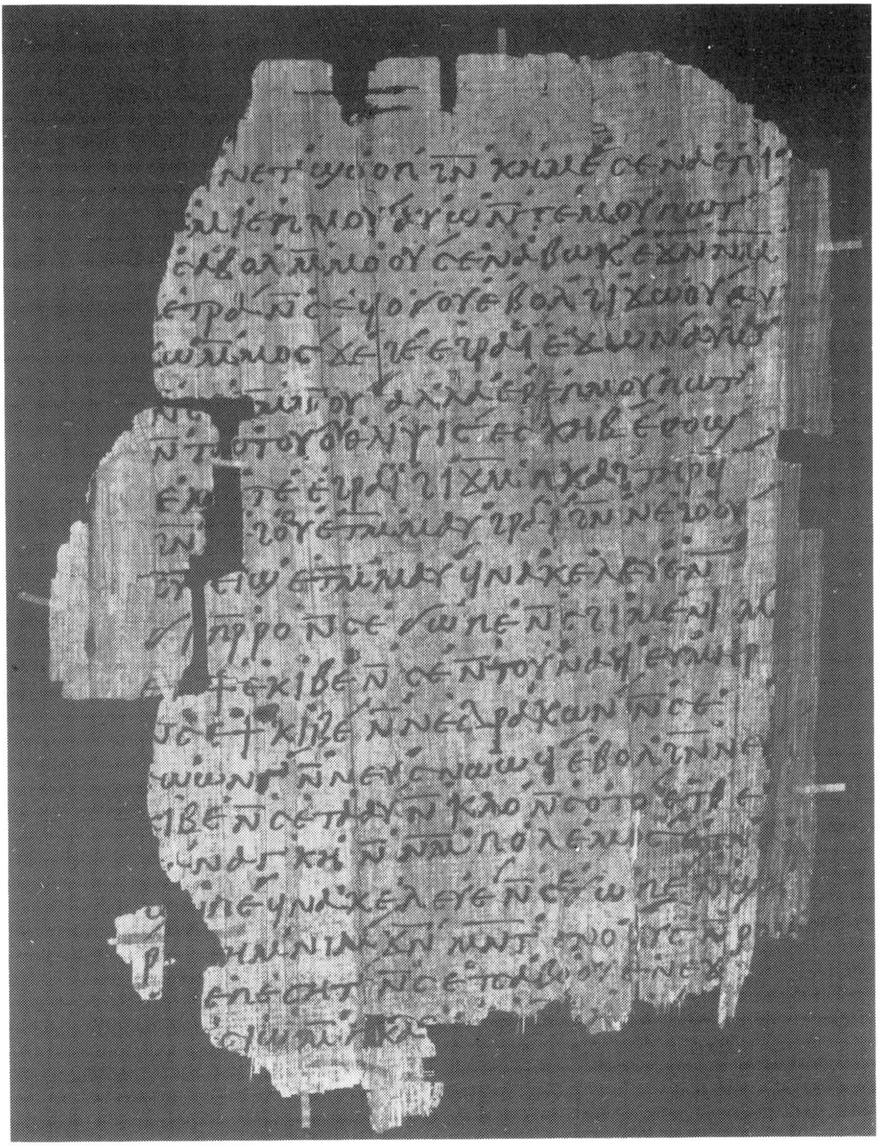

Plate XIV Chester Beatty Copic Ms Ac. 1493 (4th/5th cent) The Apocalypse of Elijah

Plate XV Chester Beatty Ms W145 (4th/5th cent) Part of a vellum roll in Greek containing a letter of St. Pachomius

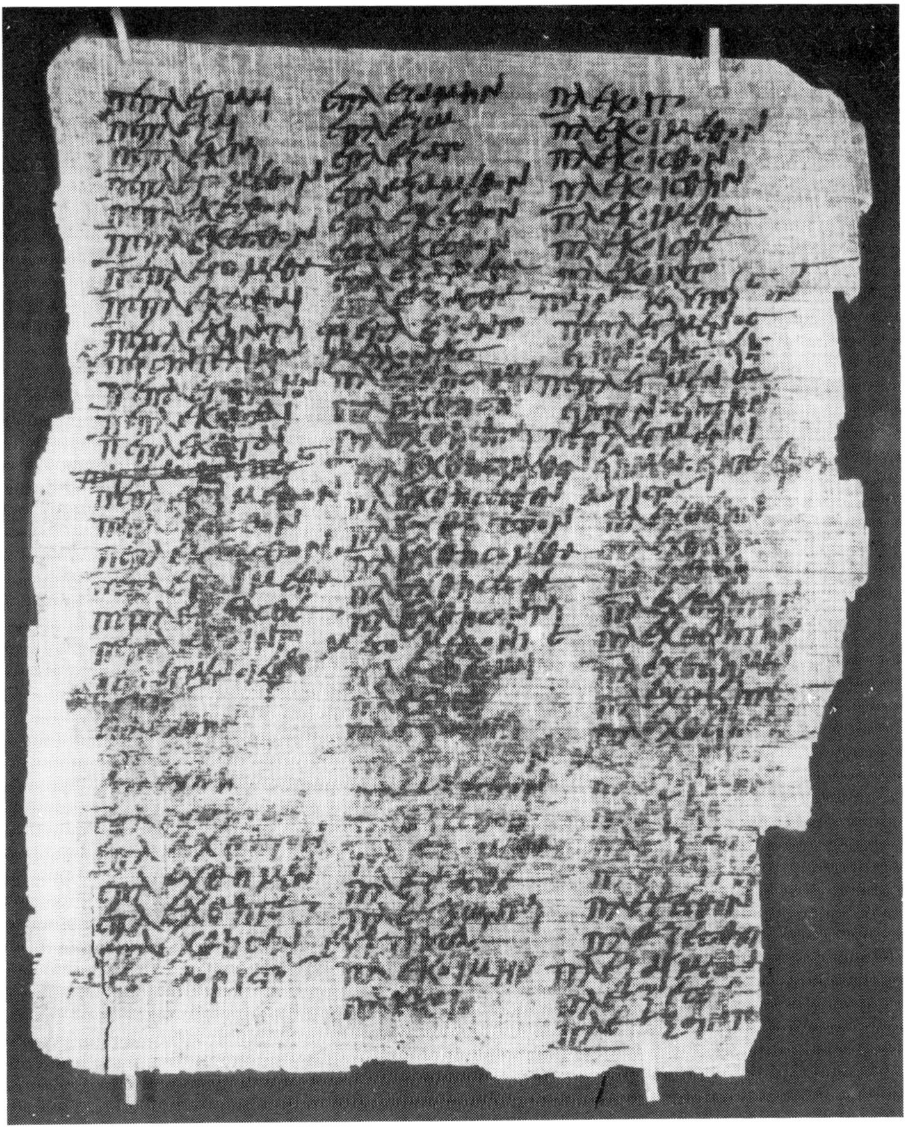

Plate XVI Chester Beatty Ms Ac. 1499 (4th cent) A page from a Greek grammar

THE COMMENTARIES OF IBN AL-BAṢĪṢ AND IBN AL-WAḤĪD ON IBN AL-BAWWĀB'S "ODE ON THE ART OF CALLIGRAPHY" (RĀ'IYYAH FĪ L-KHAṬṬ)

David James, *Chester Beatty Library, Dublin*

The importance of calligraphy in Islamic civilisation is well known. The necessity of transcribing the sacred scripture of Islam clearly and accurately gave scribes a significant role in early Islamic society as well as an enduring prestige. This prestige, together with Islam's anti-iconic attitude towards visual manifestations of the faith, meant that in the long term calligraphy was to become one of the main vehicles of creative energy in the visual arts of Islam.

Furthermore, since Islamic society was by and large a literate one, appreciation of calligraphy was widespread and the work of the masters, both major and minor, was admired and even venerated. There are numerous accounts of the lengths to which *aficionados* of the art went to acquire specimens of the handiwork they coveted, and of the large sums for which the examples of calligrapher's work changed hands, though, as is often the case, after the masters responsible had died.[1]

Biographical dictionaries and historical chronicles give considerable information on the lives of the great masters, while occasional details of the careers of many of the lesser ones are recorded even though it may be only a line giving the date of their birth and the name of their teacher and pupils, if they had any. The most famous calligraphers prior to the fourteenth century were Ibn Muqlah (d. 940), Ibn al-Bawwāb (d. 1022) and Yāqūt al-Musta'ṣimī (d. 1298). Both Ibn Muqlah and Ibn al-Bawwāb are reported to have composed a treatise on the art of calligraphy. That of the former is lost, while only the introduction of the latter's survives.[2] Very little in fact can be attributed to the masters of calligraphy from the "classic" period in the way of writings on their profession, partly because information was imparted by example and word of mouth and partly because the secrets of many crafts and professions were carefully guarded.

This is what makes the survival of the *qaṣīdah* or ode on

calligraphy by Ibn al-Bawwāb relatively unusual. Nevertheless the poem talks in generalities and conceals, rather than reveals, details of Ibn al-Bawwāb's art.

Ibn al-Bawwāb's full name was Abu 'l-Ḥasan 'Alī ibn Hilāl. His father was a minor official, a doorkeeper (*bawwāb*), hence his name "the son of the doorkeeper". He began as a painter before taking up calligraphy, in which he excelled. He was well versed in learning and became an associate of a minister at the court of the Būyid dynasty which ruled Iran and Iraq in the tenth and eleventh centuries. For a time he was in charge of the library of sultan Bahā' al-Dawlah (988-1022) in Shiraz, though most of his life appears to have been spent in Baghdad where he died in 1022. The best known example of his handwriting is found in a Qur'ān in the Chester Beatty Library, Ms. 1431, dated 391/1001. Some years ago the manuscript was the subject of a detailed investigation by the late D.S. Rice, who was at pains to prove that the manuscript was the only genuine example of the hand of the master.[3]

The authenticity of the poem never appears to have been in doubt and one of the earliest versions of it is given by no less a scholar than Ibn Khaldūn in his *Muqaddimah*.[4] A slightly later one is given by Muḥammad ibn Ḥasan al-Ṭībī, a Mamlūk official and calligrapher at the court of Sultan Qānṣawh al-Ghawrī, popularly called Qānṣūh al-Ghūrī (1501-1516) in a compendium of calligraphic styles written for the royal library in Cairo.[5] A commentary on the poem was written by two later calligraphers and it is this commentary which is the subject of this contribution.

The commentators are Ibn al-Baṣīṣ and Ibn al-Waḥīd.[6] According to the *Durar al-Kāminah* of Ibn Ḥajar, Ibn al-Baṣīṣ was Mūsā ibn 'Alī ibn Muḥammad, a native of Hammah in Syria who was born in 1253 and died in 1316. He is said to have invented a special type script called *al-Mu'jiz* which was employed in Damascus, and to have passed much of his time in rustic pursuits and composing poetry. The later Ottoman historian, Mustaqīm-zādah says that Ibn al-Baṣīṣ was called Muḥammad ibn 'Alī ibn Mūsā and was a pupil of Ibn al-Bawwāb. If this is not an error for Mūsā ibn 'Alī ibn Muḥammad, the Ottoman writer having accidentally reversed the order of the names, it must be an ancestor. Which of the two wrote the commentary on Ibn al-Bawwāb's *Rā'iyyah* is not clear, though it was probably the man mentioned by Ibn Ḥajar who was a contemporary of the other commentator, Ibn al-Waḥīd. The latter was a colourful character whose biography is recorded in detail by several Mamlūk historians. Muḥammad ibn Sharīf al-Zar'ī, called Ibn al-Waḥīd, was born in Damascus in 1249 and went to Baghdad, where he became a pupil of Yāqūt al-Musta'ṣimī before making his way to Cairo at the end of the thirteenth century. He obtained a post as secretary in the al-Ḥākim mosque, which was partly destroyed by an earthquake in 1302. The mosque was repaired at the expense of a powerful Mamlūk emir, Baybars al-Jāshnagīr (the Taster). Ibn al-Waḥīd became very friendly with Baybars, who gave him a position in the chancellery (*dīwān al-inshā'*) in Cairo. He was notoriously lazy but enjoyed the favour of the Emir Baybars. In 1304 Baybars commissioned him to produce a Qur'ān in seven volumes, to be housed in the new foundation (*khānqāh*) he was building near to the mosque of al-Ḥākim in which the Qur'ān was to be read each Friday. Ibn al-Waḥīd was given 1,600 dinars to undertake the work, which was carried out by a team of craftsmen under his direction. Rumour had it that he pocketed most of the money and spent only 600 dinars on the work. When this was brought to the attention of the emir he overlooked the matter, saying that one had to tolerate the foibles of a true genius. Although some of these "foibles" seem to have been rather startling,[7] we can see Baybar's point when looking at the Qur'ān, which happily has survived.[8]

It is not known when Ibn al-Waḥīd wrote his commentary on the poem of Ibn al-Bawwāb, but as the former died in 1311 it must date from before that year. It is found in a manuscript in the National Library, Cairo, copied at the beginning of the eighteenth century, Ms 119. This was published with an introduction in Tunis in 1967 by Hilāl Nājī, who stated that it was the only text of which he was aware.[9]

The text which is the subject of this article is located in the British Library, Ms Or 13,017, and contains the commentary of Ibn al-Waḥīd together with that of Ibn al-Baṣīṣ. This has been collated with the 1967 edition of the text published by Hilāl Nājī and with the edition published by the same scholar in 1986 in the journal *Al-Mawrid* 4, No. 15, 259-270. This latter edition is based on a copy of the commentaries of Ibn al-Waḥīd and Ibn al-Baṣīṣ in the Arif Hikmet Library, Medina. On neither occasion did Nājī consult the British Library manuscript, of which he was not aware.

The poem is usually referred to as the *Rā'iyyah* of Ibn al-Bawwāb, meaning that each line ends with the letter *rā'*, but in the British Library version it is simply called the *Qaṣīdah*, or Ode.[10] It consists of six folios of text, 24v-29v, with fifteen lines of script to each side. The poem is copied in red *naskh* script, slightly larger than the commentary which is in black *naskh*. The work is undated but appears to have been copied in the sixteenth century. It does not bear the signature of the copyist but there are a number of notes signed by one al-Muṣṭafā ibn Muḥyi 'l-Dīn. The text is quite well copied and the language of the commentary relatively simple. Nevertheless, being a technical treatise written to inform practitioners of the art of calligraphy, it does contain a number of obscure words and phrases, some of which are found in other medieval works on scribal practices and the techniques of calligraphy.[11]

There have been several Arabic editions of the poem. It has been translated in English, French and Turkish in the nineteenth and twentieth centuries.[12] The 1967 edition of the commentary by Nājī gives only that of Ibn al-Waḥīd; his 1986 version includes the commentary of both Ibn al-Waḥīd and Ibn al-Baṣīṣ. The 1986 version differs in several respects from the text of the British Library manuscript.

The Ode of Shaykh Abu'l-Ḥasan 'Alī ibn Hilāl, the scribe of Baghdad known as "Ibn al-Bawwāb", with the commentaries of Ibn al-Baṣīṣ and Ibn al-Waḥīd

Fol. 24 v *In the name of God, the Compassionate, the Merciful,*

O you who wish to excel in composing,
desiring an elegant hand, well-formed

He addresses[13] whoever wishes to write a fine hand, saying, "O you who wish to excel in composing", meaning the composing of writing, and "well-formed" meaning the well-formed construction of the script. The purpose and aim of every craft is to follow the action of nature; each word must be like a well-proportioned form. The construction of the script is divided into four: the placing, the balance, the measure and the spacing. The placing (*awḍāʿ*)[14] of the letters on the line is that devised by the Shaykh, May God Most High have mercy on him. The balance (*munāsabah*) means that there should be a proper relationship (among the letters). Measure (*maqādīr*) means that the letter *alif* should not exceed its *lām* (in height). Spacing[15] (*bayāḍāt*) means that there should be an equal distance between *alif* and *lām*, and the distance should be consistent in the remainder of the line. He says "desiring", meaning that no one will write an elegant hand unless he desires it in his heart.

If your aim in writing be true,
Pray to your Lord to ease the way.
Prepare a pen good and straight,
Easy, not hard, on the knife.[16]

Fol. 25 r His remark "Prepare" implies the preferability of old, treasured pens over those newly cut, and an insistence on their antiquity. By "straight" (*muqawwam*) he means not bent (*aʿwaj*), nor bruised (*mabṭūḥ*), nor twisted (*maftūl*) with white streaks.[17] It should be easy for the knife to trim the nib (*baryah*), not difficult. In the commentary of Ibn al-Waḥīd he says that the pen should be "straight" (*muthaqqaf*), which is derived from *thiqāf*,[18] the name for the wood from which spears and arrows are made. He also says "hard, suitable for the craft of inking" instead of "easy on the knife", which is better because the flaccid pen will compel you to make the nib short and (the ink) will quickly dry.[19] "Inking" (*taḥbīr*) means inscribing in ink. In the copy of Ibn al-Waḥīd the following verse is apparently an additional one:

When you propose to trim a nib,
Aim for medium size.[20]

He means of medium length and thickness, unless you are

writing the *ṭūmār* hand,[21] when it should be large, the opposite (of what we have said).

Examine its two ends and make your nib
at the end where it is narrow and slender.

He commands you to look at the two ends of the pen (i.e. the untrimmed reed), and whichever is the finer and thinner, make of it the nib (*baryah*), as the nib must be at the head of the reed which is the harder of the two ends, since the moisture has dried out because of the exposure of the skin and the long beating down of the sun upon it. Thus the head of the reed has become thinner
Fol. because of its compactness.[22] This verse means that what
25v he (Ibn al-Waḥīd) said about hardness is more correct than the other remark about (the reed) being easy on the knife, since that version would make a contradiction in the words of the Shaykh. When this is known, put the pen on the ground and let it roll and then stop. Make the nib at the point where it stops so the pen will not be twisted.[23]

Make the jalfah of decent size,
not too long, nor too short.

The *jalfah*[24] is the length of the nib. Scribes have differed over this, some saying, "Let it be like the beak of a dove and the straightness of an arrow". Others say, "Let it have (the length of) a thumb-joint knot". Others say, "Neither long nor short". This latter is what the Shaykh has said referring to the firmness or flaccidity of the pen. The firm pen may be long: its limit is its give-and-take, causing the consistency of the script to alter.

Its thickness[25] *should likewise be*
midway, between too much and too little.

If the pen is too thick then the points where the strokes change direction (*farakāt*) will be obscured;[26] if too little, the fluidity of the writing will decrease and, if it is an obliquely-cut pen, the vertical strokes will clash with the thickness of the horizontal ones and the changes of direction will be too thick. The round-cut pen (*al-mudawwar*) will make the vertical strokes too thick. Thickness (*shaḥmah*) occurs in the *ṣadr*[27] of the pen where it is placed on the paper and in its sliced-off part (*fatḥah*).[28] There are those who remove it, there are those who leave a substantial amount, and there are those who say that it should be average, which is the choice of the Shaykh. In the version of Ibn al-Waḥīd – may God have mercy on him – he says:

Fol. 26r *Make the split in the middle, so that*
the "teeth" on each side will equal be.

Make the nib-split (*shaqq*) in the middle of the pen so that the ink will flow down the centre and so that one-half of the pen-split will not be weak and the writing will be spoiled. If, however, the right "tooth" is a little bit thicker, that will do no harm.[29]

When you have done all that with the care
of an expert seeking a remedy,[30]
Then turn your attention towards making the point,
for the point is the crux of the task.

He begins with the nib, which has been discussed previously. Then he talks of the point (*qaṭṭah*), saying "Turn all your attention and concentration towards it, because neither the paring (*naḥt*) of the pen nor its splitting will alone produce (good) script. It is the point that creates the writing. And when the blade of the knife swerves from the position where it has been placed on the point, though it be a quarter of a hair's breadth, then the point will be spoiled and the writing will not be a success. The way to do it is to take a firm dry reed, put the knife on the nib and bring it in at an angle to (make) the *ṣadr*[31] of the pen, pressing on forcefully so that you make the point. Cut through in a straight line and it will make a sharp noise. If the point is sharp the writing will be clear: if it is not sharp it will be untidy. The point is what scribes pay attention to, and whoever understands it, understands writing and its sciences.

Fol. 26v

Do not ask me to reveal it,
it is a secret to which I shall hold.

The Shaykh is chary of explaining the secrets of wisdom except to the one of whom he approves, after the manner of the learned in protecting their secrets from the ignorant.

But the substance of what I want to say
is that the point should be somewhere
Between oblique and rounded.

Ibn al-Waḥīd said, "The Shaykh merely hints at the (cutting of) the point in this verse because of the effort he underwent to understand it, and because interest in acquiring a high degree of excellence was supreme in his day, since the benefit from this art was great. He merely hints at the major reason for perfecting it by his remark "somewhere between". After him, when people diverged from his method (*ṭariqah*),[32] due to their ignorance of
Fol. 27r (the cutting of) the point and due to the paucity of good examples of his work and the waning of interest in achieving the best from this art, I decided that it was necessary to reveal what he had merely hinted at. He spoke in generalities, concealing the detail, the meaning of which is that every identifiable style (*qalam*), like *muḥaqqaq*[33] and *naskh*,[34] is characterised by a specially trimmed nib-point. That of *rayḥān*[35] is the most oblique, gradually decreasing until *riqā'*,[36] which is the least oblique. There are several types between oblique and rounded."

So devote sufficient effort towards it,
Perhaps you will acquire what has been
handed down.

The Shaykh, May God Most High have mercy on him, emphasises the practice of the point by copying. Due to my copying good examples of his work in all styles and my comparing his different nib-types, by long experiment all has come clear to me. When al-Walī al-'Ajamī[37] cut a rounded nib his *rayḥān* style and what related to it was spoiled, but his *riqāʿ* and what related to it improved. Today the Iraqis do the opposite.

Into your inkwell you should mix
soot, compounded with vinegar or unripe grapes.

He chose soot because of its smoothness and beautifying quality, and the two extracts for their smoothness, grip, and because they were less likely to decay. Ibn al-Waḥīd said, "I believe that the ingredients should be mixed cold;
Fol. that is the recipe of al-Samʿānī,[38] which consists of: one
27v part of gallnuts (*ʿafṣ*); half a part of gum arabic (*ṣamgh*); a quarter part of vitriol (*zāj*), ground and mashed with pomegranate juice (*māʾ al-julnār*) in a mortar for some days until it ferments and is clarified. Then alum (*shabb*), pure white salt (*milḥ al-andarāʾnī*),[39] verdigris (*zinjār*), and aloes (*ṣabr*) should be added. For every *raṭl* add half an *ūqiyah* of gum arabic.[40] Let it be put in the sun for two weeks."

Ibn al-Baṣīṣ said, "The inkwell wad (*līqah*) should be of silk washed with soap and well teased out and very dry. Then take the high quality ink and pour it over the wad and stir it. The ink is produced from the following ingredients: Socotra aloes – a dirham's weight; Genoa saffron – a dirham's weight; verdigris, unground (*bi-lā ḥakk*?) – three dirham's[41] weight; pure white salt – three dirham's weight. Let the ingredients be beaten separately. Let good, sound, unpierced fresh gallnuts be taken and be crushed and broken in thirds and quarters to the weight of three *ūqiyahs*. Let them be steeped for three days with myrtle leaves and boiled until a third evaporates. Let it be clarified through a filter on to the above-mentioned ingredients and be fermented for seven days. Then take the clarified liquid and put in a glass jar. Let good, unpounded gum arabic be put with it: it will retain its essence (i.e. of the gum). Let it be blackened with Cyprus vitriol. The viscous liquid makes suitable
Fol. ink. The scribe who wishes may extract soot from flax
28r oil and use it in place of the gum arabic. It will give black-

ness and beautify it. Let pure Cyprus vitriol be added to intensify its blackness and beauty."

"When this has been done, put in the wad and when it has submerged and settled in the inkwell, if the scribe thinks that its strength is deficient he can pour in vinegar or the pulp of unripe grapes." Diluted red ochre, orpiment and camphor may be added to increase its luminosity and beauty. This is the meaning of what he says (in the verse):

Add to it red ochre which has been
diluted, orpiment and camphor.

He means iraqi ochre (*mughrah 'irāqiyah*), which has a reddish tinge, to give it bulk and arrest the drying-up of the moisture. Orpiment (*zirnīkh*) will improve its colour, keep flies away and kill them. Camphor (*kāfūr*) will preserve it and scent it.

When you have fermented it,
take some paper, smooth and sized,
Flatten it in a press to be
free from creasing and distortion.

When you have fermented your inkwell and nibbed your pen, go and take some heavy, smooth paper, sized (*makhbūr*), as he says, for polishing, on which the script will not be disjointed, the passage of the pen will be
Fol. smooth and it will not snap. If it is pressed after cutting
28v it will remove creasing and this will not affect its limpidity and polish.

The Shaykh Ibn al-Bawwāb, May God Most High have mercy upon him, has said:[42]

"Choose well three things, for on them
the splendour of fine script depends:
Ink, strong paper and a pen, which when you have
gathered them together you can be glad
And if you are missing any when the new moon appears,
by the tail-end of the month you will
have them."

Then patiently make imitation your habit,
for nothing fulfils a desire like patience,
Begin with a wooden slate,
thus does the accomplished, praiseworthy man.

The Shaykh orders the studying, night and day, of examples which he gives to the beginner which will make him understand their principles and nature. He ponders them in order to master some of them. Patience must be the basis, since without it one's desired aim cannot be achieved. Then he commands him to begin with writing on a wooden slate (*lawḥ*) to simplify matters, as he can erase anything unsuitable. He should commence with the *muḥaqqaq* and *ash'ār*[43] styles because they are firmly established. He said the first time he only commands once: that is what the clever, praiseworthy shrewd man will do.

Ibn al-Waḥīd said, "This information is for the advanced (pupil)[44] as the following verse indicates":

Fol. 29r *Then transfer to a scroll, unsheathing it resolutely,*
peeling it from its roll.[45]
Boldly stretch forth your hand to write,
nothing gains what is desired like courage.

Ibn al-Baṣīṣ said, "The Shaykh commands that after using the slate the student should prepare himself to write by sitting on one knee and half of the other,[46] taking up the pen and writing on a roll (*darj*). The roll is of paper and is for well-proportioned (*mansūb*) writing and fair copies of the Shaykh's hand. He takes an example of the Shaykh's script and transfers it to the roll in his own hand (. . . ?).[47] The Shaykh orders him to take heart, saying that one should not be afraid of writing. If one is afraid the hand will surely tremble when one writes. He says, "Boldly stretch forth your hand", which means that one should attack the matter and enter into it without fear or anxiety. Courage is desirable in everything. Most people fear that they will not be able to write as they desire, so their hands become limp in their frustration."

Do not be shy if at first
you make an error in your writing,
Fol. *The matter may be hard but then improves.*
29v *Many a time ease follows difficulty.*

The first verse appears in the version of Ibn al-Waḥīd and means that the weak, ignorant man fears that people may see his shortcomings when he begins to learn his art, so he is prevented from learning by his pride and stupidity, remaining ignorant all his life.

The second verse encourages the pupils when he finds the going slow and is despondent, by helpfully asserting that the patient man gets what he wants.

When you have reached your goal
and are happy and overjoyed,

that is, when you have reached your aim in writing and its various forms, which are several. There are two principal categories. *Muḥaqqaq* is the one with which you should begin in order to ascertain its letters. Its letters *wāw*, *fā'* and *mīm* have open loops. Its letters are well-formed (*muḥaqqaqah*) and (?*mukhtalasah*). From it are derived the *rayḥānī* and *naskh* styles in which are written Prophetic Sayings, works on grammar, language and *fiqh*.

The second category is *thulth*, which is the basis of proportioned writing (*kitābah mansūbah*).[48] When the student has mastered it he will have mastered all the letters necessary for writing. From it all other styles derive. One of these is *tawqī'āt*,[49] in which are written the proclamations[50] . . . and decrees of the sultan. From the *tawqī'āt* style is derived its sub-type (*far'*), *riqā'*, in which is written the correspondence of the royal chancellery and legal contracts.

Ibn al-Baṣīṣ said: "Then my father,[51] the Shaykh, considered the first category, *muḥaqqaq*, and the second, *thulth*, and combined them so that they fused, calling (the result) *ash'ār*, which is the seventh hand. There are those who call it *mu'annaq*. He was asked, may God have mercy on him, 'When does calligraphy deserve to be considered good?' He replied, 'When its parts are in proportion, when its *lām* and *alif* are perfect, when its paper (*qirṭās*) shines and different styles of letters (*ajnās*) are not confused, when its up-strokes and down-strokes are in harmony, and its *rā's* are distinct from its *nūns*'."

Muḥaqqaq is the style in which the letters are perfectly formed. *Tawqī*' is the style in which the letters intermingle and hang contrary to the absolute. With regard to *muḥaqqaq*, it is not purely curvilinear; it requires its letters to be suspended (in a certain way). It is not purely rectilinear, it needs correcting.

Ibn al-Waḥīd said: "His expression, agreement, ally (*ḥilf*, *ḥalīf*) means helper (*mulāzim*). Its origin is that one considered weak among the Arabs feared that people would harm him, so he took refuge with a strong party after allying himself with him. Rejoicing (*ḥubūr*) means happiness (*masarrah*)."

Then give thanks to your God
and follow His pleasure,
For truly God loves
every grateful heart.

Ibn al-Waḥīd said: "Thanking means to speak of favour, and following His pleasure means that you should agree obediently to whatever He desires of you."

Strive that the fingers of your hand
will write what is good
So that it will be left behind you
in the abode of deception.

Ibn al-Waḥīd said: "He requests that your hand write nothing that will bring God's displeasure upon you, for worldly desires which are deception.

For whatever a man does now
will confront him on the morrow
When he has to face
the inscribed record of his deeds.

Ibn al Baṣīṣ said: "Know that writing may be taken as

evidence against Man in the Next World, and as evidence in his favour. May God have mercy upon him (the author) in the Final Abode."

A Glossary of the Technical Terms Used in the Arabic Text

anbūbah
"reed" or "tube".

ash'ār
ash'ār, also called *mu'annaq*, is said by several Mamlūk authors to be a rare form of script. According to al-Nuwayrī, *Nihāyat al-Arab fī Funūn al-Adab* (Cairo 1923-55) it is a combination of *thulth* and *muḥaqqaq*. According to al-Ṭībī, *Jāmi' Maḥāsin Kitābat al-Kuttāb*, it is a combination of *naskh* and *muḥaqqaq*. See *Muqarnas* 2 (1984) 148, for another possible meaning.

aṣl
A principal script as opposed to a derived one (*far'*). See al-Qalqashandī, *Subḥ al-A'sha* and al-Nuwayrī, *Nihāyat al-Arab*, for *uṣūl* and *furu'*.

awḍā', sing. *waḍ'*
"Placings", or perhaps "rules". See al-Zabīdī, *Ḥikmat al-Ishrāq* 63, when he talks of: *awwal man waḍa'a 'l-khaṭṭ kāna ādam*, "The first person to devise writing was Adam."

baryah
The nibbed part of a reed pen. *Barā* means "to trim a pen". See Lane, *Lexicon* Part 1, 197. Lane does not mention *baryah*. It occurs also thus in the Medina copy of the text. Cf. Nājī, *Al-Mawrid* 4, No. 15 (1986) 264. Al-Zabīdī, *Ḥikmat al-Ishrāq* 73-79, uses *burāyah*. *Barī* means the act of trimming the pen.

bayāḍāt, sing. *bayāḍ*
"Whiteness", i.e. a space where there is nothing. In this case it means the gaps between the letters. Lane, *Lexicon* Part 1, 183.

darj, daraj
"Roll" or "scroll". Lane, *Lexicon* Part 3, 867.

fatḥah
See note 28. *Fatḥ* means the act of cutting the *fatḥah* or aperture. See Robertson, *Studia Semitica et Orientalia* (1920) 77; *Tuḥfat ūlī 'l-Albāb*, Nājī (ed.) 57, Rosenthal, *Ars Islamica* 13-14 (1948) 4.

farakāt, sing. *firkah*
See note 26, and al-Ṭībī, *Jāmi' Maḥāsin Kitābat al-Kuttāb* 18, for an explanation.

jalfah
See note 24. Nājī, *Al-Mawrid* 4, No. 15 vocalises the word thus. Robertson, *Studia Semitica et Orientalia* (1920) 76, gives *jilfah*, as does Rosenthal, *Ars Islamica* 13-14 (1948) 4. *Tuḥfat ūlī 'l-Albāb* Nājī (ed.) gives *jalfah*. Lane, *Lexicon* Part 2, 444, gives both variations.

kabasa, kabbasa
"To press"; "to squeeze".

kitābah mansūbah
"Proportioned writing", but the exact meaning of the term *mansūb* or *al-khaṭṭ al-mansūb*, which refers to the script developed by Ibn Muqlah, has never been properly explained. See N. Abbott, "The Contribution of Ibn Muqlah to the North-Arabic Script", *American Journal of Semitic Languages* 56 (1939) 70-83.

lawḥ
A slate or writing tablet. Lane, *Lexicon* Part 7, 2679.

makhbūr
Lane does not give a meaning for this word other than "being well seasoned or having much grease". It appears to mean "sized" from the context in which it is used in the text.

maqādīr, sing. *miqdār*
"Measurement" or "measure". Lane, *Lexicon* Part 7, 2496.

muḥaqqaq
One of the two principal scripts, being rectilinear (*yābis*) with its letters perfectly formed (*muḥaqqaq*). For examples see D. James, *Qur'ans of the Mamlūks* (London 1988) 19.

munāsabah
"Relationship". Lane, *Lexicon* Part 7, 2787, but "balance" seems to be more what is meant here.

munsaṭiḥāt
The horizontal strokes, from *insaṭaḥa*, "to be spread forth, extended". Lane, *Lexicon* Part 7, 1357, and Robertson, *Studia Semitica et Orientalia* (1920) 80.

muntaṣibāt
The vertical strokes, from *intaṣaba*, "to be erect". Lane, *Lexicon* Part 7, 2799, and Robertson, *Studia Semitica et Orientalia* (1920) 80.

naḥt
"Paring". Robertson, *Studia Semitica et Orientalia* (1920) 77. Rosenthal, *Ars Islamica* 13-14 (1948) 4.

naskh
The commentators put *naskh*, the normal scribal hand, together with *muḥaqqaq* and *rayḥān* in the rectilinear category of scripts rather than the curvilinear. For this important distinction and other remarks on the various classical hands and their derivatives, see the forthcoming article by A. Gacek, "Arabic Scripts and their Characteristics as seen through the eyes of Mamlūk Authors", *Manuscripts of the Middle East.*

qaṭṭ
"The cutting of the point". Lane, *Lexicon* Part 7, 2539. See Robertson, *Studia Semitica et Orientalia* (1920) 77; *Tuḥfat ūlī 'l-Albāb*, Nājī (ed.) 57, and Rosenthal, *Ars Islamica* 13-14 (1948) 5; al-Ṭībī, *Jāmi' Maḥāsin Kitābat al Kuttāb* 15.

qaṭṭah
The point of a pen. See also al-Zabīdī, *Ḥikmat al-Ishrāq* 79; al-Ṭībī, *Jāmi' Maḥāsin Kitābat al-Kuttāb* 16. Lane does not give this word. He does mention *qiṭṭah*, "a mode or manner of cutting a thing, such as the nib of a writing reed" (*Lexicon* Part 7, 2539).

raṭūbah
This term is used by writers on calligraphy to mean roundness or curvature. Scripts are divided into two basic categories:

al-aqlām al-muraṭṭabah (the curvilinear) and *al-aqlām al-yābisah* (the rectilinear).

rayḥān
According to some Mamlūk authors, *rayḥān* was simply a smaller version of *muḥaqqaq*. Several modern authors identify a larger *muḥaqqaq*-type script as *rayḥān*; e.g. M. Lings and Y. Safadi, *The Qur'an* (London 1976) No. 100. *rayḥān*, unlike *muḥaqqaq*, has pronounced spikes on the alif and lām. James, *Qur'ans of the Mamlūks* 19.

rikhw
"Yielding, flaccid" and *rikhwah*, "flaccidity". Lane, *Lexicon* Part 3, 1060.

riqā'
A smaller version of *tawqī'*, used for writing letters of lesser importance. For an illustration see al-Ṭībī, *Jāmi' Maḥāsin Kitābat al-Kuttāb* 78-79.

ṣadr
See note 27.

shaḥmah
See note 25. Also al-Tībī, *Jāmi' Mahāsin Kitābat al-Kuttāb* 16.

ṣiqāl
"Polishing"; "burnishing".

ṣulb
"Hard", "firm", and *ṣalābah*, "firmness". Lane, *Lexicon* Part 5, 1711.

taḥbīr
"Inking", "writing in ink"; *ḥibr*, "ink".

ṭūmār
See note 34. The original meaning of *ṭūmār* is a scroll. al-Qalqashandī, *Subḥ al-A'shā* Vol. 3, 49.

tadwīr
The act of cutting a pen-nib so that it is rounded (*mudawwar*). This has presumably the same meaning as *muṣawwab*. See Rosenthal, *Ars Islamica* 13-14 (1948) 5, where the term is explained.

taḥrīf
The act of cutting a pen-nib obliquely so that it will be *muḥarraf*, "oblique". Rosenthal, *Ars Islamica* 13-14 (1948) 5, and Lane, *Lexicon* Part 1, 551.

yarāʻah
Lane does not give this word. It appears in Wehr, *Dictionary of Modern Arabic* 1106, with the meaning "reed"; "reed pen".

Notes

1. D.S. Rice, *The Unique Ibn al-Bawwāb Manuscript in the Chester Beatty Library* (Dublin 1955) 8-9.
2. Later writers often quote from their treatises. Aḥmad ibn Alī al-Qalqashandī, *Ṣubḥ al-Aʻshā fī Ṣināʻat al-Inshā'* (Cairo 1964) Vol. 3, quotes Ibn Muqlah on the formation of the letters of the alphabet. The introduction to Ibn al-Bawwāb's treatise is given in Yāqūt's *Irshād al-Arīb ilā Maʻrifat al-Adīb* (London 1929) Vol. V, 488; Rice, *The Unique Ibn al-Bawwāb Manuscript* 5 n.1. According to Adam Gacek, Ibn Muglah's treatise does exist and is referred to in his forthcoming article in *Manuscripts of the Middle East* 2. I am grateful to Adam Gacek for this information and for other useful comments on this article.
3. Rice, *The Unique Ibn al-Bawwāb Manuscript*. Rice's conclusions to his masterful investigation have never been challenged. The manuscript was reproduced in facsimile by the Club du Livre, Paris, in 1972, and all existing copies were later purchased by ADEVA (Akademische Druck und Verlagsanstalt, Graz).
4. Ibn Khaldūn, *Muqaddimah*, M. Quatremère (ed.) (Paris 1858) tome 1/2, 347.
5. Muḥammad ibn Ḥasan al-Ṭībī, *Jāmiʻ Maḥāsin Kitābat al-Kuttāb*, S. Al-Munajjid (ed.) (Beirut 1962) 19. For other versions see Rice, *The Unique Ibn al-Bawwāb Manuscript* 5 n. 9.
6. For Ibn al-Baṣīṣ see Ibn Ḥajar al-ʻAsqalānī, *al-Durar al-Kāminah fī Aʻyān al Miʼat al-Thāminah* (Hyderabad 1931) Vol. 4, 376; Musaqīm-zādah, *Tuḥfat-i Khaṭṭāṭīn* (Istanbul 1928) 462. For Ibn al-Waḥīd, see D. James, "Some Observations of the Calligrapher and Illuminators of the Koran of Rukn al-Dīn, Baybars al-Jāshnagīr", *Muqarnas* 2 (1984) 147-157 and n. 8.
7. Ibn Ḥajar al-ʻAsqalānī, *al-Durar al-Kāminah fī Aʻyān al-Miʼat al-Thāminah* (Cairo 1966) No. 3704. Ibn Ḥajar states that Ibn al-Waḥīd poured wine into his inkwell and copied out a Qur'ān with the mixture. It seems hard to believe that such an act of mischief not to say sacrilege, could have been perpetrated. Perhaps the explanation is to be found in the poem and commentary at the point where it is mentioned that grape-pulp may be used as a thickening agent (Fol.

27r). Somewhere along the line grape-pulp (*ḥiṣrim*) may have become wine (*nabīdh*).

8. British Library, Ms Add. 22, 406-413.
9. *Sharḥ Ibn al-Waḥīd ʿalā Rāʾiyyat Ibn al-Bawwāb*, H. Nājī (ed.) (Tunis 1967) 2.
10. The poem is in the Arabic metre *kāmil.*
11. I am very grateful to Aḥmed Mustafa, the well-known calligrapher, for his comments on some of these words and expressions.
12. Baron McCuckin-De Slane, *Les prolégomènes d'Ibn Khaldoun* (Paris 1865) 403; S. Ünver, *Hattat Ali bin Hilal, Hayati ve Yazilari* (Istanbul 1958); A.J. Arberry, *The Koran Illuminated: A Handlist of Korans in the Chester Beatty Library* (Dublin 1967) xiii-xiv; F. Rosenthal, *Ibn Khaldun, The Muqaddimah, An Introduction to History*, 3 vols. (Princeton 1967) Vol. 2, 388-389.
13. The text commences with a grammatical explanation of a number of words. "*Yā* is the vocative particle, *man* is like the governing word in a genitive construct." Such linguistic points have been incorporated into the notes so as not to interrupt the flow of the text.
14. The way the letters are drawn and placed on the page according to the system of Ibn al-Bawwāb. (Courtesy of A. Mustafa).
15. This can be interpreted in more than one way but seems to mean that the distance between the two vertical strokes forming the Arabic definite article should be consistent throughout each line on the page. (Courtesy of A. Mustafa).
16. This line does not occur in Ibn Khaldūn's version of the *rāʾiyyah.* Because the line ends in the letter *nūn* it cannot have been part of Ibn al-Bawwāb's poem.
17. *khuṭūṭ bīd.* Presumably the white streaks that sometimes occur after the reeds from which pens are made have been left to soak in the water where they grew before being cut down.
18. For *thiqāf* see Muḥammad Ibn Manẓūr, *Lisān al-ʿArab* (Cairo 1891) Vol. 10, 362-363.
19. The text mentions here that *yasūgh* "fashioning" is a metaphor.
20. Arberry, *The Koran Illuminated*, "perfect symmetry"; Rosenthal, *Ibn Khaldun*, "exact symmetry". The commentary indicates that the expression *bi-awsaṭ al-taqdīr* was understood as "middling in length and shortness, thickness and thinness".
21. The large chancery hand of Mamlūk Egypt.
22. The lower part of the reed is not exposed to the sun because it is under the ground or submerged in water.
23. Allowing the pen to roll will reveal any twist in the stem. The part where the pen rests, i.e. that touching the ground, is the part cut away to make the underside of the nib. (Courtesy of A. Mustafa)
24. According to E.W. Lane, *Arabic-English Lexicon* (Reprint: Beirut 1968) Part 2, 445, the *jalfah* is the distance between the place where the paring commences (*mabrā*) and the point. That is, the aperture which opens in the underside of the reed as it is pared by the scribe's

knife. The mouth of the aperture will be long or short depending on the distance of the *mabrā* from the point. This is confirmed by F. Rosenthal, "Abū Ḥaiyān al-Tawḥīdī on Penmanship", *Ars Islamica* 13-14 (1948) 4 n. 22.

25. *shaḥmah.* This is translated as "pith" in E. Robertson, "Muḥammad ibn ʿAbd ar-Raḥmān on Calligraphy", *Studia Semitica et Orientalia* (1920) 76. However, a dried-out reed has no pith as such. *Shaḥmah* thus means the wooden circumference of the reed which may be several centimetres thick. It is worth noting that the treatise translated by Robertson, which he was unable to identify (57-58), the whereabouts of which are unknown, is identical to the *Tuḥfat ūlī 'l-Albāb fī Ṣināʿat al-Khaṭṭ wa'l-Kitāb*, H. Nājī (ed.) (Tunis 1967), attributed to ʿAbdal-Raḥmān ibn al-Ṣā'igh (1368-1441).
26. *farakāt.* When the letters of the Arabic alphabet which are based on circles or semi-circles are drawn, the pen is held at the same angle throughout. The strokes will taper to a point as they change direction. These points where the change of direction occur are the *farakāt.* If the pen is too thick the tapering of the stroke will not be clearly defined. (Courtesy of A. Mustafa)
27. *ṣadr* is the trimmed point, re-cut at an angle. See note 31.
28. *fatḥah* is the length of the cut part of the reed, in the centre of which is the *jalfah* or aperture.
29. When the nib-split is made the halves on either side of the split are called "teeth" (sing. *sinn*). In the normal way of writing Arabic from right to left, the right-hand "tooth" will take the weight, so if this is slightly thicker than the left-hand one it will strengthen the pen.
30. *ṭabb* and *ṭabīb*, "treating medically"; and "physician" has the meaning here of *labb* and *labīb*, "being intelligent" and "intelligent". *Ḥattā* is a preposition.
31. The point is trimmed by the knife coming down vertically, then the *ṣadr* is made by cutting across the underside of the tip at an angle. (Courtesy of A. Mustafa)
32. I am translating *ṭarīqah* as "method" and *qalam* as "style" or "hand".
33. *muḥaqqaq* historically is one of the earliest cursive scripts. Its main characteristic is the drawing up of the "tails" of letters like *mīm* and *wāw* under the body of the line of text. It was the main qur'anic hand throughout the Near East.
34. The normal cursive hand of everyday scribal usage.
35. *rayḥān*: a script similar to *muḥaqqaq* but with tapering verticals, "hooks" on the strokes of the definite articles, and very finely written vowels.
36. *riqā'* is a smaller version of *tawqī'*.
37. Abu 'l-Ḥasan ʿAlī ibn Zengī. He was the pupil of a famous woman calligrapher Shuhdah bint al-Abbarī, who died in 1178-79. His work was influential in fourteenth-century Egypt. Al-Zabīdī, *Ḥikmat al-Ishrāq ilā Kuttāb al-Āfāq*, A. Hārūn (ed.) (Cairo 1954).
38. This is probably an error for al-Simsimānī, i.e. Muḥammad al-Sim-

simānī, the teacher of Ibn al-Bawwāb. Cf. Rice, *The Unique Ibn al-Bawwāb Manuscript* 7.

39. Usually called *dhar'ānī/dharānī*; Lane, *Lexicon* Part 3, 958.
40. Weights and measures differed somewhat from one part of the Islamic World to another and from one century to another. In fifteenth-century Egypt the weight of a *dirham* was 3.186 grams, the weight of a *raṭl* was 458.78 grams (144 *dirhams*), and that of an *ūqiyah* 38.23 grams (12 *dirhams*). See W. Popper, *Egypt and Syria under the Circassian Sultans, 1382-1468 A.D.; systematic notes to Ibn Taghrî Birdî's Chronicles of Egypt (Continued)* (Univ. of California Publications in Semitic Philology 16; Berkeley and Los Angeles 1957) 39-40, also, W. Hinz, *Islamische Masse und Gewichte* (Leiden 1970).
41. See the previous note.
42. These verses are additional and cannot have been part of the original *rā'iyyah*.
43. According to al-Ṭībī, *ash'ār* was a specific script; al-Ṭībī, *Jāmi' Maḥāsin Kitābat al-Kuttāb* 18.
44. The printed text gives *al-kātib al-muntahā*, which makes this clear. Nājī, *Sharḥ Ibn al-Waḥīd* 20.
45. In Ibn Khaldūn, *Muqaddimah*, Quatremère (ed.) 347, this verse and the previous one are combined and there is no mention of scroll or roll (*darj*). Thus Rosenthal in his translation was unable to make sense of "unsheathing it with resolution". Cf. Rosenthal, *Ibn Khaldun, The Muqaddimah* 389.
46. This was the normal position in which a scribe sat to write. For a pictorial representation of what the text means, see D. James, *Islamic Masterprices of the Chester Beatty Library* (London 1981) 44.
47. At this point in the text which appears corrupt, there is a digression on whether the original says *muntaḍiyan* or *muntaṣiban*. The former is preferred.
48. This important sentence is missing from the British Library manuscript. It appears only in the edition published by Nājī, *Al-Mawrid* 4, No. 15 (1986) 269.
49. *tawqī'* or *tawqī'āt* is a cursive scribal hand in letters usually separate and often attached by additional ligatures.
50. The text of the British Library manuscript breaks off at this point. The remainder of the translation is taken from the edition by Nājī, *al-Mawrid* 4, No. 15 (1986) 269-270.
51. Ibn al-Baṣīṣ is referring to his own father when he uses the term "the Shaykh" here, not to Ibn al-Bawwāb.

24v. بسم الله الرحمن الرحيم

يا من يريد اجادة التحرير   ويروم حسن الخط والتصوير

يا حرف نداء للبعيد والقريب. مَن شبيه بالمضاف يريد خطاب مَن يقصد حسن الخط ويروى «يا مَن يروم اجادة التحرير» اى تحرير الكتابة و«التصوير» اى تصوير الخط وهو العام من كل صناعة وغايتها تشبه فعل الطبيعة. فيجب ان تكون كل كلمة كالصورة فى مناسبة الاعضاء. وهو ينقسم اربعة اقسام: اوضاع ومناسبة ومقادير وبياضات. فالاوضاع التى وضعها الشيخ رحمه الله تعالى والمناسبة ان تكون كلها نسبة والمقادير التى لا يزيد الفها على لامها والبياضات وهى التى تكون بين الالف واللام بياض متساو وسائر السطر بياضهُ متساوٍ. قوله «ويروم» فيه دليل على انه لا يحصل له حسن الخط حتى يقصده بقلبه

25r. ان كان عزمُك فى الكتابة صادقاً   فارغب الى مولاك فى التيسير/
أَعْـدِدِ من الاقلام كل مقوّمٍ   سهل على السكين غير عسير

قوله «اعدد» فيه اشارة الى تفضيل الاقلام العتيقة المختزنة على الحديثة العهد بالقطع وتحريض على تعتيقها. قوله «كل مقوّم» اى غير اعوج ولا مبطوح ولا مفتول ويكون فيه خطوط بيض ويكون سهلاً على السكين فى البرية غير عسير وفى رواية ابن الوحيد «كل مُـثَـقَّف» وهو مشتق من الثِقاف وهى الخبشة التى تُـقَـوّم فيها الرماح والسهام. وفى روايته «صَلْب يصوغ صياغة التحبير» عوض «سهل على السكين» وهو احسن لان القلم الرخو يضطرك الى تقصير البرية ويجفى سريعاً وقوله «يصوغ» استعارة و «التحبير» النقش من الحبرة وفى نسخة ابن الوحيد هذا البيت الآتى زيادة على ما وجدتُ.

واذا عمدتَ لبرية فتوخّـها   عند القياس باوسط التقدير

يعنى متوسطاً فى طوله وقصره وثخانته ورقته الا ان تبرى الطومار فيستغلظ وبالضد.

انظر الى طرفَيْه فاجعل بَرْيه   من جانب التدقيق والتحصير

امرك بالنظر الى جانبي القلم فايهما كان ادقّ وارقّ فابر منه لانه يجب ان تكون البرية من رأس الانبوبة فانه اصلبُ اجزائها لان رطوبته قد جفت بسبب انكشاف قشرها عنه ودوام قرع الشمس له ولذلك صار رأس الانبوبة ارقّ
25v. لتلزّزه. ومعنى هذا البيت / يدلّ على ان ما تقدّم من قوله «صَلْب بصوغ» اصوب من الرواية الاخرى وهى «سهل على السكين» لان على هذه الرواية تحصل المناقضة فى كلام الشيخ. اذا عُلِمَ هذا فينبغى ان تضع القلم على الارض فيتدرّج ثم يقف فابر من الموضع الذى وقف عليه فما تجيء البرية مفتولةً.

واجعل لجَلْفَته قواماً عادلاً   يخلو من التطويل ولا من التقصير

الجلفة طول البرية واختلف فيها الكتّاب فمنهم مَن يقول «كمناقير الحمام واعتدال السهام» ومنهم مَن يقول «عقدة اصبع الابهام» ومنهم مَن يقول «لا طويلة ولا قصيرة» وهو الذى اشار اليه الشيخ وذلك بحسب صلابة القلم ورخاوته. فالصلبة تطول وحدّها الا ان تأخد فى الخط ولا تعطى فتختلف ثخانة الكتابة.

وكذاك شحمته اعتمد توسيطها   لتكون بين النقص والتوفير

الشحمة اذا عظمت سترت الفركات واذا خفّت قلّت رطوبة الكتابة. فان كان القلم محرّفاً فرقّت منتصباتها رقّةً تنافر بها ثخانة منسطحاتها وثخنت بها الفركات والمدوّر يثخن به المنتصبات. والشحمة فى صدر القلم اذا وضع على الورق وفى فتحته. فمنهم مَن ياخذها ومنهم من يجعلها بارزةً. ومنهم مَن يقصد بها التوسّط
26r. وهو اختيار الشيخ قال فى نسخة ابن الوحيد رحمه الله تعالى /

والشَقّ وَسِّطْهُ ليبقى سنُّهُ   من جانبيه مشكل التقدير

تُوَسِّط شقّ القلم لينزل الحبر فى وسطه ولئلا يضعف احد شقي القلم فتفسد الكتابة لكن اِن عظم السنّ الايمن لم يضرّ.

حتى اذا احكمت ذلك كلّه احكام طبّ بالمراد خبير

الطَبّ بفتح الطاء والطبيب بمعنى اللب واللبيب وحتى حرف جرّ يختصّ بالظاهر.

فاصرف لشأن القطّ عزمكَ كلّه فالقطّ فيه جملة التدبير

اول ما شرح فى البرية وتقدّم الكلام فيها ثم شرح فى القطّة فيقول «اصرف اليها همتك وكلّيتك» لان النحت فى القلم والشقّ لا يباشر احدهما الخط بنفسه. والقطّة هى التى تصوّر الكتابة بذاتها. فمتى زاغت شفرة السكين عن الهيئية التى يجب ان تكون عليها عند وقعها على القطّة مقدار ربع شعرة افسدت القطّة فلم تصحّ الكتابة. وصفتُها ان تأخذ قصبة يابسة صلبة وتضع
26v السكين على البرية فوق القصبة وتميلها الى صدر القلم وتنزل عليها بقوتك / بحيث تصل القطة الى القصبة فتحزّ فيها حزاً مستقيماً ويطلع لها حس قوى. واذا كانت القطة حادّةً تجىء الكتابة صافية واذا كانت غير حادّة تجىء الكتابة مشعشة والقطّة عليها العمل عند سائر الكتّاب ومَن عرف القطّة عرف الكتابة وعلمها.

لا تطمعن فى ان ابُوحَ بذكره انى اضِنّ بسرّه المستور

انما بخل الشيخ بالتصريح به حتى لا يعرفه الا مرتاض فى فك رموز الحكمة على عادة الحكماء فى صيانة اسرارهم بالرمز عن الجهّال.

لكن جملة ما اقول بانه ما بين تحريف الى تدوير

قال ابن الوحيد «رمز الشيخ عن القطة فى هذا البيت لما عانَي فى تعرّفها من الشدّة ولانّ الهمم كانت فى طلب الفضائل عاليةً فى زمانه ولانّ جدوى هذه الصناعة كانت عظيمةً. ورمز الى السبب الاعظم فى اتقانها فى قوله «ما بين». ولما غيّر قوم بعده كثيراً من طريقته لجهلهم بالقطّة ولقلّة ما وقع اليهم من

27r جيد خطّه وقلّة الهمم / فى بلوغ الغاية فى هذه الصناعة رأيتُ كشف رمزها واجباً. وهو انه قال «جملة» فتحتها تفصيل والمعنى ان لكل قلم مسمى كالمحقّق والنسخ قطّة تخصّه. فقطّة الريحان اشدّ تحريفاً ثم نقل حتى تكون قطّة الرقاع اقلّها فصارت انواعاً من التحريف الى التدوير».

فابذُل له منك اجتهاداً كافياً فعساك تظفَر منه بالمأثور

الشيخ رحمه الله تعالى يحضّ على مزاولة القطّة بالنقل فانا لنقلى من جيد خطة الاقلام كلّها وقياسى على قطّاته المختلفة صحّت لى بطول التجربة. ولما قطّ الولى العجمى مدوّراً فسد ريحانه وما يليه وصلح رقاعه وما يليه والعراقيون اليوم بالضد.

والِقْ دواتك بالدخان مدبّراً بالخلّ او بالحِصْرِم المعصور

اختار الدخان لنعومته وتطويسه واختار العصارتين لنعومتهما وقبضهما وبُعْدهما عن الفساد. وقال ابن الوحيد «وانا ارى ان المركب على البارد خير منه وهو
27v نسخة السمعانى. وهو جزء عفص ونصف جزء / صمغ وربع جزء زاج يُطحن ويُدعك بماء الجلنار فى الماون اياماً حتى يتخلّ ويُصَفّى ويُلقَى عليه من الشب والملح الاندرانى والزنجار والصبر لكل رطل منها نصف اوقية صمغ ويُوضَع فى الشمس اسبوعين». وقال ابن البصيص «ينبغى ان تكون الليقة من حرير مغسولة بالصابون منشّفه تنفيشاً جيداً كثيرة اليباس. ثم تأخذ الحبر العال المطوّص وتلقيه على الليقة وتحرّكها. والحبر مستخرج من الحوائج المذكورة وهى حبر اسقطرى درهم، زعفران جنوى درهم زنجار بلاحك ثلاثة دراهم. ملح اندرانى ثلاثة دراهم. تدقّ هذه الحوائج كل واحد بمفرده ويُؤخَذ العفص الاخضر غير مثقّب صحيحاً سالماً من العيب ويُدقّ ويُكسر اثلاثاً وارباعاً والوزن ثلاث اواق. ويُنقع ثلاثة ايام مع شىء من ورق الآس. ويُغْلَى الى يذهب ثلثه ويُصَفّى من راووق على الحوائج المذكورة ويُخلّى سبعة ايام. ثم ياخذ ما صُفّيَ من الماء ويُجعل فى اناء زجاج ويُجْعَل معه الصمغ الجيد غير مدقوق فانه ابقى لجوهريته ويُسوَّد بالزاج القبرصى ويُعمَل من الماء المصمغ

حبراً مركباً. وللكاتب المنسوب / ان يستخرج دخاناً من زيت الكتان ويجعله 28r.
مكان الصمغ فانه يعطيه سواداً وتطويساً. ويعمل معه زاجاً قبرصياً خالصاً
ليقوى سواده وتطويسه واذا فرغ من ذلك غمره بالليقة فاذا تغمرت الليقة
واستقرّت فى الدواة فان رأى الكاتب قوايه مختلاً غمره بالخلّ او بالحِصْرِم
المعصور». ويضاف اليه المَغْرة المصوّلة والزرنيخ الاصفر مع الكافور ليزداد
اشراقاً وتطويساً وهو معنى قوله

واضِفْ اليه مَغْرَةً قد صوّلت   مع اصفر الزرنيخ والكافور

يعنى المغرة العراقية وهى تكسوه حمرة ويجعل له جسماً فتزيل مصى الرطوبة.
وبالرزنيخ يحسن لونه ويمنع الدباب ويميّته. والكافور يحفظه من الفساد ويطيبه

حتى اذا اخمرتها فاعمد الى الـ   ورق النقى الناعم المخبور
فاكْبِسْه بعد القطع فى المعصار كى   ينأى من التشعيب والتغيير

اى اذا اخمرت دواتك وبريت قلمك فاعمد وخذ الورق الجسيم الناعم.
«المخبور» فى قوله للصقال. وان لا يتقطع فيه الخطّ وان يطيب فيه مشى القلم
ولا يتقصّف. واذا / كُبِسَ بعد القطع زال عنه التشعيب ولم يتغير مأيته 28v.
وصقاله.

قال الشيخ ابن البواب رحمه الله تعالى

«تخيّر ثلاثاً واعتمد بها   فانها على بهجة الخط المليح تعين
مداداً وطرساً محكماً ويراعة   اذا اجتمعت قرّت بهن عيون
فيحلّ هلال لو تعذر بعضها   عليه ارته العجز كيف يكون»

ثم اجعل التمثيل دأبك صابراً   ما ادرك المأمول مثل صبور
ابدأ به فى اللوح اول مرّة   فكذاك فعل الماجد التحرير

امر الشيخ بمراقبة المثال الذى يمثّله الشيخ للمبتدىء ويعرّفه اصوله واشخاصه
ليلاً ونهاراً وينظر فيه حتى ينال بعضه. وجعل الصبر هو الاصل لانه اذا لم

يصبر ما يدرك قصده. ثم امره ان يبدأ به فى اللوح فى اول ما يكتب ليسهل عليه لانه يمكنه ان يمحو فيه كلّ ما جاء غير مناسب ولا يبدأ به الا بقلم المحقّق او الاشعار لانهما اقرب الى التحقيق. وقال «اول مرّة» فلم يأمر الا مرّةً واحدةً وهى البدأة. فذاك فعل الماجد الذكى الالمعى وقال ابن الوحيد «هذا الكلام للمنتهى». ويدلّ / عليه البيت الآتى. 29r.

ثم انتقل للدرج منتضياً له عن ما تجرّده من التشمير
وابْسط يمينك فى الكتابة مُقْدِماً ما قام بالمطلوب غير مجسور

قال ابن البصيص «امر الشيخ بعد اللوح ان ينتصب للكتابة. والانتصاب ان يكون قعوده على ركبة ونصف ويأخذ القلم ويضع الكتابة فى الدرج. والدرج هو الورق الذى للكتابة المنسوبة والمبيضات على الشيخ. ويأخذ خط الشيخ وينقله الى الدرج بخطه اشهى واظنّه تصحّف عليه قول الشيخ «منتضياً» بالضاد المعجمة والياء المثناة تحت بمنتصباً بالصاد المهملة والباء الموحدة. وامر الشيخ ان يجرّد عزمه ولا يهاب احداً اذا كتب. ومتى يهاب احداً فان يده تضطرب اذا كتب. وقال «ابسط يمينك بالاقدام» وهو الهجوم على الشىء والدخول فيه من غير فزع ولا ملل. فان الجسارة مطلوبة فى كل شىء واكثر الناس يخاف ان لا يأتى بالكتابة على مراده فتختل يده بخيبته

29v. لا تخجلنّ من الردى تخطّه فى اول التمثيل والتسطير/
فالامر يصعب ثم يرجع هيّناً ولربّ سهل جاء بعد عسير

البيت الاول فى نسخة ابن الوحيد ومعناه ان الجاهل الضعيف يستحى ان يرى الناس نقصه فى ابتداء تعلّمه للفن فيمتنع من التعلّم لكبره وغباوته فيبقى جاهلاً طول حياته. والبيت الثانى يحذّر الطالب عند استبطائه وضجره من القنوط ويبشّر الصابر بنيل المطلوب.

فاذا بلغتَ مناك فيما رمته وغدوت حلف مسرّة وحبور

اى اذا ادركت املك فى الكتابة واقسامها وهى تنقسم الى اقسام. من ذلك ما ينقسم الى اصلين. الاول قلم المحقّق وهو اول ما يبدأ به وذلك لتحقيق حروفه. وهو ان تكون واوه مفتوحة وكذلك فاؤه وميمه وحروفه محققة ومختلسة. ومنه يستخرج قلم الريحان والنسخ وهو الذى يكتب به الاحاديث النبوية وكتب النحو واللغة وكتب الفقه وغيرها. ومتى اتقنه الكاتب اتقن جميع حروف الكتابة. ومنه تتفرع الاقلام وفرعه يستخرج منه وهو قلم التوقيعات الذى يكتب به المناشير